"To write usefully about Intentional Commun _____ their importance to the world, beyond the spec _____ biographies weave a picture of a community, so an overview of many community histories reveals the contribution of this quiet movement to that healthy cultural diversity on which human evolution depends (as does world ecology on biological diversity). The chronicler not only reminds busy communitarians of each other, and of the vital role of their whole movement; he/she must also integrate the economic, social, and spiritual insights of Intentional Community into a larger society struggling toward its global future. By comparing two 'communities of communities,' Dan McKanan, who shows rare empathy and aptitude for accurate recording, has produced what is hopefully the first of many parts of his chronicle."

Helen Zipperlen
Camphill Village Kimberton Hills
Kimberton, Pennsylvania

"Catholic Worker, Ammon Hennacy, remarked that while he might not be able to change the world, he was certain the world would not change him. With a refreshing and critical eye, Dan McKanan explores this idea of change by introducing us to the lives and roots of several Catholic Worker and Camphill communities. The challenging question is about change. Does the gentle personalism and radical philosophy of the Worker and 'threefolding' and 'curative education' concepts of Camphill have any effect on changing our 'filthy rotten system'? Dan McKanan asks the right questions for the right reasons."

Brendan Walsh
Co-Founder, Viva House
Baltimore Catholic Worker

For everyone at Maple Hill Farm. — with gratitude,

Dan McKanan

Touching the World
Christian Communities
Transforming Society

Dan McKanan

LITURGICAL PRESS
Collegeville, Minnesota

www.litpress.org

Cover design by David Manahan, O.S.B. Photo courtesy of iStockphoto.com, Oleg Prikhodko.

1   2   3   4   5   6   7   8   9

Library of Congress Cataloging-in-Publication Data

McKanan, Dan, 1967–
    Touching the world : Christian communities transforming society / by Dan McKanan.
        p.   cm.
    ISBN-13: 978-0-8146-3175-1
    ISBN-10: 0-8146-3175-4
    1. Christian communities.   2. Community—Religious aspects—Christianity.   I. Title.
BV4405.M39 2007
267'.182—dc22   2006013850

Contents

Introducing
the Communities

Camphill is a beacon for all on the path toward social renewal. Its fundamental ideals light the way to a better future—a future where the work of healing the earth unites with the work of healing social life—where people's needs are met with love, where equality of opportunity is assured and where the individual spirit unfolds in dignity and freedom.

—Camphill Village Copake[1]

To foster a society based on creed instead of greed, on systematic unselfishness instead of systematic selfishness, on gentle personalism instead of rugged individualism, is to create a new society within the shell of the old.

—Peter Maurin[2]

It is Saturday morning, and the kitchen at the Des Moines Catholic Worker house is buzzing with activity. Church groups, Grinnell College students, and a pack of Cub Scouts appear at the door to drop off food or help serve the daily meal. There are more volunteers than necessary, but each person has a story to share. An older man, wrestling with the wounds of a recent divorce, wonders if his faith is calling him to a change of lifestyle. A United Parcel Service manager, intrigued that one of his part-time employees is a live-in volunteer at a homeless shelter, peruses the hundreds of newspaper clippings about antiwar demonstrations that line the walls. A high school senior prepares for her trip to the Worker's sister village in Chiapas, Mexico. A father discusses anarchist philosophy while his twelve-year-old son plays chess with several homeless men. A college professor, visiting to research a book on intentional communities, is invited into the game and soundly defeated. And holding court at the center of it all is Carla Dawson, who arrived at the Worker as a homeless single mother and is now often described as the community's "franchise player." Carla tells stories, barks orders, stirs soup, and greets each newcomer with a warmth that seems born of lifelong friendship.

Saturdays at Camphill Village Minnesota are usually quieter, but once a year this rural village of eighty people hosts several hundred visitors for its Open Day. Mostly residents of the nearby towns of Sauk Centre and Long Prairie, the visitors are traditional folks who work hard on farms and in offices, spend their free time with their children, and worship regularly at Lutheran or Catholic churches. As they take a hayride through Camphill's fields, the visitors learn about a lifestyle that is both similar to their own and very different. The Camphillers share their love of the land, but their farming is shaped by "biodynamic" principles that forbid the use of chemical pesticides and require that planting and harvesting follow astrological rhythms. Rather than traveling to a distant office, the Camphillers alternate between work shifts in the home, the garden, and traditional craft shops that produce wooden toys, woven rugs, and hearty cookies. Though they work as hard as their neighbors, they receive no individual salaries. Decisions about family vacations or private school tuition must be negotiated with the entire village, though there is usually enough money to go around. Perhaps most importantly, adults with developmental disabilities are at the heart of Camphill life, and on Open Day they are especially eager to show off the community that they have built up. Sarah, who has Down syndrome, rushes about, offering a boisterous hug to everyone she recognizes. Mike, who grew up on a farm just ten miles away, beams with pride as he reports on the calves and baby goats born on the farm this year. Martha rocks back and forth, clutching her Cabbage Patch doll, as she makes a joke about the name of each new person she meets. "Is your name Daniel? Daniel have to tell another joke!"

Touching the World

The Des Moines Catholic Worker and Camphill Village Minnesota, along with the dozens of communities that are like them, can be lifted up as heroic alternatives to competitive, consumerist society, or dismissed as irresponsible utopians who prefer personal purity to social responsibility. But neither of these characterizations does justice to the mixed and mingled character of life at a Catholic Worker house or a Camphill village. It is true that Camphillers and Catholic Workers live in ways that are different from those of their neighbors, sometimes heroically so. But Catholic Workers and Camphillers also live *with* their neighbors. They worship together, serve together on school boards, share vegetables and political opinions and gossip. Community members are eager to share the insights they have gleaned from cooperative living, but they are also willing to learn from their neighbors. And it is in this living together that Christian intentional communities can do the most to instill values of cooperation, equality, and love in society as a whole.

This book begins from a simple premise: a Christian intentional community can be a transformative presence in the world only if it touches the world. Throughout history, many Christians (and others) have sought to build "the kingdom of God on earth"—to forge an alternative to the violence, inequality, and fragmentation of mainstream society. In the face of militarism, industrialism, and greed, small Christian communities have lifted up such values as sharing of possessions, gentle care for vulnerable persons and for the earth, and cooperative work that honors the special gifts of each individual. But creating the alternative is only the first step. In order to make the alternative meaningful, a community must resist the temptation to cut itself off from "the world." It must be flexible enough to stay connected to the persons and institutions that comprise "the world," even as it calls them (and itself) to ongoing transformation. Christian communities should, in other words, build bridges rather than walls, opening their boundaries so that they can share their own gifts and receive the gifts of others.

The task of building bridges is difficult and risky. Indeed, communities that choose to build walls between themselves and the world can reap enormous benefits. They have a clear sense of who they are and why they are superior to their neighbors. Their members are highly motivated to stay in the community for fear of being cast out into a hostile world. One influential study has shown that communities that maintain high boundaries—for example by using distinctive language and clothing to limit contact with outsiders—are more likely to survive for multiple generations.[3] The cost of such practices, however, is that at best these communities benefit only the handful of individuals who are willing to make a total break from the world. At worst, their isolation allows authoritarianism and abuse of power to flourish unchecked, sometimes culminating in sexual exploitation or the tragedy of a Jonestown. When these tragedies are publicized, they reinforce the perception that the ideals of the Gospel are meant only for heaven. Meanwhile, other, quieter communities go about the hard work of connecting Gospel ideals to the values and practices of people in mainstream society.

I have chosen two movements to illustrate the practices of touching the world. Camphill is a worldwide network of schools and villages in which persons with and without developmental disabilities share life together, usually in an agricultural setting. It was founded by Karl König, a physician and a student of Rudolf Steiner's esoteric Christianity, who had fled with a group of friends from Hitler's Austria to an estate in Scotland. Like Camphill, the Catholic Worker movement emerged during the worldwide social crisis of the 1930s. Founded in New York City by Dorothy Day and Peter Maurin, the movement has grown to encompass nearly two hundred urban "houses of hospitality," rural farming communes, and associated ventures. The two movements have exercised little direct influence on one another; indeed, few Camphillers or Catholic Workers are even aware of the other movement. Yet they are similar in their concern for social renewal, their flexible approach to membership, their inclusion of families as well as single people, their attempt to preserve a communal Christian identity without imposing any orthodoxy on individual members, and their openness to the experiences of death and resurrection that are sometimes the consequence of their other values. These common practices provide multiple points of contact with the larger society.

Just as individual Camphill and Catholic Worker communities maintain open and flexible boundaries with the larger society, so each movement taken as a whole has a boundary that is difficult to define. Karl König declared that "the Camphill Movement is no trade-mark" and that "anyone can call himself a part of it," though he added that the "council of the Movement may have to consider whether such an assertion is right or wrong."[4] The Catholic Worker has never had such a council; it is literally true that any group of people can "join" simply by declaring their community to be part of the movement. Each movement, moreover, maintains close ties to a variety of freestanding communities that decline to affiliate formally—often because they hope that independence will facilitate close ties to the larger society. Such communities play an important part in my story, though I draw examples or quotations from them only when I am confident that comparable examples could also be drawn from the "official" communities.

Both the flexible boundaries of these movements and the comparative nature of my study create certain terminological challenges. I refer to Camphill and the Catholic Worker as "intentional community movements," and to the constituent groups of each movement as "intentional communities." But most Camphillers refer to their local communities as "schools," "villages," or simply "Camphill places," reserving the term "Camphill Community" for the inner circle of individuals who have made a lifelong commitment to sustaining the ideals of Camphill. Catholic Workers often point out that their houses of hospitality cannot be called "intentional communities" because so many of their residents are there out of need rather than conscious intention. "I myself have often thought of our communities," wrote Dorothy Day in 1964, "as concentration camps of displaced people, all of whom want community, but at the same time want privacy, a little log cabin of their own, to grow their own food, cultivate their own gardens and seek for sanctity in their own way."[5]

I have retained the phrase "intentional community" because its meanings, in contemporary usage, are so loose that it can function as a convenient umbrella. At both Camphill and the Catholic Worker, people who are not related by marriage or blood share living space, meals, daily work, and/or service on a regular basis, even if not all the people associated with each movement share all of these things. As such, they fit into a broader culture of intentional communities that includes many other groups that I might have included in this study. The L'Arche movement, founded by Jean Vanier in the 1960s, is similar to Camphill in its choice of work and to the Catholic Worker in its spiritual underpinnings. A number of freestanding Protestant communities, including Sojourners, Koinonia, Jubilee Partners, Reba Place, and Iona, have combined community sharing, family life, care for the earth, and passionate advocacy of social justice. The Christian practices of bridge-building that I celebrate are also exemplified by "engaged Buddhist" communities, by spiritually eclectic communities such as Findhorn and Sirius, and by many secular communes and cohousing communities. The Fellowship for Intentional Community works hard to help this broader spectrum of communities "touch the world" by sponsoring conferences and publishing a popular directory. And though Catholic monastic communities (including those that sponsor the colleges where I teach) do not embrace the specific bridge-building practices I will discuss, they have their own ways of touching the world. They sponsor colleges and hospitals, welcome persons of many faiths into their oblate or associate programs, and celebrate liturgies that bend the hierarchy's rules toward greater hospitality.

My choice to focus on certain movements and not on others is largely the product of circumstance. When I began teaching at Saint John's University and the College of Saint Benedict, I consulted the Fellowship for Intentional Community's directory to find communities in my neighborhood, and thus got to know Camphill Village Minnesota. That community has remained at the center of my research efforts, graciously allowing me to live with them for four extended stays as well as many shorter visits. I first got to know the Catholic Worker through the Saint Catherine of Genoa house of hospitality in Chicago, where I volunteered weekly while in graduate school. Saint John's and Saint Ben's have sent a remarkable number of alums to the Worker movement, and these individuals have provided links to houses of hospitality and farms throughout the Midwest. My analysis of Camphill and Catholic Worker communities has also been shaped by my ongoing research on similar communities rooted in the Transcendentalist and abolitionist movements of the nineteenth century. This comparative perspective has persuaded me that the world-touching practices found in Camphill and the Catholic Worker can not be traced to their unique circumstances, but represent a viable path for Christians of many times, places, and denominations.

My research method has been eclectic. Over the course of about five years, I visited around twenty Camphill, Catholic Worker, and informally affiliated communities, participating in daily life and interviewing a cross section of residents. In my interviews, I rarely tried to identify the most important leaders or even the most dedicated members, preferring to gain insights from the full spectrum of short- and long-term residents who make up these communities at any given time. I did not, however, attempt to obtain a statistically random sample. I have sought additional insights from the interviewees by sharing article and section drafts with them, and offering them the opportunity to clarify or expand on their quoted comments. I also offered interviewees the choice to be quoted either anonymously or by name. When they did not express a preference, and when no sensitive material was involved, I have quoted them by name as a way of honoring their personal contributions to the communitarian project. I supplemented my own participant observation with a wide reading of secondary sources, archival material, and movement periodicals. I have not, however, attempted a comprehensive study of either movement, and am thus deeply indebted to the more detailed studies of previous scholars.

Though I would not identify myself as a "Catholic Worker" or a "Camphiller," I have made no attempt to adopt the stance of the neutral social scientist. I was trained as a theologian and church historian, and as a result I see my own scholarly vocation as that of a critical insider—one who offers new analyses and insights from the perspective of a fundamental commitment. In this particular case, my fundamental commitment is as a Christian communitarian. I believe that Christians should be about the work of building communities that both challenge and connect with the larger society. I have chosen to lift up two movements that share this ideal and that, in my view, often succeed in realizing it. I can imagine myself joining either movement; if I could not imagine this, I would not have chosen to write about them. At the same time, the picture I offer of Camphill and the Catholic Worker will not be a simple mirror of the accounts offered by movement leaders and participants. Such accounts often stress the movement's uniqueness, its fidelity to its ideals, and the heroism of its founders, while I will accent similarities with other movements, flexibility of practices, and the ordinariness of most participants. My intent is not to downgrade the movements, but to uncover the complex process by which lofty idealism is translated into transformative presence in the world. By praising these communities for characteristics they do not always find praiseworthy, I hope to challenge them to a deeper and more creative engagement with the wider human community.

The bulk of this book will be devoted to the specific practices that allow Catholic Worker and Camphill communities to touch the world. In chapter 2, I will consider ways communities have adapted or even changed their missions in order to allow members to follow distinctive callings, with particular emphasis on the experiences of short-term community members and the "extended community" of people who participate in the life of an intentional community without giving up their place in the larger society. In chapter 3, I will identify the practices that allow people to build family and community relationships simultaneously. Chapter 4 will consider practices that allow communities to maintain their Christian identities without compromising the spiritual freedom of the diverse individuals who are drawn to their work. In chapter 5, finally, I will seek to come to terms with the short lifespans of some of the communities in this study by identifying the practices that keep them open to the possibility not only of death, but also of resurrection. To set the stage for these explorations, however, I must briefly tell the stories of each movement.

The Catholic Worker

"It all happened while we sat there talking, and it is still going on," wrote Dorothy Day in the conclusion to her autobiography. Indeed, Catholic Workers of every generation have loved to talk, and a favorite topic is the formative myth of how Day, a bohemian journalist, and Peter Maurin, a French eccentric, came together to start a movement that would put the ideals of the Sermon on the Mount into concrete practice. Born at the turn of the twentieth century, Day was raised largely without religious faith and spent her young adulthood as a socialist journalist. What she called the "natural happiness" of becoming a mother drew her to the Catholic Church, which appealed to her as the spiritual home of "the great mass of the poor." Since her common-law husband was a devout atheist, she broke off the marriage in order to join the church and have her daughter Tamar baptized, then sought to connect her old and new lives by writing on social issues for the lay Catholic journal *Commonweal*. Through *Commonweal*'s editor, she met Peter Maurin, a vagabond intellectual whom she called the "Saint Francis of modern times." In the third year of the Great Depression, Maurin knocked on her door and began "declaiming" one of the "Easy Essays" that outlined his distinctive interpretation of Catholic social teaching.[6]

Maurin, who was fifty-seven when he met Day, had been born into a huge French peasant family and educated by the Christian Brothers, an order that he briefly joined. Influenced by English "distributists" such as Eric Gill and the "personalism" of Emanuel Mounier, Maurin's social theory emphasized personal responsibility within a decentralized agrarian economy. While most American Catholics were enthusiastic about Franklin Roosevelt's New Deal, Maurin insisted that the best way to achieve the "common good" was for each person to take individual responsibility for the well-being of his or her neighbors, performing the "works of mercy" that had long been featured in Catholic spirituality. "In our own day," he complained, "the poor are no longer / fed, clothed and sheltered / at a personal sacrifice, / but at the expense of the taxpayers. / And because the poor / are no longer fed, / clothed and sheltered / the pagans say about the Christians / 'See how they pass the buck.'" In order to create a society "where it is easier for people to be good," Maurin proposed a three-part program consisting of "round-table discussions" for "clarification of thought," "houses of hospitality" in each city or diocese, and, most ambitiously, farming communes that he called "agronomic universities."[7]

From the beginning, Catholic Workers sought both to expound this ideal and to put it into practice. When Maurin knocked on Dorothy Day's door, his immediate plan was to launch a newspaper to promote his ideas. This they did quickly, though not without a significant conflict between Day's penchant for muckraking journalism and Maurin's preference for a constant republication of his program. Though Maurin withdrew from the editorial board, editor Day continued to publish his Easy Essays and pay homage to his role as intellectual founder. The resulting combination sparked the imaginations of both the young idealists who spent hours hawking the *Catholic Worker* in Union Square and the 100,000 subscribers who were reading the paper by its second anniversary.

The process of implementing Maurin's practical program was more haphazard. Unemployed persons began showing up at the door of the apartment where they were publishing the paper, and personalist principle dictated that they attend to the needs of these persons. Relying on donations from sympathetic priests and newspaper readers, they rented an apartment they dubbed the Teresa-Joseph Co-operative. Within a few years, the community included hospitality houses for both men and women (St. Joseph's House and Maryhouse, respectively) that also provided editorial offices and living space for volunteer editors and cooks. Other associates of the movement lived in nearby apartments, at a series of "garden communes" on Staten Island, or at the larger farm established in Easton, Pennsylvania, in 1936. (Both the houses of hospitality and the farms would change location several times during the ensuing years.) Meanwhile, the fledgling community sponsored a "Catholic Worker School," with topics ranging from racial justice to scholastic theology to Jewish spirituality. By September 1935, a list of "Allied Movements" added cooperatives, unions, maternity guilds, and "legislation for the common good."[8]

This mix of activities appealed to Depression-era Catholics. As Day and Maurin spoke at Catholic universities and parishes, they simultaneously raised money for the work in New York and inspired local people to start their own houses of hospitality or discussion "cells." Jane Marra, a labor organizer in Boston, started a house of hospitality there in 1935. In Saint Louis, a circle of *Worker* readers started the "Campion Book Shop and Propaganda Committee" as an alternative to a nearby communist bookstore, then added a coffee line, a house of hospitality, and a 250-acre farm. In Chicago, an African American Catholic named Arthur Falls was inspired to create a house that emphasized self-help more than the works of mercy: rather than providing soup and shelter, he created a credit union and a lending library of books on cooperatives and race relations. Another Chicago group began publishing their own local paper, though they encouraged readers to spend their first quarter on the New York *Catholic Worker*. By 1941 nearly forty communities sponsored houses in such far-flung cities as Sacramento, Memphis, and London, and farms in Minnesota, Michigan, Ohio, Pennsylvania, Vermont, Massachusetts, and New York.[9]

"Invariably," noted Worker historian William Miller, these communities "were examples of Dorothy Day's counsel: begin where you are and with what you have." Day provided them with moral and often financial support, lists of local subscribers to the *Worker*, and free publicity, but each house remained structurally independent, and for the most part Day refused to impose any organizational, ideological, or theological party line. Beginning with Arthur Falls' "Chicago Letter" of June 1935, the *Worker* published regular updates on local activities, and by November 1937 there was enough activity to fill an entire issue. Day also took pains to remind local groups that "we emphasize again the necessity of smallness. The idea, of course, would be that each Christian, conscious of his duty in the lay apostolate, should take in one of the homeless as an honored guest." This ideal of the "Christ room" in the family home has remained as integral to the movement as houses of hospitality and farming communes.[10]

Almost from the beginning, the Catholic Worker coupled its economic radicalism with fervent opposition to war. A 1934 pamphlet entitled *The Catholic Church is Anti-War* opposed both imperialist and class warfare on the basis of the just war criteria, but a few years later an editorial declared more emphatically that "The Catholic Worker is sincerely a *pacifist* paper," adding that "the pacifist in the next war must be ready for martyrdom." The primary context for these declarations of antiwar sentiment was the Spanish Civil War, in which Day's former communist comrades were fervently supporting the Republican side, while many Catholics embraced Franco and the Nationalists as defenders of the church. Some readers who admired the *Worker's* high-minded criticism of both sides were troubled when the paper retained its pacifist commitments in the face of World War II. An editorial in June 1940 contrasted their position with that of Communists who might change with a changing party line: "We consider that we have inherited the Beatitudes and that our duty is clear. The Sermon on the Mount is our Christian manifesto." In the issue immediately following Pearl Harbor, they reiterated the point in almost identical terms: "We are still pacifists. Our manifesto is the Sermon on the Mount, which means that we will try to be peacemakers."[11]

Though this stance provoked little controversy in New York City, it split the national movement in two. "Until the Pope speaks," editorialized one of the Chicago communities, "it is the right and obligation of every Catholic to form his own conscience on the issue of the war." The house in Seattle began distributing the Chicago paper instead of the New York paper, and the Los Angeles community went so far as to burn copies of the New York *Worker*.[12] Day responded with a circular letter that acknowledged the disagreement but urged those who "take it upon themselves to suppress the paper" to "disassociate themselves from the Catholic Worker movement." (She was more ambiguous about houses that dissented quietly.) "There is no reason," Day added in a more conciliatory note, "why we should not be associated together as friends and fellow workers, but there is every reason for not continuing to use The Catholic Worker name."[13]

This surprising (to some) declaration of principle provoked a variety of responses from the local Worker communities. The Chicago paper ceased publishing; the Pittsburgh community separated itself from the movement; the Seattle community separated, then returned after tempers cooled. Other communities scarcely noticed, yet the overall effect of World War II was nearly fatal to the movement. Many houses closed when volunteers enlisted in the army or were sent to conscientious objector camps; others found there was little need for hospitality in a wartime economy with virtually full employment. Half the original thirty-two houses of hospitality had closed by 1943, and only the communities in New York, Detroit, Cleveland, Rochester, and Harrisburg, with their associated farms and one independent farm in Upton, Massachusetts, continued well beyond the end of the war. The Rochester house is the only original Worker community outside New York City that survives today; it broke early from the New York model by accepting nonprofit status, and has rarely been featured prominently in the New York paper.

The fact that the Worker survived at all can be traced to at least two factors. The first is that Dorothy Day retained personal friendships with many of the Workers who disagreed with her, even corresponding with those who enlisted in the military, and was thus able to draw several back into the work following the war. These connections, in turn, allowed Day to soften her own stance. By the time she wrote *The Long Loneliness*, she acknowledged that although the presence of nonpacifists in the Worker "is a matter of grief to me . . . I can see too how good it is that we always have this attitude represented among us. We are not living in an ivory tower."[14] The second key factor was the annual retreat for Catholic Workers from across the country that Day inaugurated in 1939. In some ways, this exacerbated tensions within the movement: Father John Hugo, who took over responsibility for leading the retreat in 1941, was a fervent pacifist who also struck many Workers as "Jansenist" in his demanding piety. Still, for those who were drawn to Hugo's spirituality, the experience of a full week each year of silence and scriptural meditation could galvanize commitment to the movement and provide a sense of shared identity to Workers who labored in many far-flung places.

By the 1950s the Catholic Worker had settled into a period of slow growth and maturation, despite the tendency of historians and former Workers to write of the movement as a thing of the past. New houses—some enduring and others less so—appeared in Washington, D.C.; Portland, Oregon; Memphis; Oakland; and even London. The Worker's close connection to the

Catholic rural life movement inspired many to start new Catholic Worker farms, though most of these could be better described as alternative family farms than as the "agronomic universities" envisioned by Peter Maurin. The New York community, meanwhile, experienced something of an artistic and intellectual renaissance. Ade Bethune began contributing a distinctive style of woodcut to the paper in the 1930s, and after 1949 her efforts were supplemented by those of Fritz Eichenberg, a Jewish Quaker whose depictions of Christ standing in a breadline and of a black man on a cross continue to appear in the New York paper and on the walls of most Worker houses.[15] The newspaper also featured the writings of John Hugo and Robert Ludlow—described as the Worker's "dominant intellectual presence" between 1946 and 1954—and the more impassioned advocacy of Ammon Hennacy, a Tolstoyan anarchist who stressed the connections between Peter Maurin's personalism and various radical traditions indigenous to the United States.

Though the Worker had always advocated active "resistance" to war, it was Hennacy who pushed civil disobedience to the center of the Worker's mission. In 1955 he persuaded Dorothy Day to join him in refusing to participate in the civil defense drills that were an integral part of Cold War policy. Within a few years, New York had canceled its drills, and other Workers were finding new ways to resist. Karl Meyer, son of a Vermont congressman and a convert to Catholicism, was inspired not only to found the Saint Stephen's Catholic Worker in Chicago, but also to trespass at military installations, join a peace march to Moscow, and publish advice on how to avoid paying the federal income taxes that were used to fund the Cold War. Echoing an article published by John Hugo in the *Catholic Worker* in 1948, Meyer also proposed the burning of draft cards. This tactic caught on during the Vietnam War, as *Worker* editor Tom Cornell burned his draft card at the Polaris nuclear submarine base in 1960, on national television in 1962, and again at a mass demonstration in Union Square in 1965. Brothers Dan and Phil Berrigan, who began writing for the paper early in the 1960s, quickly moved to pouring blood on draft files, then burning them with napalm in the Catonsville Nine action of 1968.[16]

Dorothy Day responded to such actions by suggesting that destruction of property was not truly nonviolent, and reminding readers of Peter Maurin's conviction that "the works of mercy are the most direct form of action there is."[17] Still, the close association between the Catholic Worker and the Berrigans' "ultra resistance" contributed enormously to the proliferation of Worker houses. Jonah House, the Baltimore community founded by Phil Berrigan and Liz McAlister, was not officially a Worker house because it did not do hospitality, but the Berrigans' friends Willa Bickham and Brendan Walsh started Viva House Catholic Worker to provide hospitality for war resisters and others in need. Mike Cullen, founder of Milwaukee's Casa Maria Catholic Worker House, was deported after he and Jim Forest participated in an action modeled on that of the Catonsville Nine. Other Worker houses that were close to the Berrigans include Boston's Haley House, the Ammon Hennacy House of Hospitality in Los Angeles, and the Des Moines Catholic Worker, whose cofounder Frank Cordaro has declared that "we're not afraid to call the Berrigan brothers, Dan and Phil, our Rabbis and Jonah House the Mother House of US faith-based resistance to war and the ways of war."[18] Several of the communities founded during this period evolved into regional "motherhouses," instilling Worker values in young people who would go on to found new houses in dozens of cities. Ironically, at a time when many observers viewed the Worker as an "outdated idea" that was being supplanted by liberation theology, it was on the verge of an era of explosive growth.

That growth came in the 1980s. The Reagan-era cuts to federal housing programs, coupled with the deinstitutionalization of persons with mental illnesses, created a national crisis of homelessness and gave new relevance to the work of hospitality. Increasingly, houses of hospitality popped up in such small cities as Worcester, Massachusetts, or Winona, Minnesota, as well as in major metropolitan areas. Simultaneously, Reagan's Central America policies generated a stream of refugees from El Salvador and Guatemala, and other Workers were formed as part of the "Overground Railroad" that helped these refugees en route to Canada. Some of the new communities shared the movement's strong commitment to antiwar activism, while others evolved into more conventional homeless shelters whose tax-exempt status limited their activism. Dorothy Day's 1980 death and subsequent canonization process also gave important publicity to the movement. Her autobiography, *The Long Loneliness*, was soon one of the most widely assigned books at Catholic colleges, and at least a few houses were founded by people who had no previous exposure to the movement except through books.

From the 1940s onward, Dorothy Day and the New York Worker responded enthusiastically to the growth but were careful to let each new community chart its own path. They used the newspaper to share the movement's stories: anecdotes about hospitality, hagiographies of saints whose actions resonated with Worker ideals, and memories of such Catholic Worker "saints" as Maurin, Hennacy, and eventually Day herself. Occasional *Worker* columns might also admonish local leaders to attend daily Mass or establish certain "departments," but no attempt was ever made to weed out those who failed to comply. The New York paper also published and republished so many versions of the movement's "Aims and Ideals" or "Positions" that none could be regarded as absolutely normative, though any one could be borrowed (sometimes with extensive editing) by a new house wishing to explain itself to potential supporters.[19]

A hallmark of all such attempts to "define" the Catholic Worker is the (frequently humorous) acknowledgment that definition is impossible. "Ammon Hennacy," recalled a statement produced by the Austin house and reprinted by others, "often said that Catholic Workers usually are neither (Catholic nor Worker). That's a pretty good start! Anyone can call themselves a Catholic Worker, and many do." Perhaps the most popular introduction to the movement today is a cartoon produced by Chuck Trapkus in which the history and ideals of the movement are related to various school subjects. Under "Social Studies," for example, Trapkus wrote that "the Big Idea behind the CW is PERSONALISM: being personally *responsible* for everybody else's problems." But if precise definition is impossible, most Worker communities could endorse the list of four core values identified by Duluth's Loaves and Fishes Catholic Worker: hospitality, resistance, community, and spirituality.[20]

"Hospitality," said Carla Dawson of the Des Moines Catholic Worker, "means if somebody comes in and they need something to eat, or they need a shower, or they need a cup of coffee, or they need to use the phone or they need to use this as their address, we have it or we let them use those things." Put differently, hospitality means practicing the "works of mercy" outlined in Matthew 25, which the movement has consistently sought to revive. Some Catholic Workers provide overnight accommodations while others offer only a meal and a space to hang out during the day; some open their doors to all comers, while others limit themselves in order to attend more closely to each individual. But virtually all would agree that hospitality is work that everyone should do (albeit in a variety of ways), and that it should take place in one's own living space rather than in specialized shelters or institutions dependent on what Day called "Holy Mother the State." Catholic Worker hospitality, explained Tom Heuser of Saint Catherine of Genoa Catholic Worker, is "not so much focused on rehabilitating and fixing, looking at people as problems to be fixed, but rather people to be celebrated and embraced, and to journey with." Ironically, Catholic Workers do not always take sufficient credit for the fact that this spirit has now spread to many state-funded shelters and drop-in centers.

"Resistance" is an umbrella term for the many ways in which Catholic Workers oppose war and systems of injustice. Many Catholic Workers stress confrontational tactics: massive demonstrations, civil disobedience at weapons facilities, sabotage of weapons, tax resistance. A few choose to write letters to their legislators or even run for office themselves. (Given the Worker's tradition of anarchism, election-time newsletters often feature debates about the pros and cons of voting.) Perhaps most significantly, Catholic Worker newsletters and roundtable discussions introduce the full range of peace and justice issues—the war in Iraq, the ongoing dangers of the American nuclear arsenal, genocides in Sudan or Rwanda, the debate over women's ordination—to ordinary people whose first motivation may have simply been to share a casserole with the homeless.

Perhaps the most defining feature of the Catholic Worker is the conviction that hospitality and resistance are, in Donna Howard's words, "mutually empowering." "The balance between those two," she explained, "made each one possible for me. I was able to go further with each one because of the other." When she stood trial for a Plowshares Action in which she damaged a radio system for communication with nuclear-armed submarines, Donna could talk about sharing her home with persons experiencing homelessness, and about her dream that the millions of dollars spent every day preparing for war might be redirected to human needs. And when she spent time in the kitchen at the Loaves and Fishes Catholic Worker, she learned to love both likeable and unlikeable people, honing the nonviolent skills she needed to confront the war-makers of the world.

The place where hospitality and resistance, charity and justice come together is of course community. Most Workers can resonate with the closing words of Dorothy Day's autobiography, in which she wrote that "it all happened while we sat there talking," suggesting the roots of hospitality and resistance in human relationships. Many, moreover, share her fondness for the Catholic doctrine that the whole church, and indeed the whole of humanity, comprises the Mystical Body of Christ. "We cannot go to Heaven alone," Dorothy Day insisted. "Otherwise, as Péguy said, God will say to us, 'Where are the others?'"[21]

Finally, Catholic Workers place strong emphasis on the spiritual sources for hospitality, resistance, and community. "The vision is this," wrote Dorothy Day in 1940. "We are working for 'a new heaven and a new *earth*, wherein justice dwelleth.' We are trying to say with action, 'Thy will be done on *earth* as it is in heaven.' We are working for a Christian social order." This vision continues to be fleshed out in ways that are both broadly inclusive and specifically Catholic. "The leaders of the work," Day sometimes insisted, "must go daily to Mass, to receive food for the soul."[22] To this day, daily Mass-goers work side by side in many Catholic Worker houses with Jews, Buddhists, or spiritual seekers, drawn together by the common conviction that hospitality, resistance, and community are integral aspects of any authentic spiritual path.

These shared values leave room for considerable diversity. Theologically, there are Worker communities that promote an almost Tridentine spirituality, Workers that seek to combine theological orthodoxy with political radicalism, Workers that participate enthusiastically in liberal Catholic movements like Call to Action, and Workers that are more Buddhist than Catholic. Structurally, there are Workers dominated by a charismatic founder, Workers in which a central couple provides leadership and stability, Workers that are informal networks of families with distinct projects of hospitality, Workers that are controlled by volunteers who do not live at the house at all, and Workers sponsored by a religious order or even a university. Catholic Worker houses have specialized in care for adults with AIDS, babies with AIDS, single mothers, drug addicts, refugees, and sex workers; there are Catholic Worker farms that function as rural houses of hospitality, others that serve primarily as retreat houses, and still others that combine intensive farming and advocacy on rural issues. There are communities that call themselves "Protestant Catholic Workers" or "in the Catholic Worker tradition," as well as countless people who, inspired by previous Catholic Worker experiences, provide regular hospitality without declaring any identity at all. The challenges of this diversity were poignantly expressed in my conversation with Matt Daloisio, whom I met at Boston's Haley House in 2002. Characterizing the community there as predominantly Buddhist, Matt said he longed for a place that would nurture his Catholic spirituality more directly. But, he added, "How boring would it be if we all looked like the New York Catholic Worker." "The genius of the anarchist movement is that . . . it doesn't allow all of us to look the same." In all their diverse "looks," Catholic Workers have found hundreds of ways to engage and transform the larger society.

Camphill

Most Camphillers would readily agree that communities that wish to touch the world should not all "look the same." They would also agree with a principle that Dorothy Day referred to as the "primacy of the spiritual": a vital community movement must have a solid foundation in transcendent reality. One of the central challenges of the Camphill movement is thus to keep its diverse expressions connected to the original spiritual vision of founder Karl König.

König was an ethnic Jew who lived in Vienna on the eve of the Holocaust, a pediatrician with a special interest in neonatal development, and a student of the spiritual science of Rudolf Steiner, also known as anthroposophy. Each of these biographical facts influenced the community movement he initiated on a rural Scottish estate named Camphill in 1940. König's earliest companions were members of an anthroposophical study circle who had coordinated their flights from Austria at the time of Hitler's annexation. From the beginning, they understood Camphill as both a place of refuge and a "morsel of the true European destiny" that had been nearly destroyed by Hitler. Their experience as refugees made it easy for them to embrace König's desire to work with handicapped children who were "refugees from a society which did not want to accept them as part of their community." But from the beginning, the vision of Camphill was broader than the task of "curative education." The "brotherhood" of coworkers, modeled on earlier communities such as the Rosicrucians and Moravians, aspired to become the seed of a "new social order" rooted in the insights of Steiner's anthroposophy.[23]

Anthroposophy can be best understood as a strand of Christian esotericism; it places primary emphasis on the inner development of spiritual knowledge and capacities rather than on such outward expressions as doctrines and church institutions. Typically, esoteric traditions have also articulated complex theories of "correspondences" between heaven and earth, and between the natural cosmos and the human microcosm, sometimes incorporating notions of reincarnation and astrology. Esotericism has always been a part of Christianity, but there is a long history of conflict between Christian esotericists and doctrinally oriented churches such as Catholicism. Only in the modern era have esotericists been free to publicize the fruits of their spiritual researches, even as they insist that the deepest levels of spiritual knowledge are accessible only to the initiated.[24]

Rudolf Steiner, an Austrian born in 1861, was one of the most important shapers of this modern, semipublic strand of Christian esotericism. Trained in both science and literature, he came to esoteric spirituality in part through his work editing Goethe's scientific works and in part through a series of childhood encounters with unusual spiritual phenomena. For a time he found a spiritual home in the Theosophical Society, but his interest in Christian esotericism clashed with the Theosophists' emphasis on Eastern religion. In 1913 his followers organized the Anthroposophical Society; Steiner refounded this under his personal leadership a decade later. Also in 1913, Steiner began building the Goetheanum in Dornach, Switzerland. This massive, highly distinctive building, rebuilt after a fire on New Year's Eve

1921–2, continues to serve as global headquarters for the wide-ranging "initiatives" of anthroposophy.

Steiner's presentation of anthroposophy had two primary aspects. First, he articulated a complex theory of human nature and taught a series of spiritual exercises that would allow any person to develop his or her spiritual capacities. From this perspective, the heart of anthroposophy is a spiritual practice that can be freely undertaken by any individual, regardless of his or her abilities in other dimensions of life. In my interviews with Camphillers who embrace anthroposophy as their spiritual path, many highlighted Steiner's view of human nature as the key to his relevance for both community building and work with persons with developmental disabilities. What "makes a lot of sense to me," explained Jan Zuzalek of Camphill Village Minnesota, "is that the person isn't just a physical being, that there's something more and you're always trying to . . . bring out the gifts of that person."

The second aspect of Steiner's spiritual science involved his effort to apply the results of his own spiritual "researches" to concrete human problems. "There are very many people who've been clairvoyant and can tell things in the spiritual world," explained Richard Neal of Camphill Copake. "Those are usually experiences that are wonderful for the person who has them, but don't translate into a lot of real life help or opening of paths for people who hear of them." Steiner's gift was that "he was able to . . . translate spiritual experiences into an earthly form that people who didn't have that experience could work with." Often, Steiner made these "translations" in response to specific requests for help. When he was asked to help educate employees' children at the Waldorf Astoria Tobacco Factory in Stuttgart, he developed a program of education that grew into the worldwide movement of Waldorf schools. Christian ministers drawn to anthroposophy persuaded Steiner to create rituals for the Christian Community, or Movement for Religious Renewal. Steiner offered eurythmy, a form of symbolic movement, to dancers, while requests from farmers led him to develop biodynamic agriculture, which combines organic principles with astrological and homeopathic techniques for revitalizing the soil. Perhaps the two most significant fruits of spiritual research for Camphill are Steiner's method of "curative education" and his social theory, usually known as "threefolding."

Steiner developed his model of "curative education" through his early experience as a tutor for a hydrocephalic boy and his long-term collaboration with the Dutch physician Ita Wegman. At its heart is the idea that the caregiver must attend to the whole person, rather than merely the symptoms that need "fixing." Like Catholic Worker "personalism," curative education places strong emphasis on the healing power of reciprocal relationships between persons. "Simply the meeting, eye to eye, of two persons," wrote König near the end of his life, "creates that curative education which counters, in a healing way, the threat to our inner humanity."[25] Camphillers are quick to note that "curative education" is always a two-way street. "I would say a lot of people looking at this would say it's important because we're helping the person with special needs," noted Douglas Elmquist, who grew up in Camphill and now lives at a related community called Community Homestead. "My feeling . . . is that [there is] a balancing between who's helping who. I would not be the person I am today without the people with special needs."

In Camphill schools, the practice of curative education is embodied most fully in the "college meeting," at which all the persons concerned with the development of a child gather to reflect on that child's biography and current circumstances, in order that by recognizing "the child's individual nature" they will also "realize the necessary curative and educational treatment." This practice, which König identified as one of three "pillars" of Camphill, is a therapeutic discipline that requires intense spiritual preparation.[26] "It's a serious moment," explained Lois Smith, "where you're really looking to the angel of the child and the child's higher being to really speak with you." The results of this reverent attention can be both swift and profound, Lois added. "You meet the child in person, often the next day, and you're just in awe." Though college meetings are not held as consistently today as they were in Camphill's early years, in some ways the model has expanded to cover other circumstances: Camphill Beaver Run has held a "college meeting on the land," while Camphill Minnesota occasionally convenes a special group to help a coworker with a personal crisis or vocational discernment.

Steiner's vision of the "threefold social order" built on a correspondence between the esoteric anthropology of body, soul, and spirit and the French revolutionary principles of fraternity, equality, and liberty. According to Steiner, each principle corresponds to a distinct social sphere. Fraternity applies to the material, economic, or bodily sphere, in which all of us have a responsibility to care for one another's daily needs. Equality is the cardinal value in the political or "soul" sphere of decision-making, in which it is vitally important that each person has an equal voice. And it is in the spiritual sphere (that for Steiner also includes education) that individual freedom can be fully realized. Neither economic nor political institutions should be allowed to exercise any coercion in matters of the spirit. The great evil of fascism (that Steiner foretold in part) was the way it collapsed the economic, political, and spiritual spheres into its own totalitarian system. Camphill, in response, has honored the distinctions by refusing to impose any religious or spiritual tests on its members, by making everyday decisions democratically (in many cases by consensus), and by eschewing individual salaries and practicing an ethos of mutual care. This last practice grows out of Steiner's "fundamental social law," frequently quoted within Camphill: "The welfare of a group of people who work together is the better the less the single person claims for himself the profit of his labours."[27]

Karl König's application of Steiner's ideas to the life of Camphill reflected his own experiences as a second-generation anthroposophist who just missed the opportunity to meet Steiner in person. But Camphill is much more than the outgrowth of one man's vision. From the beginning other persons, as well as external social factors, have shaped the movement in profound ways—as well as occasionally causing great personal struggles for its founder. One significant early factor was the fact that König and his male associates were sent to internment camps almost immediately after their arrival in Great Britain, just as the fledgling community was offered the use of the Camphill estate. The women were thus the true "founders" of Camphill. When König was released from the camp, he was "returning to the mainstream of his life and activity," but not truly returning to Camphill because "he had not yet been in Camphill, and the life there was at first strange to him."[28]

Upon his return, König concentrated on forging the circle of coworkers into an esoteric brotherhood comparable to the medieval Templars who had first settled the Camphill estate. This process, in which König acted as a spiritual father and teacher, involved lectures, discussion, and participation in both the sacraments of the Christian Community and a new ritual called the Bible evening, at which participants shared a Saturday evening meal and then reflected together on the connections between a Bible reading and their experiences of the past week. These activities, coupled with the intense labors of building up a new enterprise, forged what became known as the Camphill Community.

The process also generated tensions. Several of the core members of the old Viennese youth group chafed under König's overpowering leadership, then left to start their own school for curative education, known as Garvald. At the same time, the work of Camphill attracted new members who were not prepared to participate in the shared spiritual disciplines of the "inner community." The result was an extended process of "social differentiation," in which the "Camphill Community" of persons devoted to Camphill's spiritual vision was distinguished from such outward administrative bodies as "Camphill Rudolf Steiner Schools Ltd." that carried administrative responsibility for the work of curative education. Though many of the same individuals were prominent in both groups, the differentiation made space, in König's words, for those "who feel themselves to belong to the impulse [of Camphill] but who wish to find a freer, less binding form for their lives."[29]

The process of social differentiation went hand in hand with the creation of new schools and villages. The earliest of these were on neighboring Scottish estates. Newton Dee, for example, was purchased in 1945 to provide a home for a group of delinquent boys. This was the first step in broadening Camphill's mission beyond work with children with developmental disabilities. A few years later, small clusters of coworkers, including Tilla König, began planting new schools in England. Camphill schools came to South Africa in 1951, Northern Ireland in 1953, and Germany in 1958. Soon König began reflecting on the future of those Camphill graduates who were still unable to find a valued place in the larger society. Their challenge, he realized, dovetailed with society's own need for a revitalization of village life. "Around each of our houses," he wrote in a 1952 report, "a very small village should grow with four or five small houses occupied by a few families finding their place in life and work."[30] This vision was realized in 1955, when Botton Village was established in northern England as the first Camphill community for adults with disabilities. Today, Botton Village is the largest Camphill community in the world, and villages for adults are as numerous in the international movement as schools for children.

Though the pattern of life is similar at the schools and the villages, village coworkers are careful to respect the adulthood of the developmentally disabled "villagers." Typically, they speak of their work as "social therapy" or "lifesharing," rather than "curative education," and they emphasize the rhythms of daily life more than intense interventions like the college meeting. König himself warned that a clinical attitude toward adult villagers would mean that "we would then become their gaolers and they would be our prisoners."[31] Lois Smith, who has lived at both schools and villages, explained that at the schools, "there is a lot more effort . . . to help the child transform and to become everything that he or she can become," while in the villages "we *have* become."

The move to adult villages in turn sparked more dramatic expansions of Camphill's mission, as some communities undertook work with persons experiencing mental illness or drug addiction, and others suggested that Camphill might become "a place of hospitality for other impulses that were in need of support." It also sparked a series of changes, some of them painful, in König's leadership. Deluged with requests for help from new initiatives,

König declared that he needed "a period of freeing myself somewhat from Camphill" in Scotland. In 1957 he delegated his administrative responsibilities to his associate Thomas Weihs, and reorganized the inner Community so as to renounce all personal authority over his companions. After a decade of shepherding the international "Movement Council," König withdrew again from direct leadership, handing authority over to six regional councils in 1964. König spent the last years of his life at the German village of Brachenreute, on the shores of Lake Constance. Finally at home in his native region, he devoted himself to tracing what he saw as his karmic connections to the history of central Europe, and reflecting on the spiritual meaning of his Jewish identity in light of both anthroposophical Christianity and the Holocaust.[32]

It was during this period of transition in König's leadership that Camphill first came to the United States, though in a sense its roots here go back even further than those in Scotland. The first American community initiative rooted in anthroposophy was the Threefold Community in Spring Valley, New York. Founded in 1926, this community embodied "threefolding" ideals through a variety of initiatives that have included an anthroposophical college, a biodynamic research center, and a retirement village structured somewhat like a Camphill. A more direct progenitor of Camphill in North America was the school for special needs children, coupled with a biodynamic farm, that Gladys and Bill Hahn established in 1938, first in Dover Plains, New York, and then at Sunny Valley Farm in Copake, New York. In 1954 the pressure of burdensome state regulations led the Hahns to relocate to Downingtown, Pennsylvania. There they received support from Alaric and Mabel Pew Myrin, wealthy anthroposophists with a special interest in biodynamic agriculture. By the time the Hahns were ready for retirement, they were familiar with Camphill's work in curative education, and they invited Karl König to consider taking over the work. Around the same time, they learned that Sunny Valley Farm had been purchased by another anthroposophist, Toni Roothbert, who was eager to offer it for the use of a new initiative.

The first clusters of Camphillers sent to North America thus encountered a lively network of sympathetic friends, with access to suitable properties in both New York and Pennsylvania. They also found a strong network of parents, many of them Jews who sympathized with Camphill's refugee roots, who were eager to place their disabled children in noninstitutional settings. Such widespread support allowed Camphill to launch villages for adults and children simultaneously: Camphill Village USA (often called Camphill Copake) was located at Sunny Valley Farm, while Camphill Special

School found its permanent home at Beaver Run, Pennsylvania. Carlo Pietzner, a member of the original Vienna youth group, was designated as leader of the North American region, and the new villages were pioneered by Janet McGavin, Hartmut and Gerda von Jeetze with their large family, Hubert and Helen Zipperlen, Mary and Asger Elmquist, as well as Pietzner's wife Ursel and sister-in-law Renate Sachs.

These Europeans were joined by such artistically inclined Americans as the architect Joan Allen and the poet and potter M. C. Richards. By the late 1960s, the trickle of new Camphillers became a tide, as both communities were well positioned to receive the hippies and searchers of the youth counterculture. Though these young Americans were rarely familiar with anthroposophy and had trouble connecting to the formalism of European culture, many found their life's work at Camphill. "It was quite a culture shock, a culture revelation," recalled Bernie Wolf, who came to Beaver Run as a practicum student from Antioch College in 1969. But the combination of cooperation, spiritual study, and meaningful work, coupled with his "deep admiration for the carrying coworkers," inspired him to return after his graduation, and soon he "settled in with no specific leaving date." "Most of the young people who came were looking for something," added Kristin Wilson, who as a Copake staff child was somewhat younger than the hippie generation. "Looking for something and a lot of them found it." The newcomers made American habits of informality and egalitarianism more fully a part of Camphill life, even as the founding generation rejoiced at the support of so many who were able to commit themselves freely to the work.

They also provided the North American region with sufficient strength to begin launching new initiatives, spearheaded both by veteran Camphillers and by local leaders interested in better care for people with disabilities. Today the North American region includes adult villages in California, Minnesota, British Columbia, and Ontario, youth guidance schools (for people in their late teens and early twenties) in New York and Pennsylvania, and several communities in the process of formation.

In each of these places, the evolving distinction between an inner "Camphill Community" and a more inclusive "Camphill Movement" has allowed Camphill to embody the ideals of threefolding while resolving the paradox that those ideals simultaneously mandate spiritual freedom and are themselves dependent on the specific spiritual insights of anthroposophy. North American Camphills are legally incorporated as 501(c)(3) nonprofits, and official authority is vested in boards of directors that include long-term coworkers, representatives of other Camphills, parents of the disabled children or "villagers," social workers, and civic leaders from nearby towns. These directors recognize that, except in times of crisis, real decision-making power rests with the "full circle" of long-term coworkers. Most "executive directors" downplay their own authority—indeed, I had spent at least two summers living at Camphill Minnesota before I realized that it had an executive director! At Beaver Run the board even agreed to invest the powers of the executive director in the Focus Group, which in turn seeks simply to "focus" issues for decision by a larger circle of coworkers. In each Camphill place, members of the inner Camphill Community have no legal power but carry the spiritual responsibility for ensuring that Camphill remains faithful to its founding vision. Should the coworkers decide to stop caring for persons with special needs, for example, the Community members would step in to block the change. More commonly, Community members simply identify areas of concern and then address them in individual ways.

As a result of the shared work of both the Camphill Community and the Camphill Association of North America (inheritor of the coordinating role once played by Carlo Pietzner), Camphill is significantly more cohesive than the Catholic Worker. The movement is marked by an easily recognizable architectural style, a standard daily schedule, and common mealtime prayers—despite the minor rift between those who say "May the meal be blessed" and those who say "Blessings on the meal." Karl König may have declared that "the Camphill Movement is no trade-mark," but new communities must still undergo an extended process of mutual discernment before affiliating formally with the Association.[33]

Still, each community takes pride in its individuality. When Camphillers found a new community, they do extensive research on local history and ecology, and incorporate local touches into the architecture and the names of buildings. They are attentive to the differences between a pioneering community with just a few houses and a grand village such as Copake, with its roughly 250 members, or the even larger Botton Village in the United Kingdom, with several independent neighborhoods and its own post office. Different Camphills also relate very differently to local social welfare authorities. When the state of New York refused to send its students to the unaccredited school at Beaver Run, its leaders moved quickly to provide teachers with formal credentials. Kimberton Hills responded to a similar challenge by "very actively working not to be licensed." Yet there was little resulting acrimony between the communities; indeed, Kimberton's Helen Zipperlen suggested that the difference simply reflected the distinction between a school and an adult village. "The finished product from the work of Beaver Run is an educated child. The finished product from here is something which is woven or milked or whatever. . . . We're licensed to sell raw milk and there's an inspector who comes to see that we do it properly."

Accidental factors also contribute to the differences among communities. Camphill Copake is shaped by the Jewish backgrounds of many of its villagers, as well as by its access to the cultural life of New York City, where it has held high profile musical benefits. Camphill Village Minnesota, on the other hand, is in isolated Todd County, far from other anthroposophical initiatives. Without a Waldorf School to attract anthroposophically inclined families, it has struggled to maintain a critical mass of long-term coworkers. But its greater independence from the larger anthroposophical movement has made it appealing to spiritual seekers and individuals whose primary attraction is to sustainable agriculture. It has also recognized the need to connect with local efforts to revitalize the rural economy. The new community hall, for example, includes a processing kitchen large enough to be used by a local farmers' cooperative (staffed by former Camphiller Kristin Wilson) and other neighbors. One of those who took up their offer, intriguingly enough, was a former Catholic Worker named Gary Brever, who had just launched Plough Share organic farm a few miles away.

Such initiatives reflect a growing awareness throughout the Camphill movement that the basic Camphill model may need to be adapted to allow for greater interaction with the larger society. Many compare Camphill to a plant that needed a certain amount of isolation in its germinal stages, but now requires greater exposure to light and air. In some places this means opening village facilities up to the broader public; in other places it means moving the community itself into more densely populated areas. At Camphill Kimberton Hills, for example, outsiders can eat at the café, shop at the craft shop or "Bring and Buy" thrift store, purchase a share in the large Community Supported garden, enroll their children in the Waldorf kindergarten, fulfill court-mandated community service, or even live at one of several rental properties maintained on site.

Camphill Houses in Stourbridge, England, on the other hand, was created as an urban alternative to the isolation of Botton Village. Villagers and coworkers live in houses within a conventional neighborhood, and many are employed outside Camphill. Some villagers even live in independent apartments, and meet the community only for the Saturday Bible evening.[34] The North American region has not moved nearly as far in this direction, but Camphill Beaver Run sponsors a "transitional program" for students ages 19–21 who live in two houses midway between the village and a nearby town.

Camphill Kimberton Hills has also spun off a few initiatives that are now fully part of the larger community; these include a natural foods store, a community action group for persons with disabilities, and two homes for persons with mental illness.

At the same time, a few Camphillers caution that large villages also have the capacity to touch the world in profound ways. "There's a growing tendency within the Camphill movement," said Copake's Peter Madsen, "to go into the world as opposed to retreating from it." But village life, Peter countered, provides a "social laboratory" because it has "a level of intensity that most people aren't familiar with." This laboratory is open to all sorts of people besides the full-time residents: the parents of villagers, the employees who work in the office, the extended family of coworkers. These people may be challenged to change their own lives by seeing a fully developed alternative. In an era when more Americans live in prison than on farms, Peter added, true villages have an important role to play in "revitalizing rural life."

Even as this fruitful debate goes on within Camphill, many creative adaptations of the Camphill model exist just outside the official movement. Some of these can trace their roots to curative education projects that predated Camphill, or to Garvald, the Scottish school and village founded by members of the Vienna youth group who broke with König in 1943. In North America, however, most unaffiliated communities have some ties to Camphill. Community Homestead in Osceola, Wisconsin, was started by a cluster of friends who had lived at Camphill Copake as children or young adults; for them, partial independence from the movement has allowed them to return to their roots while honoring their subsequent life paths. The Cadmus Lifesharing Association is a cluster of autonomous households initiated by a family that had spent many years at Camphill Beaver Run. And the founders of Innisfree Village perhaps took König's comment that Camphill is not a trademark too seriously, for their original name was Camphill Potomac. After a conversation with the Camphill Association revealed their admiration for Camphill but lack of interest in anthroposophy, they amicably agreed to a name change. It is also significant that the inner "Camphill Community" includes many members who no longer live at Camphill places, some of whom are now seeking to bring the spirit of Camphill into new initiatives or more conventional careers. Indeed, as Karl König declared, all the "single people who work in the spirit of the Movement and who feel united with it" are part of Camphill.[35]

One can find a full spectrum of Camphill variations in the small town of Temple, New Hampshire, located about a two hours' drive from Boston.

This area, which has been a hotbed of anthroposophical activity since the founding of High Mowing Waldorf School in 1942, hosts at least five distinct initiatives working with persons with special needs, three of which I had the opportunity to visit in 2002. By far the largest is the Lukas Community, a village of four or five households. Lukas was founded in 1981 by a group of parents whose children had lived at Camphill Beaver Run, but then failed to find a suitable placement at one of the North American Camphills for adults. Though Lukas undoubtedly has the "look" and "feel" of a Camphill, it has gone a bit further than many Camphills in adopting practices from the larger nonprofit world. It has an extremely clear focus on its mission of providing good care for special-needs persons that has caused it to limit its involvement in biodynamic agriculture. Though Lukas coworkers do not receive formal salaries, they are entitled to retirement benefits, eight weeks annual vacation, and two days a week entirely free of community responsibilities. (Camphill, by contrast, is only just beginning to develop a retirement strategy, and vacations are determined communally in response to individual needs.) They also are given semiprivate apartments with separate kitchens—an arrangement, according to executive director David Spears, that enhances the sense of community because coworkers are confident they can find private space when they need it.

If Lukas provides an alternative to Camphill that is slightly more like a traditional nonprofit, the other Temple communities tend in the direction of private-family homes. The Four Winds community, for example, maintains just two households, though it aspires to grow larger. Maple Hill Farm is a single household, and has no aspirations for growth. A history of schisms— the founders of Four Winds and Maple Hill initially separated from another community called Lyris, then split into two communities themselves—leads many folks in Temple to describe anthroposophy as inherently individualistic, but it also reflects a preference for the intimate scale of the household. Unlike Lukas, all these communities describe their work as "lifesharing," and they seek to balance care for persons with special needs with other life goals, rather than to maintain a clear division between personal and communal life. All of these alternatives share with Camphill a spirit of welcoming that binds communities together even as it opens up their boundaries.

Transformative Presence

Each movement included in this study thus has a distinct history and a distinct character. It may be helpful, now, to take a step back and specify more precisely the features they have in common, and the reasons they belong together in this book. Despite their differences, I would suggest, Camphill and the Catholic Worker share a community vision that balances egalitarianism with respect for differences, remains open to ongoing experimentation, and seeks to serve the larger society. Each has defined itself as Christian, while renouncing "sectarianism" and welcoming people from all religious traditions. Most fundamentally, each has practiced a discipline that I will call "transformative presence"—participating in the larger society in a way that opens new possibilities for others.

Both movements would affirm, in the strongest possible terms, that all people are equal in the eyes of God. For Karl König, the conviction that each person possesses an "eternal, imperishable" spiritual nature was "fundamental for our approach to the child. He is our brother and our sister. He is equal to every other human being and equal to us." Camphillers resist the clinical categories used by psychologists and social workers, and struggle to soften the inevitable distinction between "villagers" and "coworkers." The Catholic Worker, likewise, has always taken a fierce pride in its solidarity with even the so-called "undeserving poor," and in one version of its "Positions" affirmed "the complete equality of all men as brothers under the Fatherhood of God."[36]

Each movement, moreover, has sought to embody egalitarian principles in its internal structures. Dorothy Day advocated the "Benedictine ideal," in which leaders exercise a sensitive, quasi-parental authority, while many contemporary Workers aspire to either a formal or informal style of consensus decision-making. Camphills typically expedite the consensus process by distributing decision-making power among several individuals or groups, so that "we each have decision-making power where we work." Only very important decisions require the consensus of the entire community. The resulting structure, noted Richard Neal of Camphill Copake, is more like a "horizontal net" than a hierarchical pyramid. "To my experience," noted Bernie Wolf, "Beaver Run has never been led by any one or several people. It's always been *our* Beaver Run."

Neither movement has fully attained its egalitarian ideals. Despite Camphill's attempts to deemphasize the role of "executive director," it is significant that nearly all the people holding that position in North America have been men. Camphill work assignments also typically break down along gendered lines, primarily as a result of the choices and socialization of the people involved. Catholic Workers have a stronger culture of gender-neutral work, but both they and Camphill still attract a volunteer pool disproportionately white and middle-class in background.

Despite their commitment to egalitarianism, both movements have rejected the practice of community of goods, or holding all property in common. This may seem odd, in light of the fact that countless Christian communitarians have lifted up common property as the ultimate expression of equality. But Peter Maurin was fond of saying that property is "proper" to human beings. The Camphill practice of income-sharing is tantamount to community of goods for those individuals who come to Camphill as young adults with no property and stay indefinitely, but such people make up only a minority of Camphillers. Indeed, Camphillers who are independently wealthy are encouraged to take personal responsibility for the use or dispersal of their wealth, and not simply to hand it over to the community.[37]

Such practices reflect a concern to honor genuine human differences. Camphills and Catholic Workers must take into account both the differences between long- and short-term volunteers and those distinguishing "guests" from "Workers" and "villagers" from "coworkers." Many Catholic Workers can recall times when newcomers pushed for dramatic changes, then left as soon as the changes had been implemented. Efforts to involve guests more fully in decision-making have sometimes created a new hierarchy, in which the empowered "resident" guests exercise power over transient guests and those who only come for meals.[38] Similarly, Camphillers worry that giving decision-making authority to those with disabilities might give the more verbally skilled villagers an unfair advantage, or make villagers vulnerable to manipulation by the more charismatic coworkers.

At their best, Camphillers and Catholic Workers do not use the recognition of differences as an excuse for not empowering guests and villagers, but simply as the starting point for a discussion of more subtle ways of promoting egalitarianism. Several coworkers at Camphill Copake, for example, told me that they were working to create a "community meeting" at which villagers would be able to express their needs and preferences more fully. Having a public forum to express their concerns about staff kids riding their bicycles too fast, for example, could effect important changes even without formal democratic processes. Copakers have also recently expressed concern about the divisive effects of such labels as "villager" and "coworker," and have even resolved to abolish the once-prestigious designations of "housemother" and "housefather."[39] Place of Grace Catholic Worker in La Crosse, Wisconsin, similarly, has a policy that "if you want to volunteer here, you have to come here and eat first." This serves as an important reminder that all of us are in need of hospitality and service.

The commitment to egalitarianism thus requires constant experimentation with community forms. The early Camphillers took a cautious, experimental approach to implementing even such cherished principles as Steiner's Three-fold Social Order. "We first had to gather the experiences out of which a social order can arise in a living way through our lives together," recalled Anke Weihs. In keeping with the anthroposophical tradition of using analogies to human life stages, Karl König told the Botton Camphillers on their seventh anniversary that "we have toddled, we have played about, and in playing of course, nice things have begun to take shape."[40] Reba Mathern-Jacobson of Loaves and Fishes Catholic Worker observed similarly that "none of us grew up in a Catholic Worker house. . . . So we make it up as we go along and we get guidance from people who have walked this path before or who we are walking the path with."

Camphill and the Catholic Worker also share an emphasis on service. Indeed, they are often misperceived as service projects without a larger vision for social renewal. Yet even the manner in which they serve has been socially transformative. Largely because of Camphill, there is a now a consensus among social workers that people with disabilities should not be warehoused in institutions but allowed to share their special gifts with the world. Similarly, hundreds of homeless shelters now aspire to meet the standard of hospitality set by the Worker. Camphillers Helen Zipperlen and Claus Sproll, for their own part, seek strong ties to other sorts of intentional communities to help prevent Camphill from being reduced to a mere service provider.

Service, obviously, is a way in which a community movement touches the world quite directly, changing the lives of individuals who receive a meal, a place to live, or acceptance despite their disabilities. But service also contributes to "touching the world" in more subtle ways. It brings dedicated communitarians into regular contact with individuals whose motives are "merely" charitable, or who have a personal reason for wanting to work with persons with disabilities. A service mission can help build esprit de corps, holding the members of a community together even during the hard times when they may not especially like one another. "I can't imagine a more unsound basis to start a community," noted Copake's Peter Madsen, than the desire to "live together and have a nice life. . . . But together with people in need of special care, the intentions gained greater depth." Catholic Workers quote similar sentiments from Catherine de Hueck Doherty or Jean Vanier, while Dorothy Day herself affirmed that "the one factor which has brought the most results, which has served most to hold a group together, is the performance together of the Works of Mercy."[41] Without a service mission, communities often rely on coercive tactics or isolation from the larger society to build a sense of shared identity, thus depriving themselves of the opportunity to "touch the world."

The common commitment to service provides a clue to the distinctive understanding of Christian identity shared by the two movements. Many standard accounts of American community movements draw a broad distinction between "secular" communities like hippy communes and "religious" communities like the Shakers. Such classifications don't work well for Camphill and the Catholic Worker, for while these movements have cast their work as an effort to build the "kingdom of God on earth," they have refused to impose "sectarian" restrictions on individual members. A more helpful classification appears in the work of historian Seymour Kesten, who distinguished "colonies of individual salvation" from "colonies of social reorganization." For the first group, the primary purpose of life in community is to achieve salvation from sin; some would even go so far as to say that salvation is not possible outside community. Such communities have little interest in "touching the world," except insofar as this is part of the evangelistic project of persuading more people to follow the communal path to salvation. Kesten's second group, who may or may not be motivated by religious faith, seeks to remedy such evils as "poverty, ignorance, and inequality" by changing the social system. In these terms, Camphill and the Catholic Worker can easily be classified as "colonies of social reorganization" that happened to draw their primary inspiration from the Christian Gospel. I will explore the implications of this in more detail in chapter 4.

Perhaps the best window into what I am calling "transformative presence" is a word that might separate the movements: "radicalism." This is a favorite word among Catholic Workers, while for most Camphillers "radical" is "too loaded a term." Indeed, some of the most negative responses I have received in interviews came from Camphillers who were troubled by my early use of "radical Christian communities" as an umbrella term for the two movements. And yet there are some interesting connections between the reasons some give for avoiding the term "radicalism" and the reasons others give for embracing it.

When Camphillers repudiate the language of "radicalism," they usually have in mind an approach to social change that is either narrowly political or else overly "destructive." But for Peter Maurin, "radical" meant finding "roots" deeper than conventional politics. "To be radically right," he wrote in one Easy Essay, "is to go to the roots / by fostering a society / based on creed, / systematic unselfishness / and gentle personalism." Such an approach would draw on "a philosophy so old / that it looks like new." Most Catholic Workers would say that this "old philosophy" is the Gospel, especially the Sermon on the Mount. "The Catholic Worker *is* radical," explained Anthony Novitsky, "primarily in the sense that any group trying to live literally the message of the Sermon on the Mount is radical." Other Catholic Workers have explained that radicalism meant a "revolution from below" in which ordinary people would create new social structures rather than waiting on politicians. "We are to be announcers of a new social order and not denouncers of the old," declared Dorothy Day.[42]

It is easy to find echoes of this slogan in Camphill rhetoric. "In the midst of strife and chaos, and the dissolution of social forms and values," wrote Wanda Root, Camphill's founders "wanted to create a new form of social life. They wanted to find a way to live together based on a new understanding of man, and the ideals of freedom, equality, and brotherhood." This vision owed much to König's early involvement in the Austrian socialist party of Gustav Landauer, who had promoted a "new spirit" of socialism that relied on personal transformation as well as state action. König was also mindful of the fact that when Rudolf Steiner had attempted to build the "threefold commonwealth" by conventional political means, he was blocked by opposition from both left and right. Camphill's alternative approach was to "appear in the mantle of the task of caring for the handicapped, of caring for the land, of doing social work. In this way we are nevertheless able . . . to sow tiny little seeds here and there in as many places as possible." "The aim," König added on another occasion, "is not to preach the threefold social order, but in a humble way, to learn to understand it."[43]

Camphillers today continue to insist that social change begins with personal transformation. In explaining her discomfort with the word "radical," Lois Smith asked, "do I want to change society? I guess my first focus is to try to change myself. But I do believe that by changing myself, I can have a very strong effect on the rest of the world." Most Catholic Worker "radicals" would have little trouble accepting the premise that the personal transformation involved in personalist hospitality is the key to any meaningful social change.

This is not to suggest that the differences are purely semantic. Catholic Workers seek to "change themselves" by going to prison as well as by sharing their homes, while many Camphillers see such acts of "resistance" as an overly negative approach to social change. But insofar as Catholic Workers put hospitality before resistance, these differences are tactical rather than fundamental. The point is not to simply resist the injustices that make hospitality necessary but also to model one's resistance on one's hospitality. Some other anti-war groups, explained Joel Kilgour of Duluth's Loaves and Fishes Catholic Worker, will go to a military base and "point fingers at them and say that they [are] killers and potential killers." But the discipline of sharing his home with homeless persons, some of them likeable and some not, has helped him to remember the goodness in all people, including those caught in the military machine. "I know that they're good people. And we need to find that good in them and draw it out . . . and then always have room for them at our table." From the perspective of their common commitment to constructive change, Camphillers and Catholic Workers have much to learn from one another: Camphillers might learn that resistance can be a part of a larger constructive strategy, while Catholic Workers can be reminded not to get totally absorbed in resistance.

The common ground between these movements is thus "transformative presence"—the idea that society changes when small groups of people begin living in a new way. Camphillers and Catholic Workers reject the idea of revolution "from above," and refuse to use coercive methods—whether military or legislative—to get other people to change. Instead, they change their own lives in ways that do not cut themselves off from other people, and by so doing they make it easier for other people to change. The Catholic Worker, declared Frank Cordaro, does not live "away from the 'City of Man' in some sort of sectarian seclusion, but right in the very heart of man's brokenness."[44] And at Community Homestead, where the co-workers often work part-time in conventional careers, Richard Elmquist illustrated the principle from his own experience. "I work twenty hours a week, for a big defense contractor," he said. "Quite often what people will say to me is, you've got a great life, I don't know how you manage to make it work, I wish I could do that. I only work half time and yet I seem to be doing all right. . . . And my response to people when they say that is, you can do this too."

The point, Richard quickly clarified, was not that everyone should live at Community Homestead, or even in intentional community. But by living creatively *in* the world, he and other community members call out the creativity of their neighbors. A common hope of Catholic Workers and Camphillers is that all people who come into contact with their communities will feel free to make new choices—to choose sharing and personal growth and reciprocal hospitality. Ultimately, the "kingdom of heaven on earth" to which both movements aspire is not a project to be built, but a seed that will grow only when it is planted in every human heart.

Notes

1. Marty Hunt, ed., *Shining Lights: Celebrating Forty Years of Community in Camphill Village* (Copake, NY: Camphill Village U.S.A., 2001) 115.

2. Peter Maurin, "A New Society," *Easy Essays* (Chicago: Franciscan Herald Press, 1977) 109.

3. Rosabeth Moss Kanter, *Commitment and Community: Communes and Utopias in Sociological Perspective* (Cambridge, MA: Harvard University Press, 1972).

4. Karl König, *The Camphill Movement*, 2d edition (Botton Village, U.K.: Camphill Books, 1993) 33.

5. Dorothy Day, *On Pilgrimage: The Sixties* (New York: Curtis Books, 1972) 171.

6. Day, *The Long Loneliness* (San Francisco: Harper San Francisco, 1997) 107; "Story of Three Deaths," *Catholic Worker* 16/2 (June 1949); and *Loaves and Fishes* (Maryknoll, NY: Orbis, 1983) 3–6.

7. Peter Maurin, *Easy Essays*, 110–1, xviii, 63; and "Easy Essays," *Catholic Worker* 1/2 (June–July 1933) 1.

8. "Catholic Workers' School Program 436 East 15th Street, N.Y.C.," *Catholic Worker* 1/8 (1 February 1934) 4; and "Catholic Worker Program of Action," *Catholic Worker* 3/4 (September 1935) 4.

9. Janice Brandon-Falcone, "Experiments in Truth: An Oral History of the St. Louis Catholic Worker, 1935–1942," in Patrick G. Coy, ed., *A Revolution of the Heart: Essays on the Catholic Worker* (Philadelphia: Temple University Press, 1988) 317, 319; Francis Sicius, "The Chicago Catholic Worker," in Coy, *Revolution of the Heart*, 339–40, 346–7; William D. Miller, *A Harsh and Dreadful Love: Dorothy Day and the Catholic Worker Movement* (New York: Liveright Publishing, 1973) 114; and Day, *Loaves and Fishes*, 42, 55.

10. Miller, *Harsh and Dreadful Love*, 115; Arthur G. Falls, "Chicago Letter," *Catholic Worker* 3/2 (June 1935) 8; *Catholic Worker* 5/7 (November 1937) 1–8; and "Houses of Hospitality," *Catholic Worker* 4/8 (December 1936) 4.

11. "Not Pacifism," *Catholic Worker* 2/6 (November 1934) 4; "Pacifism," *Catholic Worker* 4/1 (May 1936) 8; "Our Stand—*An Editorial*," *Catholic Worker* 7/9 (June 1940) 1; "Our Country Passes from Undeclared to Declared War; We Continue Our Christian Pacifist Stand," *Catholic Worker* 9/3 (January 1942) 1.

12. Day mentioned the burning of the papers in an interview with James Finn, *Protest: Pacifism and Politics: Some Passionate Views on War and Nonviolence* (New York: Random House, 1967) 375, and one Los Angeles Worker, E. Virginia Newell, apologized for the incident in a letter to Dorothy Day, 22 October 1940, Dorothy Day—Catholic Worker Collection, series W-4, box 1.

13. Dorothy Day to "Fellow Worker," 10 August 1940, Dorothy Day—Catholic Worker Collection, series W-1, box 1; and Catholic Worker Editors to "Fellow Workers in Christ," 12 December 1941, Dorothy Day—Catholic Worker Collection, series W-1, box 1.

14. Day, *The Long Loneliness*, 272.

15. See Judith Stoughton, *Proud Donkey of Schaerbeek: Ade Bethune, Catholic Worker Artist* (Saint Cloud, MN: North Star Press, 1988); and Fritz Eichenberg, *Works of Mercy* (Maryknoll, NY: Orbis, 1992).

16. Dorothy Day, "C. W. Editors Arrested in Air Raid Drill," *Catholic Worker* 23/1 (July–August 1956) 1; Karl Meyer, "What Is to Be Done?" *Catholic Worker* 28/8 (March 1962) 6; Francis Sicius, "The Chicago Catholic Worker," in Coy, *Revolution of the Heart*, 355; and Miller, *Harsh and Dreadful Love*, 227, 319, 334.

17. Day, *Loaves and Fishes*, xvii.

18. Frank Cordaro, "Twenty-Five Years—Reflections from a Co-Founder," *via pacis*, 25/2 (June 2001).

19. Dorothy Day, "Letter on Hospices," *Catholic Worker* 14/10 (January 1948) 2, 8; "Houses of Hospitality—Primacy of the Spiritual," *Catholic Worker* 48/1 (January–February 1982) 3; Stanely Vishnewski, "How to Open a House of Hospitality," *Catholic Worker* 32/4 (December 1965) 7; "Catholic Worker Celebrates 3rd Birthday; A Restatement of C. W. Aims and Ideals," *Catholic Worker* 4/1 (May 1936) 1; "Aims and Purposes," *Catholic Worker* 6/7 (January 1939) 7; "Aims and Purposes," *Catholic Worker* 6/8 (February 1939) 7; "Aims and Purposes," *Catholic Worker* 6/10 (May 1939) 5; "Aims and Purposes," *Catholic Worker* 7/6 (February 1940) 7; "Aims and Purposes," *Catholic Worker* 10/6 (May 1943) 4; [Robert Ludlow], "Catholic Worker

Positions," *Catholic Worker* 20/7 (February 1954) 2; [Ammon Hennacy], "Our Positions," *Catholic Worker* 21/10 (May 1955) 5, 7; [Tom Cain], "Aims, Purposes, Positions," *Catholic Worker* 22/4 (November 1955) 8; and [Katherine Temple], "Our Manifesto: The Sermon on the Mount," *Catholic Worker* 53/3 (May 1986) 3.

20. Lynn Goodman-Straus, "What Exactly Is a Catholic Worker Person or House, Anyway?" *The Catholic Worker—Saint Catherine of Genoa, Chicago,* 5/4 (August 1993) 6, reprinted from *Jeremiah's Stutter,* Mary House Catholic Worker, Austin, Texas; and Chuck Trapkus, "A Catholic Worker Primer," available at many Catholic Worker houses.

21. Dorothy Day, "Aims and Purposes," *Catholic Worker* 7/6 (February 1940) 7.

22. Ibid.

23. König, *Camphill Movement,* 14, 15, 16.

24. For more on esoteric Christianity, see Antoine Faivre and Jacob Needleman, eds., *Modern Esoteric Spirituality* (New York: Crossroad, 1992).

25. Karl König, *Camphill Brief,* Christmas 1965, in Christof-Andreas Lindenberg, "Karl König— a portrait," in Cornelius Pietzner, ed., *A Candle on the Hill: Images of Camphill Life* (Hudson, NY: Anthroposophic Press, 1990) 26.

26. König, *Camphill Movement,* 36; and Michael and Jane Luxford, *A Sense for Community: A Five Steps Research Paper 2003* (Whitby, U.K.: Camphill Books, 2003) 16–21.

27. Cited in König, *Camphill Movement,* 44.

28. Anke Weihs, *Fragments from the Story of Camphill, 1939/40* (Coleg Elidyr Press, 1992), Karl König Archive, cited in Hans Müller-Wiedemann, *Karl König: A Central-European Biography of the Twentieth-Century,* trans. Simon Blaxland-de Lange (Botton Village, U.K.: Camphill Books, 1996) 174–5.

29. Müller-Wiedemann, *Karl König,* 192–3.

30. Cited in Friedwart Bock, "The history and development of Camphill," in Pietzner, *A Candle on the Hill,* 53.

31. Karl König, *In Need of Special Understanding: Camphill Conferences on Living with Handicapped Adults* (Whitby, U.K.: Camphill Press, 1986) 16.

32. Peter Roth, cited by Andrew Hoy, "Alternativenie," *Village Echo* [Camphill Copake], 16 July 2004; and Müller-Wiedemann, *Karl König,* 274–85, 379–429.

33. König, *Camphill Movement,* 33.

34. Michael Luxford, "The English and Welsh region," in Pietzner, *Candle on the Hill,* 115, 118.

35. König, *Camphill Movement,* 33.

36. Karl König, "Camphill essentials," in Pietzner, *Candle on the Hill,* 30; and [Robert Ludlow], "Catholic Worker Positions," *Catholic Worker* 20/7 (February 1954) 2.

37. Michael and Jane Luxford, *A Sense for Community,* 27, 55.

38. This process is eloquently described in Harry Murray, *Do Not Neglect Hospitality: The Catholic Worker and the Homeless* (Philadelphia: Temple University Press, 1990) 154–5, 208, 248.

39. Roswitha Imegwu, "Workshop in Social Therapy," *The Village Echo* (4 February 2005).

40. Anke Weihs, cited in Müller-Wiedemann, *Karl König,* 175; and König, *In Need of Special Understanding,* 13–4.

41. Dorothy Day, Circular letter to "Fellow Workers in Christ," Dorothy Day—Catholic Worker Collection, series W-1, box 1.

42. Peter Maurin, "Yes! I Am a Radical!" *Catholic Worker* 3/10 (April 1936) 1; Novitsky, "Ideological Development," 35; [Robert Ludlow], "Catholic Worker Positions," *Catholic Worker* 20/7 (February 1954) 2; and Dorothy Day, cited in Miller, *Harsh and Dreadful Love,* 6–7.

43. Wanda Root, "Camphill Villages: A Way of Life," *Village Life,* 10–1; Müller-Wiedemann, *Karl König,* 53; König, *In Need of Special Understanding,* 180; and König, cited in Luxfords, *Sense for Community,* 12.

44. Frank Cordaro, "A Midrash of the Catholic Worker Positions, part 2," *via pacis* 1/3 (January 1977).

Crafting Vocation

You will know your vocation by the joy it brings you.

—*Dorothy Day*[1]

A community that wishes to touch the world must begin by embracing the unique gifts of its members. Members who are free to develop such gifts, to sustain friendships with outsiders, and to balance community and individual work are also free to create strong ties to the larger society. This can be challenging for the life of the community, because it creates a dynamic tension between the development of the individual and that of the community. Communities that truly honor individuality are not always the most stable or enduring, and they rarely achieve the rapid economic growth or intense esprit de corps experienced by communities that demand self-sacrifice or limit members' interactions with outsiders. Camphill and Catholic Worker communities nevertheless take the risk of encouraging the full self-development of their members, in the faith that mature individuals will contribute to both the community and the larger society. They recognize that the tension between individual and community is a superficial one: at the deepest level, a strong community depends on strong members, and free and mature individuals are drawn to share their individuality with a community.

Each movement has its own vocabulary for describing the process by which individual self-development comes together with the life of the community. Camphillers often speak of "destiny," a term that reflects the anthroposophical idea that the human soul passes through a series of incarnations, each with distinct spiritual tasks. Community life provides an opportunity for each person to fulfill those tasks while also sharing in the destiny of others. Camphill's emphasis on traditional handcrafts also allows members to cultivate particular identities as weavers, gardeners, or bakers. Catholic Workers share this craft ethos—at least in principle—and frequently use the

language of "vocation," which they understand not merely as the call to ordination or religious life, but as the process by which every person finds
spiritually significant work. The term "vocation," which literally means "calling," is especially evocative in a discussion of the relationship between self
and community, because a "call" comes from outside the self, but must resonate with something already inside the self in order to be heard. Catholic
Worker and Camphill communities have developed a variety of practices
that allow their members to connect self and community in such a way that
they can touch the world with a deep inner joy.

The Call to Community

Most Camphillers and Catholic Workers begin the vocational quest even
before they arrive in community. The stories of these quests are as diverse as
the individuals who tell them, but typically they involve two elements that
might be called "crisis" and "surprise." On the one hand, the individual feels
an internal dissatisfaction with her current vocational situation, or perhaps
simply a yearning for "something more" in life. On the other hand, the path
by which she discovers that "something more" in community life is never one
that she had anticipated. External factors, often of quite an accidental nature,
play an important role. One rarely comes to community, in other words,
without listening both to oneself and to the larger world.

Brendan Walsh, for example, entered a Catholic seminary at the height
of the Vietnam War, and was naturally eager to connect his church's teachings
with his own strong antiwar sentiments. In a course on moral theology, he
was taught the classical doctrine of the primacy of conscience, according to
which even those with "erroneous consciences" have an obligation to follow
them. When the same teacher argued that the war in Vietnam met the just
war criteria, a dismayed Walsh put two and two together. "I left the seminary.
Packed up my erroneous conscience." Walsh's decision was also influenced
by his growing awareness that the diocesan priesthood does not offer the
same opportunities for community life as membership in a religious order
or Catholic Worker community. After his departure, he became deeply involved in the antiwar movement, married a former nun, Willa Bickham
(whose own experience of community in the Sisters of Saint Joseph was
much more positive), and founded Viva House Catholic Worker in Baltimore.
Brendan and Willa, along with their daughter and her family, have sustained
that community for more than thirty-five years.[2]

Walsh's experience parallels that of dozens of seminarians who have
found their way to the Catholic Worker over the years. But seminarians are

not the only ones who are led to community by a vocational crisis. Ecologist Ben Cownap reached his crisis when he was working for the World Wildlife Fund in Germany. Since "sitting in an office wasn't my idea of what ecology was all about," he moved to Camphill Kimberton Hills in order to "live ecology." Maggie Olson left a high-paying job inspecting "jet fuel nozzles for military aircraft" after her son heard a Catholic Worker activist speak at his school. Shortly thereafter, Maggie joined the Des Moines Catholic Worker as a full-time member, writing in the newsletter that "the loss of income will signal the giving up of my 'independence' to be replaced by a total giving to Christ's mercy and love."[3]

Many Camphillers come to community after experiencing vocational crises within teaching or other helping professions. Like Maggie Olson, Mary Davis learned of the community she would eventually join through her son, who attended a Waldorf school near Camphill Kimberton Hills. As her son befriended the children of Camphill coworkers, Mary found herself volunteering occasionally at the village. She was beginning a career as a physical therapist at the time, and quickly realized that the institutional setting was uncongenial. "I had work relationships," she recalled, "but we didn't really share a lot." Both the job and her own situation as a single mother forced her to spend too much time thinking about money. "I'd been feeling really frustrated with . . . chasing a dollar all the time, and paying rent and paying the bills and that was just taking, it felt like all of my energy. I wanted to try a different way of approaching things and community seemed to be a way of alleviating some of that." Even this realization did not open an easy path to community. She tried to arrange a trial visit at Camphill Kimberton Hills, but was prevented by the worst blizzard in decades. She visited Camphill Copake, but worried that her own spiritual practice of a Course in Miracles would not fit with the intensely anthroposophical ethos of that community. Then, at a Course in Miracles retreat, she met a coworker from Camphill Minnesota. As their romantic relationship blossomed, Mary realized it was time for her to separate from the Pennsylvania area where she had spent nearly her entire life. By moving to Camphill Minnesota, she found both a better way to practice physical therapy and a new chapter in her life story.

For many, the vocational crisis is intensified by factors in the larger society. The Great Depression and the rise of Hitler had a galvanizing effect on the first Catholic Workers and Camphillers, while in the 1980s the AIDS crisis pushed Tom Heuser toward a Catholic Worker vocation. As a gay man, Tom felt a strong desire to respond, so when he quit his job as a New York City budget analyst, the first thing he did was sign up to volunteer at Gay

Men's Health Crisis. After he had taken that step, Tom was surprised again and again by the turns his quest took. Due to a training requirement, it was six months before he could begin volunteering. He had been attending Friday night roundtables at the New York Catholic Worker, and "when they said that they needed some help on the kitchen, serving soup . . . I figured, well, what the hell, I had time." Soon he was there every week, then nearly every day. He moved into the Worker house for a time, then moved out to begin a nurses' aide training that was required for volunteer (and later paid) work at a nearby cancer facility. Soon Tom found himself thriving in a new "career" as a nearly full-time volunteer on a minimal income.

Then came the biggest surprise of all. Tom heard of a new Catholic Worker in Chicago that was devoted specifically to helping people with AIDS. As a devoted, lifelong New Yorker, Tom could not really imagine making a permanent move, but he had friends in Chicago, so he stopped by in January 1991. After that visit, he couldn't get Saint Catherine's off his mind, so he wrote to arrange a monthlong visit "just to explore what is going on." "I just couldn't leave New York City," Tom explained in our interview. "It was just absurd. But I thought that there was something there that I had to work out or something and that that might lead to my next step or whatever. But by the end of that month it became very clear to me that, my God, I have to move here. Apparently everyone there realized that back in January." Tom expressed the same sense of surprise in his introductory article in Saint Catherine's newsletter: "I'd be hard pressed to explain what has brought me to St. Catherine's. If anything, my stay here is simply the next step on a journey unwittingly begun when I quit my job. Each step has required surrender—to what, I don't know—perhaps the unknown. But each step has brought renewed confidence and strength to go further."[4]

The social crisis of the Gulf War combined with the personal crisis of a divorce to bring Donna Howard to the Catholic Worker. "It was a time of reconstructing my entire life," she recalled. "Everything changed. . . . I wasn't sure that I wanted to go on, and when I decided that I wanted to go on I decided everything had to match my spirituality." She dreamed of moving to a Central American barrio after her sons had grown. Then the first Gulf War began. Her sons and their friends were deeply opposed, and concerned about the possibility of a draft. They looked to her for guidance, and she realized that her quest for community did not have to wait for her parenting responsibilities to end. They searched for community together, and soon became the founding family of a new household within Duluth's Loaves and Fishes Catholic Worker community.

For many, community life is the culmination of a vocational search that begins in college. As a student at Evergreen State College, Peter Madsen felt "dissatisfied with most of what I found around me in middle-class America," so he took a four-month road trip in search of "parts of America I wanted to really embrace." Though he visited several intentional communities, nothing seemed just right. He returned to school. There he read Norwegian sociologist Nils Christie's book on Camphill. Peter was "amazed by what was described" and began asking his classmates, "Which one of us will be willing to actually live like this?" After graduation Peter decided he would be the one. His slightly careless reading of Christie's book had left him with the impression that the sort of community he described could be found only in Norway, and that he would be welcomed simply for showing up. So he showed up at Camphill Vidaråsen with only a guitar and a backpack. "I went with this incredible determination," he told me laughingly, "and was met rather coolly." Ordinarily, Camphills make advance arrangements for their foreign coworkers to have visas and work permits. Fortunately, Nils Christie himself persuaded the skeptical Camphillers to let Peter stay. He did so for three years, ultimately meeting his spouse and making a long-term commitment to the Camphill movement.

Today, Peter describes this haphazard journey as part of his destiny. At Vidaråsen, his naive utopianism was challenged by an experienced coworker who acknowledged his "complaints" about the community, but warned, "all these things you find wrong with this place, don't make the mistake of thinking that wherever you go next you won't also find those things wrong.""That really opened a large door in my soul," Peter told me, "to just go into, and have it not have to be perfect. 'Cause that's the thing I was suffering mostly. What do you mean, it's not perfect? When, why should it be?" Peter also discovered that in Norway he could make a connection to Camphill's underlying spirituality that would not have been possible in the United States. "Had I met Camphill and anthroposophy in the English language," he explained, "I don't think I would have stuck around. I would have thought, this is too weird." But as a foreigner learning a new language, he was open to the new and the weird, and began to welcome many anthroposophical ideas and practices under the impression that they were Norwegian ideas and practices. "I've seen that amongst many Camphillers," Peter noted, "that they go abroad before they take the plunge in Camphill."

The college where I teach, like most Catholic colleges in the United States, encourages vocational quests by sponsoring "alternative spring breaks" at Catholic Worker houses and other intentional communities. So it is not surprising that Mike Sersch thought he knew the Catholic Worker well by the time he graduated. He had met Workers and other peace activists from throughout the nation when he participated in the Atlantic Life Community's annual Holy Week demonstration at the Pentagon. Traveling between home and college, he had occasionally visited the La Crosse Catholic Worker, founded by an acquaintance from his home parish. He had spent two years living in the Jubilee Community, an intentional community within the dormitory system with a strong emphasis on social justice. Several of his close friends joined Catholic Workers or related communities before Mike's graduation. By January of his senior year he could say, "I want to go to a Catholic Worker, I know that's what I'm called to do."

Still, Mike had some surprises in store when he embarked on a tour of several Catholic Workers during his Christmas break. "I was . . . looking for a community in a large city that had a lot of activism, a lot of people in the house, a lot of young folks," Mike explained. "I imagined myself being in jail a good portion of the time." The Catholic Worker in Winona, Minnesota, did not meet any of Mike's criteria, but it was a convenient stopping point between two houses that did. After a "white-knuckling" drive in a snowstorm, Mike "walked in the door, and within half an hour I was tearing up, and I said, this is my home. . . . I just knew that Winona was going to be the place." The quiet peacefulness of the community, with its strong emphasis on small-scale hospitality, allowed Mike to move beyond the "unsettled and uncontemplative" life of a student activist. "It ties me down in a place that I need to be tied down in. And by that tying down . . . other gifts can come out."

For other people, the journey to community begins with a surprise, and only gradually connects back to the individual's sense of vocation. Helen Zipperlen was "an overgrown teenager" looking for the meaning of life in the organic agriculture movement of the 1950s when she offered someone a ride home from a conference in the south of England. Her companion was headed to Camphill Botton Village, which was then just six weeks old. She was captivated by the village's commitment to culture—her first task was to paint the library—and by two men who explained the threefold vision of their community. "I remember to this day the feeling, with my pink paintbrush dripping away, [that] this is what we've been talking about in organic agriculture. And these guys are telling it to me. But these are interesting guys. They're not like other people. It was my first meeting with a handicapped person. . . . They told me absolutely succinctly what this village was going to be that they were going to make." Helen spent several years in and out of Botton, then the rest of her life at Camphill Copake and Kimberton Hills.

Unlike Helen, Christine Elmquist had a definite plan in mind when she first encountered Camphill—and that plan had nothing to do with community. She had just graduated from college in England and, she recalled in our interview, "I knew exactly what I wanted to do. . . . I wanted to teach. . . . I had fixed myself up with the University of Exeter to do my postgraduate work in education, and then I'd go from there." With her plan set, she decided to take a year off from "head work," though she would have "died before I said" that she was "called" to a year of "service." Such language struck her as intolerably "God-squaddy." Still, subconsciously, that is just what she was looking for. She flipped through a directory of volunteer programs, "and in there was a list of Camphills. Just running my finger through . . . as soon as I saw the name I knew I would go there. . . . I did not want to go on those sorts of things, so I decided I would . . . make all my applications elsewhere. And then I realized, well, just a minute, that means I am counting it doesn't it?" During a visit to a Camphill in England, she was advised to apply to Copake in New York, and soon she found herself, with her "city" clothes and "punky" hair, in a bucolic village in rural New York. "I woke up and I had no idea where I was. And this huge house and the smell was so different. It was really, really odd, and they seemed like the strangest people. And I knew I had come home."

For most of the people just described, the accidental character of this "coming home" to community only reinforces the sense of spiritual calling. Carla Dawson was homeless when she came to the Catholic Worker; she stayed on to become the backbone of a thriving community. "When you live with the Worker," she says, "I think it's more present in your life that things happen for a reason. . . . you can feel it more when you live in a community." Similarly, the founder of Catherine of Genoa Catholic Worker wrote that "God sometimes seems to write straight with crooked lines. Though I had never planned on being involved in such an effort, for me the founding of this particular Catholic Worker House was one of the clearer points of intersection between God's will and my own life." By creating the spaces for just such intersections in the lives of their members, intentional communities are empowered to touch both those individuals and everyone who is in turn touched by them.[5]

Finding Vocation in Community

For a few of those who hear the communal call, the initial feeling of coming home never wears off. For most, passing through the gates of a community is only one step in an ongoing journey. They must still struggle to find the work best suited to them. At this point, the community faces a significant test. Will it simply plug the new member into whatever activity is most needed? Or will it become a companion in the individual's journey, opening itself to the possibility that the new person is "called" to bring something new and perhaps challenging into the community? At their best, Catholic Worker and Camphill communities have made the second choice, creating patterns of shared life that encourage members to continue listening for their vocation after their arrival in community.

Camphill, for example, encourages members to perform both mental and physical labor in a variety of socially stimulating contexts; as Ben Cownap pointed out, "in Camphill we're great at having three or four vocations all at the same time." The workday is divided into morning and afternoon shifts, so that one might be a kitchen helper in the morning and the chief of a candle-making crew in the afternoon. Members with a sense of vocation to gardening or baking or office work are encouraged to develop those skills, but also to try things for which they have less aptitude. Hartmut von Jeetze, whose training was in biodynamic agriculture, found that in some ways he was more effective as head of the woodworking shop, because "I was less biased as to what handicapped people face when they learn to do this work. . . . If you have learned it too well you are actually handicapped yourself." The disabled villagers also have many opportunities to identify certain tasks as their vocation. "A few of the guys," noted Ian Robb of the Camphill Copake farm, "have been milking cows for thirty years. It's a real vocation. Everyone identifies, I'm a farmer. . . . These are my cows."[6] Such flexibility is possible because the real "work" for which the villages are paid is not weaving or woodcarving, but simply caring for the villagers, who receive government benefits or financial support from their parents. This fact allows Camphill to make few compromises in its approach to work, although it somewhat limits the applicability of the Camphill model as an alternative to the industrial labor system.

For Lois Smith, Camphill provided the context for a vocational quest that lasted for years. When she first came to Camphill Copake in her mid-twenties, she had just turned down a scholarship to study landscape design. "People who know me at this end of my career," she recalls with laughter, "would probably have no concept that that could ever be on my mind." Experiences at two Camphills persuaded her that she wanted to explore the use of music as a therapeutic tool, and the Camphill network made it easy for her to pursue this quest: she traveled from place to place in Europe, visiting both

Camphills and other anthroposophical institutions for curative education, always observing how music was used in each place. This was a "seed" that allowed her to connect back to the time when, as a Jewish college student, her heart had been opened by the beauties of Christian choral music. After a stint at Camphill Beaver Run, Lois settled at Camphill Village Minnesota, where she took on both the formal role of master weaver and the more informal vocation of coordinating music for the community. The community welcomed her musical gifts and even enabled her to complete an interdisciplinary master's degree in music and therapy, and in turn Lois provides new choral pieces for almost every festival and major event in the village's history.

Since Catholic Workers are usually urban households rather than self-sustaining villages, they do not offer the same range of employments as Camphill communities. But they achieve the goal of diverse employments by other means. Many Workers divide their time between hospitality to the homeless and resistance to unjust political structures, tasks that draw on different skill sets. Others use part-time employment to cultivate their vocations as nurses, priests, or teachers. Since individual Catholic Worker communities vary widely in structure, location, and mission, the network itself allows individuals to relocate in pursuit of a vocational fit. Someone interested in agriculture might join a Catholic Worker farm; someone with a vocation in health care might start a Catholic Worker clinic or hospice.

For the young activists who are often drawn to Catholic Worker houses, the practice of hospitality provides a focal point for vocational discernment. My former student Mike Sersch, for example, reflects that "I came to the Worker as an activist learning how to do hospitality," and soon found that he had much to learn from the alcoholics, Vietnam War veterans, and other homeless people who had "been around the block so many times." "They tend to humble the college activist that comes in and 'knows' how the world is supposed to work," Mike acknowledges, adding that, "I like that." Similarly, Joel Kilgour recalls that he came to the Loaves and Fishes Catholic Worker in Duluth as "a seventeen-year-old hyper-activist who probably liked a little bit to be in the limelight and was pretty angry and cynical." The practice of hospitality helped him to root his activism more positively in the Gospels as he learned new skills. Though he does not feel as talented in talking to new guests as others in the community, Joel says that "I show my love by cooking good food and keeping the house clean and helping people find services in the community."

Even the Catholic Worker practice of going to prison for civil disobedience provides fruitful opportunities for vocational growth. "Sometimes you hear people say," veteran Worker Tom Lumpkin told oral historian Rosalie Riegle Troester, "'Well, why would you ever want to go to jail, because you'd be so much more effective outside, working and stuff!' I think that's questionable. Maybe it has to be decided by each individual at certain times in their life, but there's certainly all sorts of opportunities to minister in jail."[7] Some Workers use the time to write; in the age of email, prison reflections have become one of the most widely distributed genres of Catholic Worker literature. Some hone their techniques of creative nonviolence. Joel Kilgour, for example, once spent seven hours refusing what he regarded as the dehumanizing strip search that was a precondition of his release from jail. Then, while waiting in his cell, he spontaneously stripped naked and explained to the startled guard that "the only power he has over people is the power that they choose to give him." Still others organize movements for inmate rights, or simply share their own gifts with their companions in bondage. One creative Worker even procured a grant to buy banjos and teach lessons while at Leavenworth. "[That] is just an image that has kept me laughing for weeks," mused Mike Sersch, who told me the story. "I just imagine all these guys wearing blaze orange and playing banjo. Picking and grinning."

Camphill and Catholic Worker communities have thus helped many individuals find their life's work, and these individuals have in turn touched the world through their labors both inside and outside the community. More generally, both movements have also touched the world by holding up a holistic, balanced understanding of vocation in an epoch when both professional and working-class people are often forced into narrow, mechanistic career tracks. Simply by calling their work "hospitality," rather than "social service," Catholic Workers challenge the professionalization of care for the poor. Hospitality takes place in one's home, rather than in a professional institution; it requires no special training; and it insists on treating the "guest" as a whole person rather than a collection of symptoms.[8]

Camphillers likewise spend little time thinking about the diagnoses of the people with whom they live. Many of them have completed the "seminar" training offered at certain Camphills, but this model of training is far more holistic (with a strong emphasis on the study of biographies and the arts) than that of conventional social work. There is a semiprofessional tendency in some larger Camphills to separate out the roles of "workshop leader" and "houseparent," but also a strong desire to preserve the spirit of the early days, when "everyone still did everything."[9] Camphillers rarely use the language of "hospitality," primarily because the disabled villagers are as much "at home" in Camphill as the coworkers with whom they live—indeed, the most senior members of many Camphills are villagers. But the ideal of "lifesharing" functions for them in the same way as "hospitality" does for Catholic Workers. For Camphillers, vocation is a way of life, not a career track.

Camphill and the Catholic Worker make perhaps their greatest contribution to a renewed understanding of vocation through their attention to the vocations of homeless "guests" and disabled "villagers." For the most part, the larger society treats these persons either as helpless recipients of social services or as unskilled performers of menial labor. Indeed, many programs seek only to move them from the former to the latter role. The "problem" of homelessness or disability can be solved by providing individuals with low-wage jobs, ordinarily in the service economy, that allow them to live "independently" in apartments or group homes. This approach fails to acknowledge the real gifts that every individual is called to share with the world. Few persons with Down syndrome, for example, have a true gift for mopping the floors of fast-food restaurants, while a great many are profoundly gifted in the arts of friendship, affection, and living in the present. Camphill provides them with the chance to share those gifts, and thus lifts up a model of vocation centered in sharing rather than independence.

In addition to promoting the idea of vocation in general, both movements have touched the world by lifting up two vocations that are rarely honored in the larger society: farming and the "woman's work" performed in the household. This has not occurred without struggle. Many people inside as well as outside the Catholic Worker movement take it for granted that Peter Maurin's vision of the "agronomic university" was a complete failure, and it is true that few if any Catholic Worker farms have been the sort of self-sustaining, medieval-style villages that Maurin had in mind. Camphills come closer to that ideal, but they rarely make significant income through farming. The ideal that caring for people goes hand in hand with caring for the land is difficult to put into practice, as many serious farmers find their work to be all-absorbing. A few communities have even suffered painful schisms because they could not agree on the true character of that balance.

Still, many of the most powerful stories of vocation come from those who feel called to care for the land. One Camphill farmer, for example, recalled that as a Peace Corps volunteer, she was expected to teach local people things she scarcely understood herself: "I was supposed to be teaching agriforestry and soil conservation, and I didn't have any experience. . . . When I left there I wanted to . . . find out the things that I wish I would have known when I was there." Her quest eventually took her to Camphill, where she feels able to attend to the complex dynamics of one piece of land. "My commitment is to the land," she reflects, and Camphill allows her to "really get to know a place very, very, very well. You do things and you very clearly pay for your mistakes, and you learn."

When I visited Catholic Workers in Worcester, Massachusetts, local movement historian Mike Boover described a local Worker who maintains both a rural "retreat outpost" and an unofficial house of hospitality for a few homeless men near the Mustard Seed Catholic Worker. With his guests, he cultivates a large urban garden on a vacant lot once occupied by a crack house. "He's a great farmer," says Mike. "He knows what he's doing. It's perhaps the best urban garden in all of Worcester. And he cans—the guys can a ton of stuff. . . . Year round. It's pretty remarkable. Again, the whole thing unspoken. Nothing spoken. Except for me. Loud mouth that I am."

Like agriculture, household labors have been both a source of idealism and division within Camphill and Catholic Worker communities. Both movements can be understood as feminist insofar as they challenge the conventional gender division of labor, but in each case the approach contrasts sharply with that of mainstream liberal feminism, which has sought to give women greater access to the "men's sphere" of paid, professional employment. The communities, by contrast, seek to enhance the social valuation of "women's" work in the household, sometimes (though not always) also encouraging men to share more fully in that labor.

At Camphill, housekeeping is a prized vocation, with substantial work shifts devoted both to the preparation of meals and to cleaning. Though these shifts are usually carried by women, they are at least free from the double burdens of mainstream women who work full-time jobs but receive little household help from their husbands. Camphill's concern for homemaking can be traced back to its founding: it was the women who first created a community at the Camphill estate, while Karl König and the other men were interned as potentially dangerous German nationals. "The men," recalled Anke Weihs, "had been able to devote themselves in a unique way to spiritual research in the camp, [while] we had been stoking boilers, washing laundry, tending children and working the garden." The "stormy wedding feast" that followed the men's return convinced everyone that a "balance between the archetypal masculine and feminine elements is fundamental to the well-being of any community."[10]

Though Camphill continues to balance its "masculine" and "feminine" elements, it often distinguishes them in a way few feminists could approve. Camphill Minnesota, for example, once hosted a professional-style conference on homemaking, with workshops on everything from the latest microfiber washcloths, to the significance of personality types for homemaking, to ways of working constructively with the spiritual beings that inhabit dirty toilets and dusty corners. But the socially transformative potential of this gathering may have been limited by the fact that no Camphill men chose to attend. (I was present for about half of the conference, though my primary role was to cook meals for the participants!) At Camphill Kimberton Hills, Ben Cownap told me that while he and his spouse have divided housework equally, other Camphill women resent having to carry the "drudge work" of the household while their partners enjoy more varied work shifts. Homemaking is a true vocation within Camphill, but the movement could do more to help all its members hear the call.

Homemaking responsibilities are genuinely shared within the Catholic Worker movement, although they are not always performed with the consciousness and intentionality found in Camphill. In some Worker houses, especially those whose culture has been shaped primarily by single men, there is almost an aesthetic of slovenly housecleaning and bad soup. Increasingly, though, a new generation of family-centered houses offers a powerful alternative to a society driven by fast food and expanding workweeks. Peter Maurin Farm in Marlboro, New York, and SS. Francis and Thérèse Catholic Worker in Worcester, Massachusetts, are patient but persistent in introducing homeless guests to organic vegetarian cooking, while St. Martin de Porres in Hartford keeps a huge basket of fresh fruit for neighborhood children, and sponsors a food-buying club that provides fresh organic vegetables during the summer months and other items year round. Such simple practices are important first steps toward making the cultivation of home a freely chosen vocation rather than a burden arbitrarily imposed on just one gender.

Vocations in and out of Community

For some community members, the vocational quest leads ever deeper into the life of a particular community. Lois Smith's identity as a musician and weaver, for example, helps to cement her connection to Camphill Minnesota. For others, perhaps for most, the path of vocation leads through the community and out into a new role within the larger society. The ethos of vocation is thus a risky one for a community that values its own survival more than the larger social good. Communities that wish to touch the world, by contrast, must develop patterns of life that honor and empower short-term members as well as those who choose a lifelong commitment to community.

The first step in honoring short-term volunteers is making sure they are financially able to leave the community. Thus, neither movement expects new members to surrender their savings. But this is helpful only to the minority who have savings. Since Camphillers and Catholic Workers do not pay into Social Security or retirement accounts, there is a danger that some will remain in community out of economic necessity rather than a genuine calling. The Camphill Association of North America has begun to address this challenge by creating a retirement account that will benefit even those coworkers who choose to leave Camphill. The Catholic Worker, for its part, often encourages volunteers to hold part-time jobs outside the community that can ease the transition to life outside. Though departing Catholic Workers may find themselves in precarious circumstances, life in the movement is equally precarious, and thus there is little economic pressure to remain.

Making it economically feasible for community members to leave is just the first step in empowering them to go wherever their vocation takes them. An equally important practice is that of lifting up viable models of short-term commitment. Individuals must feel they are valuable contributors to the community, regardless of whether their commitment is for a year or a lifetime. They must be incorporated into decision-making in a way that, on the one hand, honors their idealism and fresh perspectives, and on the other hand, recognizes that the long-term members will have to live with any drastic changes in community structures.

Camphill has approached these challenges by maintaining a distinct category of membership for those who plan to stay only for six months or a year. Within North America, these "young coworkers" are typically Europeans who are performing alternative military service or taking a year off between high school and university. Some come with a strong interest in agriculture or disability issues; others have a Waldorf education or personal connections to the Camphill movement; still others are motivated simply by a desire to see the world or avoid the army. Camphill fosters their vocational explorations by offering a diversity of experiences, placing them under the mentorship of experienced houseparents, and offering introductory workshops on anthroposophy and developmental disabilities. As changing immigration laws make it more difficult for Europeans (and, much more so, those from the developing world) to gain visas, Camphill has adapted the young coworker model to include Americorps volunteers.

Some Catholic Worker houses have evolved similar structures for welcoming young people. Catherine of Genoa Catholic Worker in Chicago had a link with Action Reconciliation Service for Peace, a German organization that placed volunteers in countries that had opposed Germany during World War II. These volunteers, whose backgrounds were very similar to those of Camphill's young coworkers, typically stayed for a year and a half. Anathoth Community Farm has a formal internship program that attracts college students and recent graduates with an interest in peace organizing or environmental sustainability. Many Catholic Worker houses have been willing to accept Americorps volunteers, even though this is a partial compromise of their traditional resistance to government support. Others have found that they attract a steady stream of young activists and drifters, even without a formal strategy for recruitment.

The young coworker model offers both gifts and challenges. On the one hand, it allows an enormous number of people to gain a taste of community life, empowering them to bring little bits of Camphill and the Catholic Worker into the larger society. At the same time, the resulting turnover can be daunting. Old-timers may have been jaded by bad experiences with unmotivated newcomers, and have low expectations of all newcomers. Or they may pine for the old days when more of the newcomers were willing to make a lifelong commitment. But all would do well to heed Catholic Worker Stanley Vishnewski's observation that it is very difficult to predict which newcomers will stay long term. "Some come," he said, "saying they have found their life work, and remain a few months (or days). Others, more tentative, speak of a visit, and stay."[11]

One does not have to look far within these movements to find people for whom as little as a year of service has had a lifetime of consequences. Sara Thomsen and Paula Williams, partners at the time, spent just a year at the Loaves and Fishes Catholic Worker in Duluth. "The process of the year," explained Sara, "was really helpful in realizing . . . that we have gifts of . . . trying to renew people's spirits who are doing the in-the-trenches work." At first they felt guilty that they were exhausted rather than energized by the tasks of offering hospitality and building community with other Workers. As they watched community mates go to jail or prison for civil disobedience, they were tempted to think that "if you can't be in the trenches you're not as worthy." Gradually, though, Sara recognized "that there's just so many facets to the whole resistance and activism. . . . We grew stronger in believing that and coming to realize what our gifts were. . . . I realized that I really wanted to be doing more music related work. And . . . I just didn't have enough time living in community." At the same time, after a year of interacting with the wider community of peace and justice activists in Duluth, "we knew we had found our people." Today, Paula raises flowers on a farm outside Duluth, while Sara performs regularly at Catholic Worker demonstrations.

It is relatively easy for a community to affirm the subsequent vocational paths of people who never contemplated a long-term commitment. A more challenging practice is to affirm the unfolding vocations of those whose longer stays have made them bulwarks of the community. For those who are left behind, the departure of a valued companion may feel like a repudiation of the community's ideals or a thoughtless burdening of others with the community's work. Often, though, it is the growth made possible by community that compels an individual to leave. When I asked Donna Howard why she left Loaves and Fishes Catholic Worker, for example, she began by emphasizing that she never felt that things were not working or that she no longer belonged.

Rather, Donna explained, her participation in Catholic Worker activism planted in her "a very abrupt and shocking awareness" that she needed to participate in more radical forms of civil disobedience. "I was born right after that first use of nuclear weapons and all my life I've grieved about it. . . . I have never known what to do about the anguish." As a Catholic Worker, Donna was arrested about ten times for trespassing at the Extremely Low Frequency (ELF) nuclear facility in Wisconsin. But she sensed that sabotage would have more impact. "In an electronic moment the thought went from my brain to the middle of my belly and I thought I was going to throw up because I realized it was me who needed to do that. . . . So I came back and said, guess what, friends and family, I guess I have to do a Plowshares disarmament action at ELF."

Donna's decision left her community feeling that "there's more work for everybody else to split up. How are we going to . . . keep that house open?" She herself had had similar feelings just a few years earlier, when another community member had chosen to participate in major civil disobedience. At the time, she had responded skeptically to his suggestion that the community simply needed faith, but with the tables turned, she had a new perspective. "It's about having faith, an active faith . . . that compels you to move forward anyway, and to find solutions. To be creative and to honor someone's work if it's right, whether you're affected by it or not. . . . It takes a lot of maturity and personal strength to keep a right relationship when those [new life] chapters are popping up for one another. That's part of what we're called to do in community."

As things turned out, Donna's community accepted her decision with grace, perhaps expecting that she would return after her prison sentence. But the logic of vocation kept pushing her forward. While in prison, she realized that "we not only have to take these weapons apart with our hands and with our tools and with our votes and with everything we have available, but we have to build something that will replace the need for them." That something was the Nonviolent Peaceforce, a new organization that planned to intervene nonviolently in conflict situations. (Currently, a team is helping maintain a fragile ceasefire in Sri Lanka.) She moved back to Duluth with a firm resolve to devote her primary energies to the Peaceforce. "I was carrying this precious commitment," she recalled, that made a full-time presence at the Worker impossible. Instead, she chose to help the community by nurturing the evolving vocations of its members. "I was so deeply grateful for the support that I received. I think if we receive it from one another that's how we learn to give it. Members of this community come to me every once in a while when things are pretty rough, and we go for a walk. And we walk and talk. . . . We all try to grow together."

I heard a similar story about Deb and Ron Admiral, two long-term leaders at Camphill Copake. Unlike most Camphillers, Ron had considerable administrative gifts, combined with the ability to bridge the gap between Camphillers and the outside employees who work in Copake's administrative and development offices. "He was very gifted in that, in a brotherly way," explained fellow Camphiller Regula Stolz. "He was no dictator at all. He was a very warm, warm person." But after many years in Camphill, Ron and Deb felt called "to give a contribution outside Camphill . . . out of what they have been building up in themselves during their Camphill time. They wanted to carry that elsewhere into the world." So they moved to Washington State, taking positions in nonprofit organizations where they could share their Camphill experiences with a broader community. "That made a big difference in the village, when they left," recalled Stolz. "But we always manage to . . . fill in again."

Unfortunately, it is not always the case that Camphill and Catholic Worker communities can easily "fill in again." Many suffer greatly from what can be called the "revolving door" phenomenon. It is not unheard of for the entire membership of a Catholic Worker house to turn over in a single year, leaving the newcomers with little sense of tradition or connection to the movement as a whole. Even the "motherhouse" in New York City has had moments when virtually everyone had been there less than two years.[12] Other communities, including Camphill Village Minnesota, suffer less from turnover than from a steady decline in membership. This can make it hard to celebrate the new life directions of longtime coworkers with skills that are hard to replace. One Camphiller told me of a time when her community wrestled for months before accepting the departure of a valued farmer. "It really was a wrenching kind of thing where people didn't feel so free to say, openly, go ahead." Such attitudes can be self-defeating. "If there's a feeling . . . of holding on to everybody you've got in desperation," the same person added, "that's not going to be very attractive to people either."

The healthiest communities are those that can celebrate even when their own stability is threatened by changing vocations. "It can be a wonderful thing when people leave intentional community . . . and want to go off and do their own thing," insisted Helen Zipperlen of Camphill Kimberton Hills. "When people used to come to me and say, 'I've absolutely had it! I'm going to leave,' I said 'I'm not interested. . . . I'm interested in where you're going and what you're going to do. Sit down and tell me about it.'"

The Extended Community

At times, the path of vocation leads neither into nor out of community, but instead meanders along its boundaries. A person may feel "called" to participate actively in the life of a community, but not to live in it. Another may wish to live in community, but maintain ties to an outside vocation through part- or even full-time employment. Still others seek to maintain the social and emotional ties they forged in community after they have moved out. Such practices lower the boundaries that distinguish the community from society as a whole. As a result, they can force communities to question their complacent sense of superiority to "the world" and to face the risk that they might simply dissolve into that larger society. Such risks are well worth it, however, for practices of "extended community" are among the most powerful tools communities have for touching the world.

There are as many models of extended community as there are Catholic Workers and Camphills. Some extended community members are simply friendly neighbors who share in community activities. The Maple Hill Farm community early on made a connection to a nearby family that was caring for both a developmentally disabled aunt and an elderly grandmother. It was a natural thing for Maple Hill to incorporate the aunt into their Special Olympics team, and on one occasion, they even welcomed both the aunt and the grandmother into their own household for four months while the father of the family received treatment for a brain tumor. During my visit to Community Homestead in Wisconsin, similarly, I heard stories about Oskar, the old farmer who had once owned the community's farm and still lived on the property. Shortly after the community's founding, Oskar quietly began to participate in gardening projects. He is so old that he can barely walk, one community member told me, but in the summer he is out on his tractor for ten hours a day, making his contribution to the community's well-being.

Another model is the "satellite household" consisting of former community members or ideological fellow travelers. When Harry Murray conducted his sociological study of the New York Worker in the 1980s, he identified about half a dozen Workers who had moved from the house of hospitality into individual or shared apartments, some of them actually rented by the Worker itself. Other people, identified by Murray as "friends of the house," had such longstanding relationships with the community that it was hard to discern if they had ever actually lived there.[13] Similarly, when John and Kathe McKenna, founders of Boston's Haley House, returned to Boston after a few years away, they purchased a small apartment building across the street from Haley House, making the extra apartments available to friends of the house or Workers who needed a break from the intensity of community life.

Camphills generally find it difficult to sustain satellite households because their community life is more self-contained. After spending two years at Camphill Village Minnesota, for example, Mark Steinrueck bought a nearby farm with his wife Johanna. At the time, Mark was running a bakery in Minneapolis, and his hope was to be connected to the village but still have the freedom to try new things. For a time, they "were almost like an extended part of the community." But the sense of connection waned. "You can live right next door, but if you're outside you could be a million miles away," laments Mark. "It seems the moment you leave, it's like you died." Mark has since settled at Community Homestead in Wisconsin, a community that has had more success in maintaining satellite households for families that are discerning whether to become permanent members of the community. Camphill Minnesota, meanwhile, purchased a house directly adjoining its land, and this has served as a transitional space for families moving out of the community.

A few communities have had the good fortune to attract nationally known scholars and artists into their extended community. The New York Catholic Worker's roster of friends includes child psychologist Robert Coles, Jewish liberation theologian Marc Ellis, and Quaker artist Fritz Eichenberg. Dorothy Day befriended Joan Baez through their shared support of the United Farm Workers and, by Day's report, Baez maintained a Christ room for "an old ex-prisoner" in her Bay area home.[14] Camphill Copake has maintained ties with classical musicians Andre Watts and Richard Goode, as well as with Pete Seeger, a neighbor in the Hudson River Valley.

Other communities or activist organizations can also function as part of the extended community. Camphill founder Karl König maintained a longstanding friendship with Dr. George MacLeod, the Church of Scotland minister who established an ecumenical lay community at the ancient monastery of Iona.[15] Camphills typically have strong partnerships with local Waldorf schools, biodynamic farms, and other anthroposophical initiatives. Catholic Workers are often connected to so-called "resistance communities," which are usually nonresidential associations of people committed to civil disobedience directed against militarism. A resistance community in Boston met regularly at Haley House through the 1980s, while the Atlantic Life Community hosts an annual gathering for Catholic Workers and others from throughout the East Coast. Catholic Workers also work in partnership with the many Catholic religious orders that have articulated strong peace and justice commitments. The Duluth Workers, for example, often worship at the McCabe Renewal Center, the social justice ministry of the local Benedictine community of Saint Scholastica.

By far the most numerous groups of extended community members are the regular volunteers and financial supporters—church groups who commit to cooking a meal once a week at their local Catholic Worker house and local professionals who serve on Camphill boards of directors. Some community founders even credit such people with "giving birth" to the community. Just as Gladys and Bill Hahn prepared the way for Camphill Copake and Beaver Run, so a retired schoolteacher named Helen Tichy encouraged Frank Cordaro when he launched the Des Moines Catholic Worker. "I've been reading the *Catholic Worker* since the 1940s," she told Frank, "and I never ever thought I'd see a Catholic Worker in Des Moines." Though Helen never moved into the Worker house, she has been among its most faithful supporters for twenty-five years, attending its weekly Masses into her nineties.

Less obvious cohorts are the employees who work for intentional communities without being fully integrated into the community's residential life. Though the practice of hiring outside can create tensions with community ideals of economic sharing, North American Camphills have long depended on employees to bring administrative, fund-raising, or secretarial skills that supplement the interpersonal or artistic talents of the coworkers. Since these employees are more likely than the Camphillers to have local roots, they link the community to its neighbors, often bringing their family and friends to open days or other public events. At times, Camphill employees embrace aspects of the community spirit: one longtime secretary at Camphill Minnesota went on to create a family-style retirement community. More recently, such communities as Camphill Beaver Run and the Lukas Community have relied on paid staff as teachers and workshop leaders, in some cases allowing long-term coworkers to move out of the community while continuing to work there.

A final variation on the theme of the extended community is the practice of allowing residential community members to hold part- or full-time jobs outside the community. Probably the majority of Catholic Workers maintain some employment, whether to purchase cigarettes, health insurance, or piano lessons for their children. These Workers take to heart Dorothy Day's admonition that donations to the Worker are intended for the poor, and should not pay for more than the basic necessities of life. But employment also allows them to pursue vocational goals or develop friendships with non-Workers. One early model for this style of Catholic Worker vocation was Jacques Travers, whose career as a college professor allowed him to sustain a Brooklyn house of hospitality for several decades.

Outside employment is less common for Camphillers, but residents of Community Homestead cherish their practice of allowing members to maintain careers outside the community. "I think everybody needs their own individuality," Sheila Russell explained to me. "Those that feel they want to and need to keep [working in a] particular field" are supported at Community Homestead "because that's part of them." "There's a horrible picture that's out there," added Richard Elmquist, "that belonging to community is a real sacrifice, and one's got to live a life of poverty and . . . giving it all over. I think that's to a certain extent true, but that can be a really scary thing. And especially if you're either in or you're out." Communities that require a 100 percent commitment, Richard suggested, prevent many people from becoming involved at all. By allowing individuals to be part in and part out, Community Homestead "provides an opportunity for people to grow into it. To really find out what it's like. Or also to grow out of it."

Extended community, in any of these forms, contributes greatly to the maintenance of community life and even more to a community's capacity to touch the larger world. At the most basic level, extended community members perform much of the daily work of the community. At Baltimore's Viva House Catholic Worker, the live-in community members have developed a well-oiled system for coordinating up to a dozen daily volunteers who help them serve lunch, restaurant style, to two hundred hungry people. "An example [is] today's meal," Brendan Walsh told me during my visit. "We're going to serve fish cakes, salad, potatoes, and fruit. And we put that together. But a number of people made sandwiches that we're going to be giving out so that people can take them home with them." Brendan mentioned seven groups that had made sandwiches, in addition to the volunteers who came to help serve the meal, and concluded, "That's just today. We're a little light on workers today, mainly because school's out."

Most Camphills lack such elaborate systems for bringing volunteers into the community. But ever since the 1970s, the family and friends of one Copake villager have come to the community for biannual "work weekends," during which they complete major projects that might otherwise be neglected. The Camphillers of Minnesota look forward each spring to the visit of a villager's father who comes with a large truck full of sand to repair the village's potholed dirt roads. Other extended community members offer villagers part-time jobs that allow them to develop skills and experience life outside the village. One villager has a regular gig doing laundry for a former community member living in a nearby town, while another is responsible for sweeping the local police station.

Extended community members do more than provide free labor and material support, however. In many cases, they are an integral part of the emotional and cultural life of the community. The Loaves and Fishes Catholic Worker is close to at least half a dozen couples or individuals who previously lived in the community and continue to live within easy walking distance. These folks maintain a friendship network that is as evident at a community folk dance as a downtown peace vigil. And about five years ago at Camphill Village Minnesota, short-term volunteers from Europe encountered some neighbors speaking German at the local cooperative grocery. They turned out to be the high school German teacher and her German-born husband, people who likely would have felt rather isolated in economically depressed rural Minnesota. Since then, Jürgen and Lu have visited Camphill almost weekly to play folk music and socialize.

Sociologist Harry Murray observed that extended community members of the Catholic Worker built stronger friendships with individual "guests" than the live-in community members, who had to relate in a balanced way with all the people who come for food or shelter. Extended community members have their own houses, to which they can invite their new friends, and access to social circles that are often inaccessible to persons experiencing homelessness. They also lack the direct power over the guests that can inhibit friendships. As a result, Murray notes, "the deepest, longest Worker-guest friendship I know of has been between a part-time volunteer and a guest."[16]

In addition to building friendships, extended community members have filled leadership roles in some communities. A significant number of Catholic Worker houses have been founded by extended community members who provide long-term leadership and continuity, while live-in volunteers stay only six months or a year. That has been the case from time to time in New York City, and it is also the pattern in Winona, Minnesota, where cofounder Jim Allaire has served on the community's core decision-making team and also maintains an astonishingly comprehensive Catholic Worker Web site. The same model has proved successful at Place of Grace in La Crosse, Wisconsin, where the founding families have been able to sustain a vibrant sense of community in part because they came into the project with well-established friendships and a capacity to spend a large portion of their waking hours at the house.

In other cases, reliance on extended community has not worked well. The original houses in both Saint Louis and Milwaukee closed in part because their founders could not find young men to live there after the beginning of World War II. "Our chief problem," one Saint Louis founder wrote to Dorothy Day, "is that there is none of us except Bill Camp who sleeps, eats and breathes Catholic Worker day and night."[17] Similarly, the European Camphills that allow workshop leaders to live outside sometimes experience friction. "They would just come in for the workshop part," said Nicola Hobson, who experienced this model before coming to the United States. "But then still behave as if they were living inside. They came, and before it even started they would have a cup of coffee and just chat. So they would have a community life without actually committing to the whole thing."

Such reservations demand to be taken seriously. Still, the *ideal* of the extended community as a meeting ground between community and society—however this manifests itself in practice—is now well established in both the Camphill and Catholic Worker movements. The fortieth anniversary commemorative volume of Camphill Copake, for example, proclaims, "Our future depends on how we meet the world around us. For too long we felt separate, and much has changed. Partnership has replaced isolation. . . . Those Camphill places that succeed in joining their work with the work of others around them are the healthiest and most alive."[18]

The most profound gift of the extended community is not what it does for the community, but the way it offers a bridge between the ideals of the community and the realities of the larger society. At the Des Moines Catholic Worker, Ted Walker told me that the community has made a special effort to encourage occasional volunteers to bring their professional skills to the house. A nurse comes to do checkups for the guests, and a haircutter schedules appointments at the house every other week. And once a month the house hosts a "Scribes and Pharisees" Mass for local lawyers. By introducing lawyers to homeless people, Ted explained, the community seeks to break down stereotypes on both sides. "The neat thing . . . is that the lawyers come, most of them are prosecutors, and the only time most of these people would see these lawyers is when they're trying to get them. It's very important for the lawyers to be seen as someone to help them . . . [and] not just [as] horrible person[s] wrapped up in their job[s]." Ted also mentioned that his own supervisor at UPS had begun volunteering. "He thinks this place is great. . . . You definitely get the different perspectives." One Worker slips him articles about unions and the exploitation of labor, while he could hardly miss the antiwar posters that are everywhere in the house. "I think it takes a while for someone to understand all the different connections that go on within this house and this community."

Practices of extended community also help intentional communities connect to the more organic patterns of community that already exist in their neighborhoods. From the beginning, Catholic Worker hospitality drew much of its inspiration from the traditional practices of Italian and Hispanic immigrant families in New York City. "I understood [Peter Maurin's concept of hospitality] well," Dorothy Day explained, "because I had lived so long on the Lower East Side of New York—and the poor are noted for their hospitality. 'There is always enough for one more,' my brother's Spanish mother-in-law used to say. 'Everyone just takes a little less.' Poor families were always taking in other needy ones."[19] Similarly, when Brendan Walsh and Willa Bickham started Viva House in a changing neighborhood in Baltimore, they quickly discovered that their neighbors were already doing hospitality—raising six children but also opening their home to boarders and other folks in need. Friendship with this family helped them provide a child-centered environment for their daughter Kate, an only child.

The "bridge" of extended community is also evident in the work of those who maintain ties after years at Camphill or the Catholic Worker. After Kristin Wilson left Camphill Village Minnesota, she became a staff person for a local farmers' cooperative. But personal friendship kept her close to the village, and when Camphill built a new processing kitchen she arranged for it to be used by the cooperative farmers. Today the Camphillers work hard in packaging organic vegetables and other farm products from many of their neighbors.

The transition from full-time Catholic Workers to extended community also proved fruitful for Steve O'Neil and Angie Miller five years after they had founded Loaves and Fishes Catholic Worker. Their departure allowed Angie to pursue a lifelong calling to be a foster parent, something not possible in the chaotic environment of a Catholic Worker house of hospitality. At the same time, it was a struggle for them to leave a community to which they had given so much of themselves. They buffered the transition by moving just a few blocks away. For about a year Steve volunteered at the house about twenty-five hours a week, Angie handled community finances, and they hosted the weekly community meeting in their large living room. But they found that they could not sustain this level of involvement without living at the house. Angie got more involved with foster care and Steve with a transitional housing program, while both of them felt less emotionally connected as the people with whom they had lived also moved out into the surrounding neighborhood. Occasional misunderstandings persuaded them that it was unfair for them to carry the same weight in decision-making as live-in community members. The gradual pace of these changes, however, allowed Angie and Steve to listen closely to their own needs and desires as well as those of the community. Still part of a neighborhood community of current and former Catholic Workers, they remain open to the possibility of recommitting to Loaves and Fishes later on.

Through extended community, both Camphill and the Catholic Worker are building broad movements of people committed to a new vision of society. For Catholic Workers, this often means taking "charitable" volunteers and introducing them to the radical work of "resistance." The charitable work we do—the Christmas party or taking in homeless folks—that's popular work," explained Chris Allen-Doucot of Saint Martin de Porres Catholic Worker. "A lot of the folks that have become part of our extended community, we initially have met through the charitable work. And now they'll join us at vigils and demonstrations. They'll get me invitations into their church or into their different groups to make presentations about the war against Iraq. They'll lobby their congressperson and write letters and things like that."

Camphillers are reluctant to suggest that they know what is best for society as a whole, but they can still see ways in which their extended community contributes to Karl König's vision of "social renewal." At Maple Hill Farm, a single-household community modeled on Camphill, Dietmar Emmert makes sure that the disabled villagers participate in community cleanup days: "We like to help and be present to the town. What it means for other people to see Eric make his very best effort to carry that brush together and put it on the pile. We sort of reintegrate, make [our neighbors] aware of these people again, but not only as a burden. . . . You can just see these seeds . . . beginning to take root in some way." Extended community can thus be seen as a form of social homeopathy, using very small actions to effect fundamental changes in the ecology of society. By "extending" their communities to touch their neighbors, Camphill and the Catholic Worker ultimately touch all of society.

Identifying with the Community

All the practices I have described in this chapter make it easier for people to combine community life with a strong sense of individual vocation. They can also make it difficult to articulate one's relationship to the community itself. If each movement is flexible enough to include people who live "inside" and work "outside," people who live outside and work inside, people who stay for a month and people who stay for a lifetime, who is truly entitled to call him- or herself a Camphiller or a Catholic Worker? Even the formal definitions that exist within some of these communities do little to clarify who exactly is "in" or "out." Long-term Camphill coworkers are encouraged to join the inner "Camphill Community." But its members do not carry any extra authority in the day-to-day decision-making, and in some cases do not live at Camphill at all. The definition of a "Catholic Worker" is even fuzzier, as Dorothy Day herself testified: "On the one hand, there are the editors, who are called 'Catholic Workers.' On the other hand, there are *The Catholic Worker* readers. . . . When our readers agree with us, they are Catholic Workers. When they disagree, they are readers of *The Catholic Worker*. It is a fluid situation."[20]

During my community visits, I was repeatedly surprised by the reluctance of my interviewees to label themselves. "When you first asked me if we could talk," Tom Heuser said forthrightly, "I thought, I hope [to] God he doesn't ask me if I consider myself a Catholic Worker. Because I don't know." Tom went on to say that he doesn't consider himself a Catholic Worker in the narrow sense because he is no longer closely affiliated with a specific house. But "in a broader sense . . . the Catholic Worker has never left me. I'm . . . extremely grateful for that, and I also feel cursed and hounded and pursued." Others struggled similarly to make sense of the fact that they had been profoundly transformed by the movement even though they didn't quite fit their own image of a Catholic Worker. Even Duluth's Joel Kilgour, one of the few who accepted the label without hesitation, stressed his ongoing efforts to live into it. "When I think about the Catholic Worker I think first of the people who were in this community when I first encountered it, and they were a really amazing group of folks. . . . Now it's kind of left to me to try to carry on that tradition. And I don't know how well I do it."

Donna Howard, one of Joel's inspiring mentors, told me that she struggled to identify her role after moving out of Loaves and Fishes. Since she initially left to perform a Plowshares action, the community was "happy to claim me for that period of time because we believe that's part of the community work." When she didn't return to the house after her release from prison, however, she wrestled with an idea that she "had heard voiced really frequently, that you're not a Catholic Worker unless you're living in the community, in one of the houses, now. . . . That was pretty frightening to me. I felt like the door was going to hit me on the backside." She sought to maintain her connection both by remaining involved in the activities of the house and in pursuing its core values through her new work with the Nonviolent Peaceforce. But her language still carried a question mark. "Usually, I fudge a little bit by saying that I have a relationship with the Catholic Worker movement, or that I come from the Catholic Worker tradition, or that I participate in the work of the Catholic Worker community in Duluth. I usually just add a few extra words there . . . but inside I think I'm a Catholic Worker."

Many Camphillers use similar "fudge" phrases to describe their relationship to both Camphill and anthroposophy. "I think the older generation felt easier about calling themselves [anthroposophists]," Lois Smith told me. "I feel easier about saying I work, I try to work out of anthroposophy." "I'm a student of anthroposophy," echoed Melanie Sabra. Such language reflects an intriguing mix of humility and critique. On the one hand, Lois, Melanie, and others like them do not wish to imply that they have mastered the spiritual indications offered by Rudolf Steiner. "To call oneself an anthroposophist is a huge thing," said Melanie. On the other hand, they fear that labels create unnecessary barriers. "I think it's a generational thing," Lois explained. "Our generations have this deep need and wish to bring [together] the separate little things that people think [they] are." Others worry that abstract labels might distract from the concrete tasks of shared life. Don Wilson, who spent fifteen years at Camphill Village Minnesota, consistently refused to join the inner Camphill Community. "That was something I resisted out of principle. . . . Don't ask me what the principle is. . . . As far as I was concerned I was a member of this Camphill community as much as I could ever be." Other deeply committed coworkers told me that they "didn't know that much about" the process of becoming a Camphill Community member, that they "never felt that [they] really needed to become one," or that they filled the criteria König had enumerated for the Community and thus felt little need to join officially. Though such sentiments are certainly not universal, even those who are Community members often struggle to recall who else in their village belongs.

Camphillers also emphasize the ways in which their movement has evolved from a strong sense of common cause to greater emphasis on individual needs and self-development. These observations may be tinged with sadness, but there is also a sense that this evolution is inevitable and ultimately good. Indeed, Michael and Jane Luxford have identified this process as an expression of Rudolf Steiner's own "Sociological Law." According to that principle, the earliest social units tend to sacrifice the interests of the individual to those of the association, but as societies develop they place more and more emphasis on the emancipation of the individual. Ultimately, wrote Steiner, "the greatest ideal of the state will be not to control anything. It will be a community, which wants nothing for itself, but everything for the individual." This means, in the words of Copake's Wanda Root, that "it's incredibly important that people who are here are here out of their own freedom. We always say that people should stay here as long as they can serve the needs of the community and the community can serve their needs."[21]

The question of identification and membership is interwoven with that of lifelong commitment. During my community visits, I found many people who had lived in community for years or even decades and had no plans for moving on. But few of these could say unequivocally that they were committed for life. "Right now this is what makes sense in my life," said Mark Steinrueck of Community Homestead. "I can't speak for five years from now, ten years from now. I could change, the community could change." "Camphill will be in me for the rest of my life," reflected Peter Madsen, "[but] there's so many variables in it, which sap my confidence in being able to say, yeah, I'll be here until the dying day." Jan Zuzalek, who has spent almost her entire adulthood in Camphill, recalled that she had originally recoiled at the thought of committing for even an entire year. And Joel Kilgour gave a long list of reasons for staying permanently at the Duluth Catholic Worker, but still hesitated to say for certain that he would do so: "I'm really connected to Duluth. I grew up here, this is my home, it's a beautiful place, and I can't imagine being too far from Lake Superior. . . . Besides the Resurrection, that's my rock. . . . I want to root myself here and be with the people who are struggling here and make a commitment of that. I can't say that I'll be here forever, but for a while."

Such reflections inevitably turn back to the ongoing discernment of vocation. "I don't have any indication in my heart of hearts that I'm supposed to move on," explained Brian Kavanagh of the Hartford Catholic Worker. "But I also know that I wouldn't have been here in the first place if I hadn't maintained some kind of openness to the possibilities." Brian is fortunate to be part of a movement that has found so many ways of helping its members stay "open to the possibilities" by listening to the divine voices in themselves and in the world. Practices that encourage individual vocation can destabilize and complicate the lives of intentional communities, but they are also what give those communities life. As Richard Neal of Camphill Copake put it, "in the long run, community lives from the individual wanting community with the other individual. It's the only thing that works."

Notes

1. Quoted by Pat Jordan, in Rosalie Riegle Troester, *Voices from the Catholic Worker* (Philadelphia: Temple University Press, 1993) 144.

2. Brendan Walsh, "Be of Conscience (a little) more careful than of everything," *Enthusiasm* [Viva House Newsletter], March 1993, 8–11.

3. Maggie Olson, "Community," *Via pacis* 7/2 (April/May 1983) 8.

4. Tom Heuser, "From New York to Chicago," *The Catholic Worker—Saint Catherine of Genoa, Chicago* 3/4 (December 1991) 5.

5. Al Mascia, "My, How Time Flies!" *The Catholic Worker—Saint Catherine of Genoa, Chicago* 9/2 (Summer 1997) 2.

6. Hartmut von Jeetze, in *Camphill in America . . . in their own words* (Summertown, TN: Village Media, 2002); Ian Robb quoted in *Camphill Village: Inside a Special Place*, Chronicle, Channel 5 WCVB—TV, Boston, September 13, 2000.

7. Tom Lumpkin, cited in Troester, *Voices*, 204.

8. This thumbnail account of the differences between hospitality and professional social service is based on the extensive analysis of Murray, *Hospitality*, especially 4, 21, 47, 230–1.

9. Müller-Wiedemann, *Karl König*, 179.

10. Anke Weihs, cited in Müller-Wiedemann, *Karl König*, 174–5.

11. Quoted by Dorothy Day, "On Pilgrimage," *Catholic Worker* 44/3 (March–April 1978) 2, 7.

12. Murray, *Hospitality*, 109.

13. Murray, *Hospitality*, 113.

14. See Robert Coles, *Dorothy Day: A Radical Devotion* (New York: Perseus Books, 2000); Robert Coles and Jon Erikson, *A Spectacle Unto the World: The Catholic Worker Movement* (New York: Viking, 1973); Eichenberg, *Works of Mercy*; Marc H. Ellis, *A Year at the Catholic Worker* (New York: Paulist Press, 1978); and Dorothy Day, "On Pilgrimage," *Catholic Worker* 39/7 (September 1973) 1.

15. Müller-Wiedemann, *Karl König*, 160–1.

16. Murray, *Hospitality*, 230.

17. Brandon-Falcone, "Experiments in Truth," 325.

18. Lawrence Hunt, "Our Future in the World," in Hunt, *Shining Lights*, 119.

19. Day, *Loaves and Fishes*, 8.

20. Ibid., 135.

21. Rudolf Steiner, cited in Michael and Jane Luxford, *A Sense for Community*, 176–7 (see also *A Sense for Community*, 63); and Wanda Root, in *Let Each Light Shine: A Portrait of Camphill Village* (Princeton, NJ: Films for the Humanities and Sciences, 2003).

Making Room
for Families

What we've tried to create here . . . and what I think the Catholic Worker is all about, is this understanding that we're *all* family. We are all sisters and brothers.

—*Marcia Timmel*[1]

What's most rewarding [about parenting in community is] that I get to be with my kids so much. . . . What's most challenging [is] that I don't get enough time with my kids.

—*Peter Madsen, Camphill Village USA*

Perhaps no human vocation is more popular than family life. People feel called to an endless variety of careers and activities, but most are also drawn to share their lives with spouses and children. Families can inspire our highest idealism and demand our absolute fidelity. These qualities can enrich community life, but they also challenge it. Just as practices that encourage individuals to pursue their own vocations may lead some members out of community, so practices that honor family mean that members will relate to the community in a new way—if at all—with each new stage of their families' development. Still, Camphill and the Catholic Worker have insisted that they cannot be most fully themselves without the presence of families.

Indeed, the fact that most communities refer to themselves metaphorically as families suggests the range of gifts that families bring. One gift is universality: by including families, a community affirms that its model of shared life is open to all people at all stages of life. It is not a specialized activity for people with a unique calling, but an alternative social model for people of all vocations. Families help communities recognize that individual relationships of all sorts—friendships as well as spousal, parental, and sibling relationships—are a source of strength for the community. Far from competing with the community for the individual's loyalty, such special ties can knit the entire community together. Perhaps most importantly, families offer communities the gifts of change and mortality, teaching them to honor their own developmental processes and even face their own deaths.

Families provide the primary context in which people are born, grow, and die. The inner mystery of family life is that the ultimate end of a family is unknown to its members. Parents commit themselves to the well-being of their children even before they know anything about those children or what *they* will experience as well-being. Parents prepare for goods that will be fully realized—they hope—only after their deaths. Similarly, spouses make absolute commitments on the basis of only partial knowledge. In healthy families, these commitments are both absolute and absolutely negotiable. Family life is organic, and so its structures must constantly change.

The same might be said of a community, insofar as any community is composed of individuals whose developmental paths cannot be fully known to one another. But it is easy to lose sight of the organic character of a community. The family exists precisely for the purpose of being the matrix of birth, growth, and death. Communities often exist, ostensibly, to promote some more "spiritual" ideal. Because a community's lifespan is not predetermined, and may exceed that of any of its members, it is easy to forget that it cannot live forever. From a Christian perspective, this is an insidious illusion, for Jesus promised not that we would live forever but that we would find eternal life on the far side of death. In his own life, he did not so much avoid death as live without fear of it.

Healthy families thus help communities live without fear of death. Often they do this best in times of crisis. When families go through their own developmental crises, they often spark developmental crises for their communities. A valued member may marry and discover that her new spouse cannot find a suitable vocation within the community. A family that joined to find a safe space to raise children may leave because the children, now adolescents, find rural life to be stifling. For the community, this is an opportunity to let go of what is dying and embrace what is being born. By forcing communities to experience death, families invite them to experience resurrection as well—either through a renewal of life within the community or through the dispersed activities of children and families who carry seeds of community life beyond its borders.

In this section, I will explore practices that allow communities to embrace family crises in ways that "make room" for growth. Sometimes this "making room" is literal: a community may need to set aside physical space for each family to nurture itself. Sometimes it is metaphorical: a community may need to relax its emotional demands on new parents, or change the rules to accommodate restless adolescents. Sometimes, a community simply needs to make room for a family to move on. In each case, making room creates new opportunities for touching the world.

Patterns of Family and Community

My claim that both Camphill and the Catholic Worker embrace families may surprise some readers, for the Worker is often perceived as a movement for single people. Dorothy Day left her common-law marriage when she became a Catholic, and she struggled to balance her responsibilities as the mother of Tamar with her role as leader of a community that served homeless men from New York's Bowery. Peter Maurin, who had once contemplated life as a Christian Brother, was single throughout his life. The New York houses of hospitality, as well as those in other major urban areas, have attracted volunteers who are disproportionately young, idealistic, and single. When one interviewee told me that Dorothy had not encouraged families to be part of the Worker, another (himself a father) called out from the next room, "She sure didn't!"

But families have always been a vital part of the Catholic Worker. Families were prominent among the founders of early houses of hospitality, though not all moved into the houses they founded. And Day was clear that one did not need to live at a Catholic Worker house to be part of the movement. One might simply open up a spare bedroom, or "Christ room," to any person in need. Many *Catholic Worker* readers did just that, while families anchored two of the most enduring early houses. In Detroit, Lou and Justine Murphy sustained two houses of hospitality and a small farm while raising six children. In Cleveland, Dorothy and Bill Gauchat began similarly, then shifted their efforts to care for children with disabilities. No houses outside New York were featured as prominently in the pages of the *Catholic Worker* as these two communities.

The Worker farms that proliferated during the 1940s and 1950s were also more often family farms than "agronomic universities." The farm in Upton, Massachusetts, devolved into a cluster of families by the 1950s; an extended family network still occupied eight houses there in the 1980s. Holy

Family Farm, started in 1947 by the Heaney and Paul families, suffered a major setback with the death of Larry Heaney, but Ruth Heaney and her children stayed on the land for decades. Julian and Mary Jane Pleasants ran a Catholic Worker house in South Bend, Indiana, from 1941 to 1944, then moved to the countryside to raise their children in company with other families inspired by the Worker.[2] The heritage of these farms continues at Strangers and Guests Catholic Worker Farm in Iowa, anchored by Brian Terrell, Betsy Keenan, and their family.

The rapid growth of the movement since the 1960s has generated a new consciousness among Catholic Worker families, who now have many successful models from which to choose. Like the Murphys in Detroit, the Walsh-Bickhams of Viva House in Baltimore have anchored a thriving community for decades. Family-centered communities in Worcester, Massachusetts, and Hartford, Connecticut, are often cited as shining examples of the current vitality of the Worker movement. Elsewhere, Catholic Worker "communities" may consist of clusters of family households, each doing its own sort of hospitality while cooperating in resistance work or running a soup kitchen. This has been the model in San Francisco, Cleveland, and Portland, Oregon. In such places as La Crosse, Wisconsin, a group of families sustains a house of hospitality as "extended community," while short-term volunteers provide live-in staffing.

Yet another model has been developed, paradoxically, by those who left the Worker to start their families. When Tom and Monica Cornell married, for example, Tom immediately moved out of the Worker house. "I didn't want to be so closely involved in the Catholic Worker community after I married," Tom explained to interviewer Deane Mowrer. "A family is a community of its own." But the hot water and shower available in the Cornells' new apartment attracted a Worker guest almost every night, including some who stayed for years at a time. Through a series of subsequent moves, Tom and Monica continued to find ways to "work as Catholic Workers." In Newburgh, New York, they used their house "as a kind of neighborhood center for street kids" while Tom worked for the Catholic Peace Fellowship. In Waterbury, Connecticut, Tom received a salary to run a local soup kitchen, which in turn allowed the family to sustain a house of hospitality in a former convent. Eventually, the couple "retired" to Peter Maurin Farm, which is sponsored by the New York house. They have been joined there by their adult son; their daughter and her family lived for a time in nearby Newburgh. Like other Worker families, the Cornells exemplify a willingness to adapt the Catholic Worker model again and again as their own family changed. [3]

The pattern of family life at Camphill is a bit simpler. The movement was founded by a circle of young adults, many of whom formed families, and families have played a central role ever since. Camphill took the traditional family structure for granted and sought to model the community on it. "What is most important to begin with," wrote Karl König, "is to create a true social environment for these children. Not to establish an institution with big dormitories and classrooms but rather a family of children, helpers, nurses and doctors, where one's own family becomes the nucleus of the larger family."[4]

Most Camphills today are organized into households headed by "houseparents," who function as surrogate parents not only for the disabled "villagers" but also for the "young coworkers." Not all houseparents are literally parents: at Camphill Village Minnesota, the role has also been carried by a single experienced coworker, by two single people, and by a lesbian couple. Still, each household strives to maintain an extended family atmosphere. And it is rare for more than one family with children to reside in the same household. Parents retain considerable freedom to determine the shape of their family life, and then to invite others to share in it.

Despite their differences, both Camphill and the Catholic Worker have seen themselves as extended family, often using the metaphor of "family" to describe people who share living space or close emotional ties but are not related by blood. This ideal of extended family requires deliberate cultivation, but in many cases it also builds on the preexisting relationships of people who are blood kin or long-term friends. Camphill Copake's founders, for example, included not only Carlo and Ursel Pietzner, but also Ursel's sister Renate Sachs, whom many remember as "the heart of our Village in the truest sense of the word."[5] Many children who grew up there eventually married one another or young coworkers who arrived at Copake during their teenage years. These couples, in turn, became founding members of Camphill Village Minnesota and Community Homestead. In the early years of the Catholic Worker, similarly, Dorothy Day drew on the familial support of her brother John and his wife Tessa, just as contemporary Catholic Workers draw inspiration from Phil Berrigan and Liz McAlister, Phil's brother Dan Berrigan, and the activist children of Phil and Liz. For many Camphillers and Catholic Workers, these family networks provide a shining example for what the entire community movement—and the entire society—might become.

Mutual Gifts

When asked about raising children in community, most Camphill and Catholic Worker parents begin by describing the gifts that community brings to families—and the gifts that families bring to community. Some talk, for example, about the ways shared life reinforces values of love, compassion, and simplicity. "We don't have to explain why we don't watch TV to our children," noted Camphiller Sonja Adams. "You can go into any house and the same philosophy" of child rearing is present. If carefully managed, the presence of people who are poor or disabled can also engender a sense of compassion. "To me," said Lawrence Purcell, who cofounded a small Worker community in Redwood City, California, "the trick is to love your kids so much that you want what you have for them with the homeless. Not like you want to treat your kids like you treat the homeless, but that you want the homeless to have what your kids have."

Michele Naar-Obed, who has spent several years in prison or jail for civil disobedience, said that "it's very important that [my daughter] experience one way or another what most of the world experiences." But she also highlighted the importance of balance: when the family lived at Jonah House, which does not directly serve the poor, Michele placed her daughter at an "inner-city African American Catholic school" with many poor students; at Loaves and Fishes Catholic Worker, the stresses of hospitality led the family to place Rachel in a more middle-class school. "She experiences all of that," Michele concluded, "and sees that, and begins to recognize that her privilege is just that—it's a privilege." Chris Allen-Doucot, whose Saint Martin de Porres Catholic Worker is in an impoverished African American neighborhood in Hartford, contrasted his children's experiences with those of their cousins. "Their cousins, on both sides, are all being raised in very white middle-class places. They don't have friends that are black or Hispanic or poor. Our children do. But our children also have friends that are white or middle class or wealthy. So I hope that they're benefiting from exposure to different cultures and different classes—because I think every culture has something to offer us."

Camphill parents are fond of telling anecdotes of how their children take people of all backgrounds and abilities at face value. "They have had an incredible variety of social relationships that children of that age normally wouldn't have," said Mark Hobson at the Lukas Community, and this has heightened their "empathy for people. . . . At the Quaker meeting we have a lady who speaks incredibly loudly, she is epileptic, and the other children were complaining, and Anna, my eldest, said, 'Well, that's Hannah. That's how she talks.'" Sheila Russell came to Community Homestead well after beginning to parent, and as a result she has been able to observe the ways children of various ages imbibe community values. The younger children, she told me, don't notice the differences in ability, but "accept people for who they are" and are even "thrilled" to introduce their friends from school to villagers in the community. Her older daughter, by contrast, struggled to make the adjustment to community life, but eventually was able to appropriate the community's vision at a more intellectual level. She "actually put . . . Community Homestead on her website," Sheila said proudly.

Communities can offer children a sense of purpose and choices as well as compassionate values. At Camphill Village Minnesota, children are equally free to spend the long summer days working on a tractor, cultivating friendships in the summer kitchen, or studying math at a camp far removed from community life—and I have seen different kids make each of these choices. Some Catholic Worker kids have developed their own strategies for extending hospitality to neighborhood children, some love the excitement and pageantry of protests, and some quietly withdraw from it all. "Whatever you do," Catholic Worker parent Brian Terrell acknowledged, "adults impose their lives on their kids." But he went on to contrast the Catholic Worker with both mainstream society and movements like the Amish that reject that society wholesale. "Our kids . . . know enough about the real world . . . if they want it they can join it, and they would have the tools to do okay in it. . . . I don't know what our kids are going to decide but I think they're going to make those decisions knowing a lot more options than a lot of other folks will."

Community parents also value their communities' flexible approach to time with children. When I asked Mark Hobson of the Lukas Community about his experiences of parenting, he quoted an interview with John Lennon. "He was saying, it's crap what they say about quality time. Children want quantity. I like that." Peter Madsen, who cares for the garden at Camphill Copake, spoke glowingly of the pleasures of having his sons out in the fields with him and his work crew. "Though it doesn't make my work any easier really, it's very nice to have them with me and seeing what pop is doing, understanding what work is, learning how to help. . . . My favorite moments are when he just plays alongside and does his thing in the midst of us doing our thing. . . . This is archetypal, you know." Catholic Worker Chris Allen-Doucot added that the Catholic Worker approach to parenting has made it easier for his own parents to accept his radical lifestyle. "My parents . . . are still not too thrilled about this lifestyle . . . But . . . they do appreciate [the fact] that Jackie and I are both home almost all the time with our kids. They're not being raised in a daycare center [like their cousins]. . . . They're being raised by us."

They are also, in many cases, being raised by an extended family of adults and children who are diverse in age, ability, and cultural background. This circle of mentors and helpers is especially valuable to single parents. Nadine Holder came to Community Homestead shortly after the birth of her daughter, and moved in with the large family of Richard and Christine Elmquist. "The main gift," she told me, 'is that I don't feel like I have to do everything so right, and that [my daughter's] development totally depends on me. . . . There's a broader base of influence to try and copy from or think about." Carla Dawson of the Des Moines Catholic Worker told a similar story of the benefits of raising her children in community with other single moms. "That was a big plus, because we always watched each others' kids, we always did things together." The experience broadened Carla's understanding of the word "family." "I still find the term that most people use for families so shallow," she explained. "Like Eddie's in my family. . . . And Irving who's no relation to them, is probably like a father. . . . He saved my son Josh, because Josh had his days and nights mixed up when he was born, and my son Jules had just started kindergarten. I was kind of crazy for six months because I didn't have enough sleep. . . . And Irving used to get him, get him his bottle, change his diaper."

The community circle can also broaden one's sense of the parenting vocation. Observing the way people parent at Community Homestead helped Sheila Russell question the "old-fashioned way" she had learned from her own parents, as well as the standard advice of medical professionals. "It's actually helped me to look at . . . different solutions" to problems, Sheila told me, adding that she still feels free to choose the older strategies when that seems right. Joanne Kennedy, who was raised in the "lower upper class" of southern California, encountered a different style of parenting when she lived with Carla Dawson at the Des Moines Catholic Worker. "Carla's a parent for these kids' lives," Joanne explained. "She's got to face some really tough things. She's got to teach her kids some lessons I don't even know how to teach, about what it means . . . to be without a father and poor and black in America. . . . I learned a lot about . . . [how] you just sort of deal with everything each day as it comes." These contrasting experiences served Joanne well as she raised her own son Jonah in the intensely communal environment of the New York Catholic Worker.

Beneath all the praise for parenting in community lies a critique of parenting practices in the larger society. This is especially the case for Catholic

Worker Brian Terrell, who told my research assistant that "the problem today is not that the nuclear family's fallen apart." The nuclear family itself, he went on, is an innovation that has existed for only about one hundred years, and "it's an experiment that's failed. It's the mess from that experiment that we're dealing with." The debate over whether single women can parent effectively is misguided, because neither one nor two people can provide a child with everything he or she needs. It requires a supportive community, which is what Brian has tried to provide his children through the Catholic Worker network.

This critique suggests some of the distance between contemporary community parents and the founders of Camphill and the Catholic Worker. For the most part, Dorothy Day and Karl König were not dissatisfied with family life as they had experienced it. Their goal was to create a new society while leaving traditional family structures largely untouched. Many contemporary communitarians, by contrast, are responding to a crisis of family life, which they see as enmeshed in a dysfunctional industrial economy. They are drawn to community because it allows them to create a pattern of family life that, in their view, would not be possible otherwise. This does not mean that they never experience a tension between family and community! But they grapple tenaciously with that tension, because giving up on the struggle means losing both their family and community ideals.

Thus far my analysis has focused on the benefits community life offers to families. Community parents are quick to point out that the benefits also run in the opposite direction. The practices of nurture that are staples of family life, for example, can easily overflow to infuse an entire community with nurturing care. "If I'm in that caring, fatherly mode," explained the Lukas Community's Mark Hobson, "then I can also care for other people." Both Catholic Workers and Camphillers have observed that the presence of children, and especially of babies, can have a profoundly positive effect on persons experiencing homelessness or disability, many of whom yearn to have children of their own. "A child's presence enlightens the atmosphere," said Suzette Ermler, a single woman at the New York Catholic Worker. "There were people—women in particular—who were really brought out of their shells by playing with Georgie [a child who had lived at Maryhouse briefly]." Camphiller Jan Goeschel, who said that he couldn't "really imagine this place without families," noted that "the extended family situation is what makes this place different from a good institution. The house that the students live in is also really the home of the people [who care for them]."

The presence of families can also break down the barriers between those who "serve" and those who are "served" within an intentional community movement, an important function insofar as the goal of Camphill and Catholic Worker communities is not so much to "serve" the homeless or the developmentally disabled as to share life with them. Children blur the line between "Workers" and "guests," "coworkers" and "villagers," in part because they themselves fit into neither category and in part because they can make their parents vulnerable, in need of help from the "guests" or "villagers."

Joanne Kennedy, for example, came to the New York Catholic Worker as a sort of "fix-it" girl—someone who had a knack for getting struggling communities back on their feet. Just after the birth of her child, however, it was Joanne who was off her feet with mastitis. This gave several guests the opportunity to exercise unrealized gifts for nurture and community-building. Camphillers Bill and Laura Briggs learned a similar lesson shortly after the birth of their first daughter. Though Angela had some serious and frightening health problems, she also drew out the nurturing gifts of developmentally disabled adults who would never be able to have children of their own. Laura came particularly to rely on an older woman who was both developmentally disabled and deaf. "You couldn't ask for a better nanny," said Laura. "She was just a natural. You could tell how she would pick them up and hold them. If I was busy cooking, she would go and change the diapers, which she loved to do. She helped me through being able to do that, but I think also being able to mother children was something she really longed to do and was never able to. . . . It was such a wonderful thing for her and so appreciated by us."

These positive effects reach beyond the boundaries of a community, allowing it to build alliances with neighbors and mainstream social institutions. "Children, you know, are great community builders," Willa Bickham explained to Rosalie Riegle Troester. "If you have a child, you go walking around the neighborhood and talk to everybody." Willa's daughter Kate was born around the time Willa and her husband Brendan Walsh founded Viva House Catholic Worker as a sanctuary for Vietnam War resisters as well as homeless persons. Kate's presence allowed them to be perceived not just as radical peaceniks, but also as ordinary folks with a commitment to the neighborhood. She provided the initial point of contact with the next-door neighbors, a large family who frequently took in relatives or friends. That friendship deepened Brendan and Willa's understanding of the Catholic Worker's role in reviving the extended family tradition. Starting her own family at Viva House a generation later, Kate also saw how parenting can break down barriers between a radical movement and mainstream society. "When you have a baby, it is the best drawing card you could ever get for getting to know people. . . . You can go out in the backyard and everyone wants to talk to you. It's a good unifying point because most people have kids, so they can relate to your experience."

Parenting experiences can also bring a greater sense of honesty to Catholic Worker activism. Shortly before the Gulf War, Mike Miles participated in a major protest at one of the Army bases that was to be used for troop deployment, and as a result he spent Christmas in jail. When the war started just weeks after his release, the children were devastated. "We thought you were going to stop the war," they complained. Adults, Mike's spouse reflected in our interview, can "rationalize" such a situation by saying that "effectiveness isn't really what we're about," but the "very basic questions" posed by the children forced them to dig deeper into their reasons for doing resistance work.

For many community parents, this digging deeper results in more enduring commitment to the community. "The Catholic Worker," explained Brian Terrell, "is not supposed to be . . . something for somebody getting out of college and wanting to do something for the poor for the next couple of years. . . . Ultimately it's supposed to be a revolution. It should be something that people will come to for their life and will want to raise their kids in." "So many people in the world are in families," noted Claire Schaeffer-Duffy of Saints Francis and Thérèse Catholic Worker. "That's their reality. So for the Catholic Worker to embrace so many families, it's a very powerful witness."

The flip side of this witness is that families challenge communities to adjust their lifestyles to what Claire called the distinct "tempo" of family life. Families that stay long-term in community may make significant changes, limiting the scope of the community's hospitality work and chastening hopes of bringing about a revolution within a few years. But even that can be a gift, as Dorothy Day observed in describing the growth of one family at Maryfarm in Easton, Pennsylvania. "Before long Jim Montague got married. He and his wife had one baby and then another. By the time there were three of them we were able to compare our own progress with the growth of a family, and we began to get it through our heads that our ideals would only be achieved slowly—even more slowly than the development of a child. We had wanted to see them burst forth full-fledged, on their feet, as did the young calves and goats we delighted in watching."[6] The rhythms of family life are also the rhythms of genuine social change.

The Challenges of Parenting in Community

Though most community parents can sing the praises of shared life, they are equally eloquent about the challenges. Some of these have to do with the environment in which communities exist. The rural setting of Camphills and Catholic Worker farms can be isolating for some families, especially as nature-loving ten-year-olds turn into more socially oriented teenagers. The urban neighborhoods of most Catholic Worker houses of hospitality pose even more profound challenges. Claire Schaeffer-Duffy of Worcester recounted two instances when she was nearly hit by an angry guest during a pregnancy. "I used to dread the summers," she added, "because all the [neighborhood] kids . . . seemed so wound up and quick to become hostile." Claire's solution was to "hover over them," joining in basketball games to provide a model of someone "not feeling threatened by a point or two in a game." This kept her own children from being targets, as well as making "a small offering for these children whose lives . . . were so bereft of attention and affection," but it never entirely freed her from worries.

Faced with the real dangers of urban life and an activist awareness of global war and poverty, Catholic Worker parents often worry that their children will grow up too quickly. "You get beleaguered looking . . . at the cruelty," Claire Schaeffer-Duffy said, and in response she is "adamant about them taking music classes and pursuing the arts and being creative because it's kind of a statement of life." At the other extreme, Peter Madsen and some other Camphillers worry that their communities are so sheltered that their children may not grow up at all. Peter wants his children to have "one foot on land and one foot on the boat," and so he is deliberate about visiting friends who are working traditional careers and paying mortgages. He has also introduced a "farmer's market" at Copake, requiring households to exchange money for produce from the garden, as a way of introducing community kids to the economic structures of the larger society.

Another struggle for both Catholic Workers and Camphillers has to do with schooling. Catholic Workers are committed to living in solidarity with the poor, but they are rarely willing to subject their own children to the dysfunctional urban schools that are the fate of many poor Americans. Fortunately, their knowledge of "the system" allows them to access the best the public school system has to offer. The Schaeffer-Duffy children have attended racially and economically diverse magnet school programs, supplemented with private music lessons that Claire paid for by cleaning houses and writing articles. Most Camphillers are delighted to gain easy access to Waldorf schools, but parents at Camphill Village Minnesota have struggled in ways similar to the Catholic Workers. Without a local Waldorf school, parents must choose between the public schools of one of Minnesota's poorest counties, a conservative Lutheran parish school, and homeschooling. Different parental choices have very different economic implications for the community, though in general the community has maintained a commitment to doing what seems best for each individual child.

Underlying all such challenges is the question of how much parents impose their own lifestyle choices on their children. Though community parents are quick to point out that all parents do this, most recognize that the issue deserves their serious reflection. One of the differences between voluntary poverty and involuntary poverty, Catholic Worker Terry Bennet-Cauchon pointed out, is that in the former case children may blame their parents. "I'm basically their oppressor if I'm forcing them to live a life of poverty that isn't natural. They know they don't have to live this way. It's *our* choice, not theirs."[7] As a result of this reflection, most community parents are willing to make compromises on the issues most important to their children.

Community parents struggle even more with challenges rooted in the internal dynamics of community life. Because communities abolish the clear distinction between "work" and "home," many parents struggle with divided loyalties. The most challenging thing about parenting in the Catholic Worker, said Lawrence Purcell, is "being stretched between the commitments of a Catholic Worker . . . and the responsibilities and commitments to your family. You never feel that anything is done well or enough." Peter Madsen aptly expressed the dilemma with his comment that the greatest gift of parenting in community is being with his children so much of the time, while the greatest challenge is not having enough time with the children. The rhythms of life in community are simply different from those in conventional, career-driven society, and as a result community parents are hard-pressed to measure the quality and quantity of their family time against that of their mainstream peers.

Just as the benefit of combining work and home is coupled with the challenge of divided loyalties, so the benefit of having the support of an "extended family" brings the challenge of dealing with community turnover. In most communities, children develop very close relationships with unrelated adults, then see those adults move out of their lives within a few years—or a few months. Greg and Michele Obed, who have raised their daughter at three different communities, worry that she "struggles with the idea of change" because "there's been so much change in the relationships she's formed." Another family they know gave up their Catholic Worker house after enduring twelve years of comings and goings without ever seeing a sustaining community crystallize. "So many people come and go," mused Des Moines's Carla Dawson. But after running through a long list of significant people who had passed through her sons' lives, Carla added, "but that way they get to know a lot of people who live all over the world, too."

Another challenge linked to the positive experience of "extended family" is that community parents may lack the parental privacy most Americans expect. As a Camphill parent, Nancy Potter told me, "you always feel like you're on, you're being observed, you're in a fishbowl." For Chris Allen-Doucot, sharing a household with other adults has meant having to struggle to preserve the specialness of his role as parent. He doesn't like "other people parenting my children, reprimanding them perhaps in front of me." Community Homestead's Nadine Holder, by contrast, said that her challenge was "that it's really easy to just let that [the primary parental role] go." Raising her daughter in the same household with Christine and Richard Elmquist and their four children, "it would be really easy for me to just have Maya slip into the spot behind [Christine's] last child." But Nadine recalled her own experience growing up as part of the extended community of Threefold Community in New York. After her father's death, her mother justified working twelve-hour days "because she felt like the community would carry us a little bit." But Nadine missed the security of attachment to one special person. As a parent, Nadine was thus willing to "put those boundaries up again and draw [Maya] back in."

A special set of challenges awaits those parents who do not begin to live in community until their children are school-age or older. "It's a real soul movement to open up," explained Mark Hobson, "to let someone share your private space." Sylvia Bausman came to Camphill Copake as a single mother with four young sons, and she reflected that when one brings "children from a nuclear family into such a situation, no matter how wonderful the environment is, you let them go into this new pond and they are not in paradise."

There is a special consciousness of this issue at Community Homestead, which includes two families whose children have lived in community most of their lives and two whose children came to community as teenagers. The parents of the latter families are quick to acknowledge that the other children "have been more into the community than our children have been." "It was a little bit difficult at first," explained Garth Riegel. "The idea of sharing your house and not having, from their perspective, as much money as they thought they should have available for clothes, family entertainment . . . was something they could complain about as young teenagers." Of course, Garth added, it is developmentally appropriate for teenagers to feel "deprived." "As they get older all of our kids have expressed interest in participating in community life." Indeed, at the time of our conversation Garth's son was spending a year at Camphill Kimberton Hills, before beginning college, and another child was thinking of following suit. When teenage children lead their parents to community, moreover, the results can be extremely positive.

Most of the parents I spoke to recalled moments of tension with community members who were not parents. On the one hand, they valued these people as role models and occasional babysitters for their children. Yet they often discovered that singles had vastly different expectations about life in community—and far more energy to spend on community meetings and endless discussions. Camphill's young coworkers, conversely, occasionally resent their subordination to houseparents who, if they are also parenting their own children, may be less "hands-on" in their household responsibilities.

If parenting alongside single people can be challenging, parenting in close quarters with other parents can be explosive. Different parents have different approaches to discipline, and may take offense if others violate their parental prerogatives. Even if the adults keep their own boundaries clear, the children's sense of justice may be violated by too much awareness of the different rules in different families. "Sometimes it's a real pain," said Douglas Elmquist of Community Homestead, "because not everybody in this community raises their children in the same way." Reflecting on the same phenomenon, Joanne Kennedy observed that the very idealism of Catholic Worker communities can exacerbate tensions. "It's interesting that we're not easy on each other. . . . Part of what brings people to the Catholic Worker is their critical nature. You have to be critical of the society in order to have ended up here. . . . And we can be critical to each other. [Some people will say that] those kids are crazy, they never spank their kids and those kids run slipshod over everything. [And others] will say I wouldn't ever beat my child." Such tensions are greatest when families share household space. After rhapsodizing on the joys of parenting in community, Copake's Peter Madsen acknowledged that "if there were two sets of parents under one roof, I have my doubts as to how appreciative I would be of it." Given the importance of space for their well-being, the families that do best in Camphill and the Catholic Worker are those that have learned to "make room" for themselves.

Reconciling Family and Community

When I asked Willa Bickham and Brendan Walsh about raising a daughter at the Catholic Worker, they responded by drawing a diagram to show how their living space had evolved over the years. In 1985 they purchased the adjoining row house from the city for back taxes. This allowed them to devote the first floor of both houses to their soup kitchen ministry, while creating a private family apartment upstairs. The return of Kate and her husband Dave to Viva House, just before my visit, led to a new series of physical changes. "It's very difficult to raise a family in the Catholic Worker," Brendan stressed, "unless you make real space for raising the family within the family."

The Camphill practice of dividing a village into distinct households means that families rarely have to share living space with other families. Increasingly, though, there is a sense that families also need physical separation from the disabled villagers and "young coworkers" who share their households. At Camphill Minnesota, the newest residential building was designed so that half of the upper floor could function as a distinct family apartment, largely inaccessible to other household members.

The Lukas Community took a further step toward family privacy by including a small kitchen within the family apartments that are part of each household. This gives each family a place for private breakfasts, or meals on their days off, though they are still expected to share a large daily dinner with the entire household. The arrangement also prevents an awkward situation that can be observed at many Camphills: most parents allow their teenage children to prepare their own meals if they don't wish to eat with the entire household, but since they have no separate space to do so, they can often be seen eating their private meals just feet away from the large common table. Still, Lukas coworkers see their own arrangement as a trade-off. Nicola Hobson, who had lived in Camphill before coming to Lukas, said that "I don't know which one is better. If I ask my selfish one, I say this is great. If I think of the whole place, I think living closer together would be more fulfilling." Indeed, a necessary complement to the practice of "making room" for families is a willingness to let the pendulum swing back toward more shared space. Camphill Minnesota's recently completed community center, for example, includes a large dining area where the entire village shares a meal once a week.

Both Camphillers and Catholic Workers often talk about letting go of the initial expectation that they would do everything with the entire community in order to create intentional family time. When Sonja Adams became a parent after several years at Camphill Beaver Run, she quickly learned that "you can't be involved in the same way anymore with the students and with the coworkers than you were before you had your own children. You have to maybe let go some things" and rely more on other people. Trudy Pax, on the other hand, came to Camphill Minnesota after her family was established, and she recalled that "we were so excited and thrilled about Camphill, that this was going to be our family. . . . We went overboard in neglecting the family or assuming that . . . that was going to be wonderful for them too, to suddenly have four more people [in their household]. And then we saw our mistake and pulled back and started having family meals and times all together."

Roswitha Imegwu, who grew up in one Camphill and raised her own children at another, changed the rules in a different way: rather than setting aside special time for family, she made a special effort to incorporate the entire household into family activities. "If we were reading stories in the evenings," she explained, "we would do that in the living room so that anyone else who wanted to share in that story could do that." Years later, when she asked her grown children what they had most appreciated about their childhood, they recalled precisely "those times that we were together as a bigger extended family." Noting that her own affinity for the extended family model was shaped both by her Camphill childhood and the time she spent as a young adult in West Africa, Roswitha acknowledged that younger Camphillers have a tendency to a "more exclusive family life." "I sort of understand it," she said, "but . . . there's a part of me that's also a bit sad about that." Many of the changes, observed Regula Stolz, were in response to reports from children who had grown up in Camphill, some (not all) of whom "remember it very painfully." For nearly all Camphillers, this awareness of hard lessons learned tempers any nostalgia about the "good old days," even as both new and old coworkers are concerned not to let the pendulum swing too far in the direction of family privatization.

For Catholic Worker parents, changing expectations have as much to do with money as time. Voluntary poverty is a pillar of the Catholic Worker philosophy, but it can feel very different for parents. Many Worker parents choose to work part-time jobs to pay for their children's health insurance, music lessons, or family vacations. "I think I've kind of erred on the side of living a little too well for a Catholic Worker," Terry Bennet-Cauchon explained to Rosalie Riegle Troester. "I don't want to enforce a strict extreme poverty upon my children and have them grow up and resent it and reject it and go live lives of conspicuous consumption when they leave here." Bob Lassalle-Klein, who was also interviewed by Troester, elaborated the point by distinguishing "being *for* the poor, being *with* the poor, and being *like* the poor." Middle-class people who try too hard to be "like" the poor may burn themselves out and leave the movement altogether. His own choice was to live for and with the poor, "making practical accommodations because, for us, the important thing is to stay."[8]

Such accommodations should not be seen as concessions to middle-class sensibilities, but as the creative means by which Catholic Worker parents "become the change they want to see in the world" by combining the vocation of parenting with that of solidarity. Such parents, Lawrence Purcell pointed out, are faithful to the example of the movement's founder. "Dorothy Day was great at taking care of her soul. . . . She made time to write. She traveled a lot. . . . She made money by traveling and considered that her money that she could pay for her daughter's needs with." The key, in other words, is to do what one "needs to do," rather than submitting without reflection either to the parenting practices of mainstream society or to an abstract ideal of voluntary poverty.

Catholic Worker parents also "make room" for their families by transforming the missions of their communities to accommodate changing family circumstances. When Lawrence Purcell got married, for example, he and his spouse chose hospitality to battered infants as a mission that would fit with the beginning of their own family. Angie Miller and Steve O'Neil, on the other hand, found it too stressful to worry about other people's children, and so their Catholic Worker house switched its emphasis to homeless men. Viva House transformed its mission repeatedly, responding to neighborhood needs while allowing Brendan and Willa to balance parenting and hospitality. In each case what might be seen as a concession to family needs wound up enriching community life by bringing in an entirely new ministry.

It is more difficult for Camphill parents to change the mission of an entire village. But many Camphillers do choose to move from one village to another in response to the changing demands of parenting. Peter Madsen and his spouse began their family at a pioneering Camphill in Russia, where few other families were present. When their oldest son approached the age of four, Peter explained, "we started to feel like we were depriving him of something for the sake of our idealism." Their son was "the darling of the village," but he had few opportunities to learn to play and negotiate with other children, and there was no clear plan for his kindergarten. In addition, Peter was exhausted from the strain of building up a new community garden. Peter and his spouse, who is German, considered returning to the Norwegian Camphill where they had met, but it seemed unfair to introduce a fourth language to their sons, who were already struggling to master English, German, and Russian. Around that time, they learned of an opening for a gardener at Copake, which seemed the perfect solution to their dilemma. It also allowed them to build a bridge between the new Camphill in Russia and the very established one in America. Peter arranged for his brother, a filmmaker, to do a film on the Russian village that he now uses to help raise money in the United States.

Relocation within a movement can be especially helpful in light of the fact that different models of community are best suited to children's developmental stages. Many Catholic Worker parents, for example, are drawn to the farms because of the dangers that urban houses of hospitality present to young children. But the rural environment of a Camphill or a Catholic Worker farm can be isolating for teenagers, who may be more drawn to the energetic activism of urban communities. Unfortunately, not every community movement has developed such a broad array of alternatives. Camphill in the United States has just begun to contemplate the creation of urban households, although Camphill in Britain has moved much further in that direction. As a result, the opportunities for "making room" in these movements, though wide, are not unlimited.

Letting Go

Given the limited range of choices within each movement, some parents choose to move their families out of community altogether, at least for some part of their development. Though such decisions can be heart-wrenching, they should not be viewed as defeats for either the family or the community. Indeed, one of the most profoundly transformative practices for families in community is that of simply letting go of the rigid ideal that every family must live in community for every moment of its life.

Sometimes this happens abruptly, in response to a crisis. One family moved out of a Catholic Worker house almost immediately after their nine-year-old daughter tried to run away from home in protest against "living with so many people." Though her mother caught up with her only three blocks away, the incident coincided with other events that highlighted the importance of strong family ties: one of the parents had a brother who was dying of AIDS, and they also knew several people who were bitterly resentful of the neglect they suffered during community childhoods. Moving out of the Catholic Worker also allowed them to begin doing foster care, which proved to be a "form of hospitality that really includes our kids." It also helped them deepen their appreciation of the "gray zones" of intentional community. "I think some folks in the Catholic Worker view life in a very black and white fashion," said the father. "You're either a Catholic Worker or you're not. You're living a simple lifestyle or you're not. . . . And we've probably always been a little bit more in the gray zone."

Even the Walsh-Bickhams, who were so creative about adapting their style of community life to their family's needs, moved their living space out of Viva House for a few years during their daughter Kate's early adolescence. In 1979 they reached a "fed-up, stagnant period." They considered simply handing Viva House over to their friends at Jonah House, but, as Willa wrote to a Catholic Worker friend, "we don't want to go backwards, we don't want to cop-out, we don't want suburbia." Ultimately, they decided to continue running Viva House while living elsewhere. After five years, though, they realized that a live-in community was needed "in order to continue and increase the work of the house." When the adjoining row house became available, they jumped at the chance to establish a more private family apartment within the structure of Viva House.[9]

At times, parents must balance the needs of very different children in deciding whether to remain in community. At Camphill Village Minnesota, for example, one family left for a variety of reasons, among them the fact that their more introverted older child was not deeply engaged in community life. Their younger child, however, was an extrovert who was actively involved in several community workshops and had even, for a time, published a community newspaper along with one of the villagers. By moving just a few miles away, the parents made it possible for her to preserve an independent connection to the community, and she began to spend larger chunks of time there as she moved into her teenage years.

Such decisions almost always respond to specific circumstances, and the parents who make them are careful to avoid generalizations about the compatibility of family and community. The father whose daughter ran away from home, for example, added that "we've seen people who've been raised in Catholic Worker communities who are just wonderful people and continue to do great work. I know it can be done. It didn't work for us." Many parents who find community life to be ideal for their families are quick to acknowledge the circumstances that might induce them to leave. "I've always said," Jeremy Brett of the Lukas Community told me, "that if the kids feel, or if I feel that the kids are getting ignored or affected adversely by their surroundings, then I'd leave."

Community parents can be fiercely critical of those who use their children as an "excuse" for leaving community life, without acknowledging the range of factors that go into such decisions. "[It puts] a terrible burden . . . [on] these kids [to say], Mommy and Daddy left the life they loved for us," explained Brian Terrell. For his own part, Brian is quick to correct people who think his family moved from the Davenport house of hospitality to a farm for the sake of the children. "It was a tough thing when we moved here, taking our kids away, because they loved the community. . . . The whole scene was really a good one for them." But Brian was burned out from eleven years of intense hospitality, and he "wanted to give the rural aspect of the Catholic Worker a try."

Brian's criticism underscores the importance of seeing each stage of family life as an opportunity as well as a challenge. There *are* times when the needs of children provide the primary reason for moving out of a community. But such a move can be helpful to children only if, rather than blaming the children, parents take creative responsibility for bringing communal values into a new arena. Such creative decisions open up new possibilities for both the family that leaves and the community that is left. They remind everyone that "touching the world" does not depend exclusively on the efforts or stubborn stick-to-itiveness of community members. Rather, it is the wayward path of both personal and familial vocation that allows many people to build genuine bridges between the community and the larger society.

Parents also let go by acknowledging that their adult children may not choose community life. The parents I spoke to were virtually unanimous in wanting to open as many paths as possible for their children. "I don't think our hopes and dreams were different than any other parents," said Willa Bickham. "You nurture and give the opportunities to grow and develop. . . . Whether or not [Kate] ever became a Catholic Worker wasn't important for us." "I tried to raise my kids," reflected Garth Riegel of Community Homestead, "so that they would make choices about what they would want to do as their life's work in terms of the ideals that they had developed themselves." At the New York Catholic Worker, Joanne Kennedy said that she didn't want to "pressure" her son in any particular direction, but that she hoped he would "find something that makes him as fulfilled as the Catholic Worker has made me."

The deeper hope of many community parents is that their children will continue to carry the community's values. "I hope to raise two very tolerant, loving, young, spirited, free children," said Nicola Hobson of the Lukas Community. "I hope that living in community and having had to adapt to a lot of different people with a lot of different abilities will help them in that way." "My dream for my children," echoed Chris Allen-Doucot, "is that they will grow up with a sense of integrity and honesty, and . . . a natural . . . desire to serve and to work for justice. . . . If they wanted to be a Catholic Worker that would be great, but if not—if they want to become an auto mechanic, that would be great. But they could be an auto mechanic and still serve the common good." Noting his pride that his son's best friend is African American,

Chris added that "part of our dream is that my kids, when they're older, can help to be a force to integrate the society."

This sense of hope for the wider society suggests that Camphill and Catholic Worker parents share their communities' aspiration to be a transformative presence in society. For this reason, some parents even prefer that their children *not* remain in community. "I really have encouraged my kids to step out," said Roswitha Imegwu of Camphill Copake, "to go and do something outside. . . . If you want to be in Camphill that's fine, but it should be a free decision, not because you can't think of anything else to do." Elaborating on this point, Peter Madsen explained that he had come to Camphill freely, and that he "would only wish the same for any of my children. That they wouldn't feel obliged to have to live like this, neither would they feel so limited by what they grew up with here that they couldn't manage in the conventional world. That would be also tragic. 'Cause there's plenty to learn everywhere." Peter made it clear that he saw this sense of freedom as crucial not only to his children's well-being, but also to that of Camphill and indeed the world. "A true modern community can only be created out of individuals freely willing themselves to do it," Peter said. Communities that live from authority or from tradition are "petering out," leaving a tragic gap that must be filled by community life in a new key. "The modern world is asking of people that they can freely commit themselves, out of their own free will, their own freedom." If Peter is right, parents and communities must practice letting go of their children, so that those children will in turn have the freedom to renew both communities and society.

Growing Up

In fact, the children of Camphill and the Catholic Worker have already begun the renewal of society. As I spoke to the adult children of community, I discovered that relatively few identify entirely with their communities of origin, and even fewer repudiate them altogether. Most have negotiated their own ways of being connected to the community, whether by moving back and forth between community life and a more conventional lifestyle, by living in a slightly different sort of community, by serving as an advisor to the community, by doing similar work, or simply by residing nearby. Nearly all community kids endorse the values that led their parents to community life, even if they choose to embody those values in significantly different ways. Their experiences of intentional community, in short, have empowered them to negotiate the boundaries between community and society with creativity and grace.

Don and Kristin Wilson, for example, both grew up at Camphill Copake. Though they had positive childhood experiences, neither anticipated that they would continue to be part of Camphill after high school graduation. Instead, Don traveled to Mexico with a group of friends, and then moved to a biodynamic farm in Wisconsin to pursue an interest in agriculture he had developed at Camphill. Kristin began an apprenticeship with a weaver who lived near Camphill Kimberton Hills. Once Kristin and Don had left the communal framework of Camphill, they both began to miss it. On a family farm, Don recalled, "I felt really isolated . . . in a little way trapped." Kristin had a "wonderful" experience with the weaver, but also realized that she didn't want the "loner's life" of the craftsperson. They both jumped at an invitation to join the new Camphill in Minnesota, even though the founders were their parents' friends and, according to Don, "kind of that same generation we called hard-cores and made fun of when we were a little younger." Once in Minnesota, they married and began a family of three children.

Though the Wilsons were happy at Camphill, after fifteen years they moved to the nearby town of Long Prairie. One reason for the move was their sense that they had not completed the individuation process in relation to Camphill. "It was almost like we never left Camphill," said Don. "We both did very briefly. It wasn't enough." Don was troubled that he couldn't respond when people suggested that Camphillers didn't know what life was like in the real world. "They were right," Don admitted. "I didn't know what it was like to live outside. Whether it's the real world or not, that's debatable." Since their departure, Don and Kristin have worked out a comfortable existence on the edge of both Camphill Minnesota and the larger movement. The village still provides an important friendship network. Their son Tim has spent much time with peers at Camphill; their daughter Alice, now a young adult, has lived for brief periods at both Copake and Camphill Minnesota. Kristin, though not Don, is a member of the inner "Camphill Community," and takes that commitment seriously. Through her work with a local farmer's cooperative, she plays a vital role in keeping Camphill connected to the rural agricultural economy. "It's really nice to be able to still be involved and be connected and have friends," Kristin told me. "I wouldn't say that we'd never go back to Camphill."

Unlike Don and Kristin, their childhood friend Johanna Steinrueck *did* anticipate spending her life in Camphill. Ironically, Johanna has never lived in Camphill as an adult. Her transition into the larger American society began when she enrolled in pottery school at New York's Alfred University. In part because her parents were immigrants as well as Camphillers, Johanna's adjustment was rocky. "I was blind," she said. "I sometimes feel that I grew up twice. I grew up once in Camphill, my first eighteen years. And it took another eighteen years to start all over again outside of Camphill." The first time she got a paycheck for a part-time job, she didn't understand what the money was for. The individualism of art school contrasted with the communal craft ethic of Camphill, but she stuck it out to graduation—mostly to prove to her parents that she knew what she wanted to do with her life. Then, needing to pay off her college loan, she took a job in Minneapolis, near her parents and some Camphill friends. Soon enough, "circumstances took over"—she married Mark Steinrueck, who had also grown up at Copake, and had a son. For a time, Mark and Johanna lived on a small farm that was part of the extended community of Camphill Village Minnesota, but they spent more time in Minneapolis's Uptown neighborhood, where Johanna remained after their divorce.

Johanna continued to deplore the "rugged individualism" of American society so much that, unlike her parents, she never applied for American citizenship. But she also absorbed much of American culture. "I'm a hybrid," she told me. "There's a lot of American influence. . . . I think for myself. And don't like people shoving anything down my throat. . . . Also, I like my freedom." This love of freedom shaped Johanna's decision not to live in a Camphill community. Though the decision was largely "circumstantial," it also reflected her conviction that "you can't move back in life." She wanted to be involved in Camphill "on my terms," and for Camphill itself to be the sort of place where people can move more freely between the community and the larger society, gaining insights and experiences from both places. "I'm not schizo," Johanna explained. "I want to find a way to be connected to Camphill where I don't sacrifice my very hard struggles and what I've gained." She has found that way, in part, through her relationship with Community Homestead, a community founded by several of the people with whom she grew up at Copake where her ex-husband still lives.

Unlike Kristin, Don, and Johanna, Kate Walsh-Little did choose to return to the community where she grew up. Kate's parents founded Viva House a year before her birth, and Kate and her husband Dave returned there the year they were married. This outcome represented a significant development in Kate's sense of identity, for during her teenage years she had shown little inclination for the community lifestyle. "I just didn't want to be a part of it," she recalled. She liked shopping for clothes more than protesting war. Even at the height of her rebellion, though, Kate never questioned the values that had led her parents to the Catholic Worker. "Whenever we would talk about things, it just made so much sense to me what they were saying and what they believed." By the time Kate got to college, it no longer seemed uncool to live out these values. At Fordham, she joined a community home whose members explored a wide range of social justice activities. After her marriage to another campus activist, they thought about creating their own Catholic Worker in the Bronx, but then realized that "there's a good thing going down there [in Baltimore]. We'll go down there."

If Kate found the return to community life easier than Johanna Stein-rueck, this is partly because she was able to be a Catholic Worker on her own terms. When they came to Viva House, Kate and Dave did not simply fold themselves into its soup kitchen ministry. Instead, she said, "we both decided to do our own thing within the Catholic Worker." Kate, an elementary school teacher, set up an after-school tutoring program, while Dave ran a legal aid clinic. Viva House purchased a new building and rearranged its existing facilities to accommodate the new programs and provide a private family apartment for Kate, Dave, and their infant daughter. Kate was especially pleased to be raising a child in the same community context that shaped her, but she was also careful to safeguard her individuality. While hoping that her daughter would come to embrace Catholic Worker values, she was emphatic that she "has to decide what she believes, and I have to be happy with that."[10]

Jerry Mechtenberg-Berrigan, who grew up near Kate at Baltimore's Jonah House, had a teenage rebellion that in some ways put hers to shame. While she was out buying clothes, he was "fanatic for a long time about fast cars," and once broke a street lamp during a "faith and resistance" retreat. Exaggerated stories of his antics, in fact, continue to circulate among Catholic Workers. But even at the peak of his rebellion, Jerry did not question his parents' underlying values. "I knew," he said, that "nuclear weapons . . . were still there, and that was still a deadly thing. And that [resistance] was good work to do. I did take issue with the fact that we were the ones doing it." Respect for his parents' values allowed him to forge a series of connections that gradually drew him back to community. He took three college classes with Peter Gathje, a religious studies scholar who has written on Jonah House. Required to complete an off-campus internship, he remembered that his old Jonah House companions Mike Miles and Barb Kass had started a farm in Wisconsin based on the Catholic Worker model, and so he spent a pleasant spring tapping maple syrup with them. Being in Wisconsin also gave him an opportunity to visit another Jonah House friend, John Heid, at Duluth's Loaves and Fishes Catholic Worker. In Duluth, said Jerry, "I . . . fell in love with the area and . . . the model of community. In reconnecting with these old friends I found the next step in life after college." Jerry spent several years at Loaves and Fishes, and has since lived at the Hartford Catholic Worker, Jonah House, and Anathoth Community Farm.

As Jerry grew into an adult identity as a Catholic Worker, he blended Kate Walsh's respect for individual belief systems with a deep reverence for his parents' legacy. Like them, Jerry is personally committed to civil disobedience, but also admires Catholic Workers whose primary focus is direct care for the poor. It is harder for him to affirm his friends who have chosen a middle-class lifestyle, but he is not willing to condemn them. "We're all doing our best," he said simply. "That's the important thing." Jerry's refusal to judge others, he explained, stems not from an attitude of "I'm okay, you're okay," but from a humble sense of the limits of his own commitment and an awareness that "the truth is bigger than any one of us."

Despite their varied paths, Jerry, Kate, Johanna, Kristin, and Don share a nuanced approach to their communities of origin. Like most Camphill and Catholic Worker kids, they are deeply committed to communal values, but—to a somewhat greater degree than their parents, and a much greater degree than the stereotypical communitarian—they express those values in what Robert Bellah has called "the 'first language' of American individualism."[11] They are reluctant to make judgments about how other people should live their lives, and tend to justify their own life choices in terms of personal priorities rather than ultimate principles. They are comfortable with mainstream social movements, such as feminism and gay liberation, that place a strong emphasis on individual self-determination. (One Catholic Worker parent referred to feminism as the "putrescence of bourgeois values," then acknowledged that his own daughter was a strong feminist.) Many prefer a generalized "spirituality" to dogmatic or institutional "religion." (Dorothy Day was puzzled by her grandchildren's preference for "Zen breathing exercises" over Catholic devotion.[12]) With regard to both spirituality and lifestyle, they have little affinity for the sort of absolutism that can characterize a community in its founding years.

This is not terribly surprising. At one level, it simply reflects the low boundaries separating Catholic Worker and Camphill communities from the larger American society. Most of the community kids I spoke to, for example, were educated in the American public schools, where they imbibed the liberal values shared by most members of their generation. But there are also several liberalizing factors internal to the life of Camphill and the Catholic Worker that help community kids integrate the special values of the community with the more individualistic and inclusive values of the larger society.

Community life can lead to greater individualism for anyone who stays past the initial years of intense enthusiasm and esprit de corps. Ironically, it can be easier to remain faithful to a particularistic belief system if you don't try to live out your beliefs in the company of other people. Once people live together on a daily basis, their ideological unity may be dissolved by the reality of what Mike Miles and Barb Kass referred to as "personal preferences"— the fact that each individual embodies the shared beliefs in a slightly different way. "Some people," says Mike, "get up early, some people get up late, some people like classical, some people like punk, some people like meat, some people are vegan." The nitty-gritty of community life is mostly about finding ways to accommodate those unanticipated differences.

The liberalizing tendency of community life can translate into a liberal, even permissive style of parenting. Parents who have learned to accommodate the "personal preferences" of other community members may be inclined to grant similar respect to their children's preferences. This is especially the case when it comes to religious formation. Community parents often neglect formal catechesis, in part because their children resist it and in part because they figure it is not necessary to teach abstract ideas so long as these are being practiced concretely. The effect of this "osmosis" is that community kids' spiritual values are deeply rooted but correspondingly vague.

Another liberalizing factor is that children growing up in community typically have strong relationships with several adult role models. This gives them an appreciation for different value systems and ideologies. It is not simply a matter of taking or leaving their parents' values, but of sorting through the strengths and weaknesses of several different ways of life. At both the Catholic Worker and Camphill, moreover, kids have an opportunity to form close ties to adults who do *not* necessarily endorse the core values of the community. Short-term community members come for a wide range of reasons, while the homeless "guests" who live at Catholic Workers and the developmentally disabled "villagers" who live at Camphills hold the full spectrum of religious and social views. These people may have an especially strong influence on children, who do not initially recognize the line distinguishing "Workers" from "guests" or "coworkers" from "villagers." In many communities, moreover, guests or villagers are the people with the most time to spend hanging out with kids. Don Wilson, for example, recalled countless Saturday afternoons when he shared coffee with a villager before walking leisurely to the barn to milk the cows together. Such relationships give community kids a real appreciation for values and worldviews that are different from their parents.'

Camphill and the Catholic Worker are also cosmopolitan. Camphill's European roots are nurtured by a steady flow of "young coworkers" from Europe, who befriend the staff kids and invite them for visits to Europe. The Catholic Worker has a smaller presence in Europe, but many Catholic Worker kids today have traveled to movement gatherings throughout the United States, or participated in solidarity trips to the Two-Thirds World. Because community parents are often highly educated but officially impoverished, they are adept at garnering scholarships and unusual educational opportunities for their children. They also tend not to pressure their children to attend college immediately after high school, which gives them a chance to travel and clarify their values before getting locked into a particular career path.

When community kids leave home, they usually take advantage of community networks, staying at other Camphills or Catholic Workers, or simply with individuals who have been associated with the movement. These networks allow community kids to make a clear separation from home and family, because they know they can go almost anywhere in the world and find an open door. Through this process, community kids learn to separate their parents' values from their parents themselves, for they will invariably encounter younger and more accessible people who share the same values. This is what happened to Kate at Fordham, to Jerry in Wisconsin, Duluth, and Los Angeles, and to Johanna, Don, and Kristin in Minnesota.

Ultimately, the key to community kids' sense of individuality may be their sense of rootedness. Again and again, the people I spoke to linked their personal freedom to their strong connections, both to their parents and to the communities that had formed them. Jerry can move from community to community because he knows that "Jonah House will always be home to me." Many Camphill kids postpone college in favor of world travel because they know they can find a welcoming home on virtually any continent. And the experience of community is one that community kids take with them, no matter what their particular life choices. Reflecting on her peers at Copake, Kristin Wilson noted that they have taken various life paths, and yet "I think it's fair to say that all of them definitely are committed to [Camphill]." After more than twenty years away from Camphill, Johanna Steinrueck still said that "I love Camphill 'cause it's my home. It's my heart. . . . I have never left the community within."

In this sense of rootedness, community kids differ from their parents, many of whom came to community as the result of personal uprooting. The founders of Camphill were war refugees who had seen their most cherished values trampled on by European fascism, while the young people who joined communities in the 1960s had rejected, or at least seriously questioned, the deepest values of their parents and their society. Most community kids, by contrast, lean on the community as a secure repository of values. If they sometimes rebel against their parents' lifestyle, this is precisely because they feel so secure about their values. In all of this, they are much like the majority of Americans. Despite our national obsession with adolescence, most Americans come out of their period of rebellion with their parents' core values intact. But for community kids, this typical American-ness can become a profound gift to the community movement. They are uniquely poised to build bridges, translating their parents' seemingly unAmerican values into an idiom that ordinary Americans can understand.

Johanna Steinrueck, for example, has committed herself to bridge-building by advising the movement on how to recruit more American coworkers. "I want to create a situation in the future," she said, "where there's more interchange, without Camphill losing any of its integrity. . . . I've got all this insight into two different worlds, and there's so much good in both." Johanna's service to the movement also serves her individual self-interest: "I want to do it for myself, very selfishly, so I can fit in."

Jerry Mechtenberg-Berrigan told a story that encapsulates the gift that community kids can offer. While in college, Jerry made friends with several students who admired his parents' resistance work, but had more conventional goals for themselves. Though this created some moments of judgment, Jerry persisted in the friendships, and in the summer of 1999 he got together in Chicago with several friends, including one who had recently purchased his first home. As they were leaving a bar at two in the morning, this friend stole the bar's American flag, took it outside, and burned it on the street. "I was talking to [him] about it later," said Jerry, "and he was like, look. I do my thing. I study. I own a house. I still know that your parents are doing these things. . . . And I know that when you do a lot of these actions you do a lot of planning first. And I know that this was spontaneous. But . . . I had to do it." Jerry's point in telling this story was not to promote spontaneous flag-burning as an ideal activist technique, but to highlight the way he had become a bridge between his father's deliberate activism and his friend's more spontaneous approach. Jerry was impressed by his friend's action "because he did something controversial and unpopular and . . . was personally clear on the matter. . . . He did what *he* had to do." Jerry's ability to respect his friend's individual choices made it possible for his friend, in turn, to participate in his own way in the work of the Catholic Worker movement. Jerry says that "to have this happen was a gift for me," but I think the gift goes further. If Karl König's dream of a new social order is to be realized, if the Catholic Worker is to succeed in creating a "new society within the shell of the old," it will be in part because community kids have helped their neighbors connect to the community movement in countless individual ways.

Notes

1. Marcia Timmel, cited in Troester, *Voices*, 291.

2. Julian Pleasants, cited in Troester, *Voices*, 22.

3. This account draws on my own interviews, Rosalie Riegle Troester's interview, Dorothy Day—Catholic Worker Collection, series W-9, box 3, folder 23, and Deane Mowrer's interview, 5 June 1968, Dorothy Day—Catholic Worker Collection, series W-9, box 1, folder 10, p. 31.

4. Karl König, unpublished manuscript, in Karl König Archive, cited in Müller-Wiedemann, *Karl König*, 149.

5. Margrit Metraux, in Hunt, *Shining Lights*, 34.

6. Day, *Loaves and Fishes*, 54.

7. Terry Bennet-Cauchon, cited in Troester, *Voices*, 295.

8. Ibid.; and Bob Lassalle-Klein, cited in Troester, *Voices*, 296.

9. Willa Bickham to Peggy [Scherer?], 24 July 1979, Dorothy Day—Catholic Worker Collection, series W-4, box 6, folder 9; Open Letter from Viva House, Feast of the Assumption 1979, Dorothy Day—Catholic Worker Collection, series W-4, box 6, folder 9; and Brendan Walsh, "Community," *Enthusiasm*, Spring 1984, p. 6, Dorothy Day—Catholic Worker Collection, series W-51, box 1, folder 19 (titled "Newsletters").

10. Since the time of our interview, Kate has had two more children, and her family has moved a short distance away from Viva House while continuing to participate in its activities.

11. Robert Bellah et al., *Habits of the Heart: Individualism and Commitment in American Life*, updated edition (Berkeley: University of California Press, 1985) 20.

12. William D. Miller, *All Is Grace: The Spirituality of Dorothy Day* (Garden City, NJ: Doubleday, 1987) 188, cited in Geoffrey Gneuhs, "Radical Orthodoxy: Dorothy Day's Challenge to Liberal America," in William J. Thorn, Phillip Runkel, and Susan Mountin, eds., *Dorothy Day and the Catholic Worker Movement: Centenary Essays* (Milwaukee: Marquette University Press, 2001) 218.

Keeping the Faith

The Camphill Movement, however, has no intention or desire to develop into a sect. It should therefore not be regarded as a sectarian community. It is far from it. For the Camphill Movement, Christianity is an indispensable part of its life and work; it works out of Christianity, not for Christianity.

—*Karl König*[1]

I would say that I went through a conversion into a real church. And that real church was the Catholic Worker. What I was raised on was not the real church. Everything was fairy tales—no reality.

—*Kathleen Rumpf*[2]

Both Camphill and the Catholic Worker draw their models of community from Jesus' vision of a society transfigured by sharing, love, and nonviolence. Yet they are not conventional "religious communities." They are not vowed religious orders, and they are certainly not parishes or congregations. Instead, they have sought to honor the diverse spiritual paths of their individual members while remaining in dialogue with traditional, noncommunitarian Christian institutions. This is a delicate balancing act, both because of the variety of backgrounds of people who are drawn to community and because community life allows its members to express their faith in ways that are quite different from those found in conventional congregations. At their best, though, both Camphill and the Catholic Worker have articulated a distinctive Christian identity, welcomed the stranger who does not share that identity but is willing to share the work of community, honored the wayward spiritual journeys of all their members, and maintained a constructive and critical dialogue with conventional religious institutions. Each of these practices has helped them to touch the world in mutually transformative ways.

Articulating a Christian Identity

Most Christian churches—whether local congregations or entire denominations—articulate their identities in terms of creeds and sacraments. To "be" a Catholic or a Methodist or a Presbyterian means, primarily, to profess the shared faith of the church (perhaps by reciting the Nicene Creed) and to participate in its common rituals (perhaps by receiving the Eucharist on a weekly or monthly basis). Even those evangelical churches that claim "no creed but the Bible" and shun the traditional sacraments assume their members will hold certain beliefs and participate in some defining rituals, such as the altar call or "making a personal decision for Jesus." And most churches maintain membership lists that draw a fairly clear line between those who are in creedal and sacramental communion and those who are not.

The communities included in this study use none of these methods. Many host Christian services that involve creeds and sacraments, but not all community members participate. Yet these communities do have their own methods of articulating a Christian identity. For the most part, these focus not on creeds and sacraments, but on *work*. To be a Camphiller is to participate in the work of curative education or social therapy; to be a Catholic Worker is to participate in the work of hospitality and resistance. To suggest that an organization defined in such ways is a "Christian" organization implies a particular understanding of the meaning of the word "Christian." In some cases, this understanding is only implicit; in other cases, a community may make its understanding explicit by lifting up the Sermon on the Mount, the Works of Mercy, or the ideal of God's kingdom on earth as the basis for its shared work. In either case, the resulting Christian identity attaches more firmly to the community than to the individual. A community that does Christian work is a Christian community, but it cannot presume to speak definitively about the spiritual or religious identities of those who participate in that work.

For Catholic Workers, the understanding of Christian work flows directly from the Gospel. "Our manifesto is the Sermon on the Mount," declared Dorothy Day repeatedly in the pages of *The Catholic Worker*. With Peter Maurin, she developed a complete social program from the "works of mercy" listed in Matthew 25. Just as Jesus told the sheep gathered at the judgment day that "whatever you did for one of these least brothers of mine, you did for me," so Day and Maurin believed they could reconstruct society by feeding the hungry, giving drink to the thirsty, welcoming the stranger, clothing the naked, caring for the sick, and visiting those in prison. (Following medieval tradition, Day and Maurin coupled these "corporal" works of mercy with such "spiritual" works as "comforting the afflicted.") Their commitment to nonviolent resistance was likewise rooted in Jesus' "cheeky" example of loving one's enemies. At a time when few lay Catholics read the Bible and Catholic social teaching depended primarily on Thomistic philosophy, the founders of the Catholic Worker unapologetically based their movement on the Gospels and the prophets.

This is not to say that Day and Maurin were averse to doctrine. As individuals, they were convinced that doctrinal fidelity to the Catholic magisterium could go hand in hand with a radical discipleship rooted in the Gospels. They were even more convinced that participation in the church's sacraments was a necessary source of strength for discipleship. In the early years, Day tried to make such participation normative, at least for the movement's leaders. "Any appearance of success is fictitious," she wrote to local leaders in 1939, "if leaders who can work in the different cities do not make daily Mass and Communion the foundation of their work." In the same year, Day replaced the movement's biennial colloquium with an annual retreat. Under the guidance of Father John J. Hugo, who began serving as leader in 1941, the retreat consisted of a full week of silence, with readings from the lives of the saints and, especially, the Gospels. Some Workers (and some church officials!) found Hugo ascetic and Jansenist in his emphasis on giving up material pleasures, but Day insisted that "no material work is being accomplished by the Catholic Worker, in any part of the country, that is as important as this retreat. . . . If you are part of The Catholic Worker movement, it is your obligation." Those who attended reported that Hugo had helped them "to reach the goal of really living the way Christ wanted us to live. Living the Sermon on the Mount." Though Hugo stopped giving retreats at the Catholic Worker farm in the 1960s, individual Workers attended his retreats in other places right up to his death in 1985.[3]

Day's efforts to make retreats and daily Mass defining marks of the Worker were balanced by her insistence, shared with Peter Maurin, that the Catholic Worker was and would remain a *lay* movement. Both anticipating and building on the emerging theology of the laity expressed in Pius XII's *Mystici Corporis* (1943) and Vatican II's *Lumen Gentium* (which defined the church primarily as the "whole people of God"), Day believed that lay Catholics should lead the church's engagement with the world. "We never felt it was necessary to ask permission to perform the works of mercy," Day explained in *Loaves and Fishes*. "Our houses and farms were always started on our own responsibility." She gladly accepted spiritual counsel and donations from priests, but chastised the newspaper editors if they ran too many articles by the clergy. She bristled when neighbors treated the Workers as if they were monks and nuns, writing that "I am impatient at this lack of understanding. This is work for *lay people to initiate and to manage.*"[4]

Day and Maurin also dissented from the traditional view that the "counsels of perfection"—often summarized as "poverty, chastity, and obedience"—applied only to priests and members of religious orders. Shifting the emphasis from celibacy to Gospel nonviolence, they insisted that "the law of holiness embraces everyone and admits of no exception" and that "the precept of perfection is incumbent on all." And Day *was* happy to publish articles by priests if they developed this theology of the laity. In one article, Father Paul Hanly Furfey argued that a "maximum" moral standard should be the goal of all Christians, while Father John Hugo advocated a "totalitarian Christianity" in which everyone would submit to the rigorous demands of the Beatitudes.[5]

In part because of the emphasis on lay independence, the Worker consistently attracted volunteers who shared Day's understanding of Gospel morality but not her sacramental or doctrinal commitments to the church. And from the beginning, both Day and Maurin had an ecumenical sensibility. According to one early Worker, Maurin had preferred the name "Christian Worker" as an expression of this, and his Round Table discussions always included non-Catholic (and non-Christian) participants. "They were," Day recalled, "the beginning of our work for peace among religious groups. We could all meet together . . . in our search for the common good." Day's personal connections to Jews and Marxists made it easy for her to believe, as Vatican II would eventually affirm, that in some mysterious way they were also part of Christ's Mystical Body.[6] Accordingly, when such persons wanted to join the Worker in performing the works of mercy, Day welcomed them with open arms.

As the Worker's concrete witness attracted a steady stream of non-Catholic volunteers, the church as a whole was changing in ways that would have a big impact on the movement's self-understanding. In many ways, the Second Vatican Council, held in the early 1960s, was a victory for the Worker. It affirmed themes that Day and Maurin had been talking about for decades: the centrality of the laity, the importance of biblical study, the connections between the liturgy and social justice, and the doctrine of the "Mystical Body of Christ" as a basis both for ecumenism and social transformation. Almost as soon as the council had closed, however, a rift emerged over its proper interpretation. Some Catholics saw it as a correction of the defensive conservatism of the nineteenth century, but also as a reaffirmation of the classical Catholic understanding of hierarchical authority and the centrality of the liturgy. Others hoped it would be just the first step in an ongoing process of democratization and radicalization that would eventually lead to the ordination of women, the elimination of the hierarchy, and a pluralistic embrace of other religions. For the most part, Dorothy Day found herself in the first group. The more radical liturgical changes, she worried, reflected a "contempt . . . for the faith of the inarticulate ones of the earth," and she could muse nostalgically about the old Latin hymns that "take so much breath that I wonder why my grandchildren have to go in for Zen breathing exercises."[7]

Many Workers, like Day's grandchildren, found themselves in the group that saw Vatican II as a stepping-stone to more radical changes. By the 1960s and 1970s, many Worker houses sponsored lay Masses or more fanciful expressions of radical Catholicism. In one case, recalled Tom Cornell, a Worker from Chicago "held up a cup of coffee and a donut and said, 'These are my body and blood.' Meaning, 'Hell! Let's take it *all* out of the church! The reality is just this—just the bread line and the resistance to the war.'" Such practices were deeply painful to Day, as her close associate Jim Forest recalled. "It was heartbreaking for her, later in her life, to see that there was very little reverence left in the Catholic Worker movement," Forest told Rosalie Riegle Troester. "A lot of the people coming to the Catholic Worker movement couldn't . . . wouldn't open themselves to her love of the church. They thought things that were precious to her were ridiculous."[8]

Nevertheless, Day made few attempts to rally the movement to her version of Catholicism. Instead, she gradually dropped even the insistence that *leaders* of the movement would be in full communion with the church. By the 1960s, she affirmed simply that the newspaper's editors "are mostly Catholic . . . and if they are not, they agree that without brotherly love there can be no love of God."[9] In a few cases, she retained the names of ex-Catholics on the masthead even after they asked her to remove them. It is not clear exactly why Day became so reluctant to force non-Catholics or ex-Catholics out of the movement. It may be that she regretted the way her strong stance on pacifism had alienated many supporters during World War II. Even so, the juxtaposition of her strong stance on pacifism with her flexibility about Catholic identity had a lasting effect on the movement's identity. To this day, one can hardly be a Catholic Worker without practicing the works of mercy. Many Workers are pacifists, and those who are not keep pretty quiet about their views. But non-Catholics, ex-Catholics, rebellious Catholics, and ultraorthodox Catholics are all prominent in the movement, and all seem equally convinced that they have a right to be there.

Given Day's refusal to impose a theological party line, today's Catholic Worker houses articulate their religious identity in a wide variety of ways.

At one extreme, Ann O'Connor and Peter King of Unity Kitchen in Syracuse have denounced those Worker communities that support gay liberation or sponsor lay-officiated Eucharists. Repeatedly, they have called "our Catholic Worker brothers and sisters to decision! . . . If you are not Catholic in union with the Church, don't call yourself a Catholic Worker, because you are not one." But O'Connor and King speak for very few Catholic Workers, even among those who are quite orthodox in their theology. The founders of the Houston Catholic Worker, Mark and Louise Zwick, are more typical of the Worker's orthodox wing. Both in their newspaper and a recent book, they have called the movement's attention back to the Catholic saints and theologians who inspired Day and Maurin. But they have also distanced themselves from O'Connor and King's sweeping criticism of the movement, writing that "we weren't comfortable taking an approach of attacking others in the movement. . . . We wanted people to know of the greatness of the founders and what the movement had to offer in pulling together a vision for our times."[10]

The New York houses have generally taken a similar stance. Jane Sammon, one of the paper's most prominent editors for many years, cautioned in 1984 against too easy suspicion of the "institutional church." "This institution," she wrote, "which has been built, added on to, and rebuilt again and again, is capable of arousing our deepest longings for unity, goodness, and purity of intention." Still, these words appeared in a basically sympathetic account of the theology of Leonardo Boff, written when he was being disciplined by the official church's Congregation on the Doctrine of the Faith.[11]

At the other extreme, many Worker communities privilege personal spirituality over the founders' orthodoxy in articulating their identity. The presence of several Buddhists at Boston's Haley House in the 1980s led the community to describe itself as "a spiritually based community nurtured by the Catholic Worker tradition." Several other communities have chosen similar language; St. Catherine of Genoa Catholic Worker in Chicago called itself "a faith based community providing hospitality to the homeless living with AIDS, ARC or HIV, in the spirit of the Catholic Worker Movement founded by Peter Maurin and Dorothy Day." A handful of Workers use a lower-case "c" in "catholic" as an expression of ecumenical openness. The Duluth Catholic Worker, more gently, prints this self-description in many of its newsletters: "Not all are Catholic, not all are Christian—but all are encouraged to make progress along their spiritual path. We set time aside for prayer and meditation, rotate leadership in Sunday evening liturgy, and seek to provide an environment for spiritual growth." And members of Saint

Martin de Porres Catholic Worker in San Francisco once wrote that "we are a very ecumenical group, some go to Mass, some pray to Allah by the back bathroom, some ride bikes, God is a major topic, but so is many things. We have memorial services for our guests that have died, but our major form of prayer is wringing our hands together saying the sky is falling, the sky is falling."[12]

What holds this diversity together is a sense that the social vision of the Sermon on the Mount is relevant even for those who don't share the doctrinal claims of Christianity. Most versions of the "Catholic Worker Positions" thus rely more on Gospel quotations than official Catholic teachings. Ammon Hennacy's 1955 rendition, for example, affirmed that "the spiritual basis of the Catholic Worker movement stems from the Sermon on the Mount," while a 1979 update specifically cited "the Sermon on the Mount (Matthew 5:38-48) and the call to solidarity with the poor (Matthew 25:31-36) as the heart of the Gospel message."[13] Few Workers would disagree that it is the practice of Gospel-based nonviolence and the works of mercy that holds them together, whatever their theological disagreements. Sarah Jeglosky of Saints Francis and Thérèse Catholic Worker spoke for many when she wrote, in their community's first newsletter, that "we were drawn together by a common desire to live the Gospels. The Beatitudes gave us the incentive to perform the works of mercy."[14]

Many Camphillers could echo these words. Like Peter Maurin and Dorothy Day, Camphill founder Karl König had a special affinity for the twenty-fifth chapter of Matthew, with its suggestion that Christ can be found in any needy person. As a young Jewish boy in Vienna, he often walked past a hospital gate inscribed with the words, "Whatever you did for one of these least brothers of mine, you did for me." Years later König would work diligently to clarify how his community could honor this Christian moral principle while remaining open to the world. "The Camphill Movement," he wrote, "has no intention or desire to develop into a sect. . . . For the Camphill Movement, Christianity is an indispensable part of its life and work; it works out of Christianity, not for Christianity. Thus it is not an organization for the purpose of disseminating Christian faith." The same distinction applied to the specifically anthroposophical understanding of Christianity: "It is not our task to propagate [Steiner's] teachings; our endeavours are to help and to heal. We know that we can do so when we teach, treat, educate and carry out our work in the light of his indications."[15]

Though this nuanced account parallels Catholic Worker explanations of their relationship to Christianity, it also builds on Steiner's reluctance to identify anthroposophy as a "religion." By calling it a "spiritual science" instead,

Steiner made at least four important points. First, anthroposophy is directly concerned with the spiritual realities underlying the material world, including angels, elemental beings, and the "etheric" and "astral" bodies associated with each person. Second, it is based on experimental or "scientific" encounters with these realities, rather than on "religious" appeals to faith or authority. Third, anthroposophy draws on the spiritual insights of many different "religious" traditions, even as it places these within the overarching framework of Christian esotericism. It is, in the terms used by some theorists of interfaith dialogue, an "inclusivist" rather than "exclusivist" or "pluralist" tradition, "including" other traditions within its own frame of reference. Anthroposophy, finally, has implications for all dimensions of human experience—politics, economics, education, medicine, agriculture, the arts—rather than only for the communal rituals usually designated "religious." Indeed, anthroposophy has inspired one movement, the Christian Community, that does see itself as religious—indeed, it is also known as the "Movement for Religious Renewal." But its link to anthroposophy is no more intimate than that of educational or agricultural initiatives. One can be a full-fledged anthroposophist through individual spiritual practice, without participating in the communal rituals of the Christian Community.[16]

Drawing on the principles of "spiritual science," König believed that Christianity entailed not only moral principles of the sort found in the Sermon on the Mount, but also an elaborate set of truth claims about humanity, the world, and God. He also believed the source of these truth claims was not authoritative dogma but the spiritual experiences of Rudolf Steiner—experiences that were, in principle, open to any sincere seeker. These truth claims inform much of what goes on at Camphill: the way the cycles of the day and year are celebrated, the approach to care for the person with disabilities, the techniques used in tending to land and animals. This is what König meant by "carry[ing] out our work in the light of [Steiner's] indications." All Camphillers are expected to participate in this work, but the truth claims themselves are not binding on them. No one is required to "be" an anthroposophist or a Christian.

This distinction seems to have developed gradually during Camphill's early years. Just as Day at first assumed that Catholic Workers would be practicing Catholics, so the early Camphillers began their shared life as an anthroposophical study circle. There was at first little question of how to include non-anthroposophists. "König based his work and his impulses upon Rudolf Steiner," recalled Anke Weihs. "This meant that his young assistants had also to be pupils of Rudolf Steiner, something which happened without coercion or the imposition of will, for we were fully aware that our destiny had led us to Karl König and that work with Karl König meant work with Rudolf Steiner." König assumed that this "Community" would remain a close-knit circle of mutual accountability. Moreover, he was personally very much drawn to the specifically "religious" expression of anthroposophy. He had a close connection to the leader of the Christian Community in Great Britain, and in 1942 they worked out an agreement that made the Camphill Community as a whole a member of the Christian Community. König's journals even suggest that he expected Camphill to become a new sort of religious "Order." In 1945 he composed a "First Memorandum" for members of the Camphill Community, which at that time included all of the non-handicapped coworkers. This document declared that Community members were motivated by "love for the children" and "devotion to Christ," and would "fashion their lives according to the striving toward the Spirit of the Age as it was revealed by Rudolf Steiner and is manifest in the sacraments of the Christian Community as well as in the meditative communion of the individual who wrestles for self-development."[17]

As a wider group of people were drawn into the work of Camphill, König found that he had to modify both his expectations of the inner "Community" and his assumption that that community could be coextensive with Camphill as a whole. By 1948 more than two hundred fifty people were involved in the work of Camphill, and many of these were not inclined to participate fully in the life of the inner Community. König's "Second Memorandum" thus dissolved the earlier agreement with the Christian Community and declared that "the Camphill Community withdraws into its own sphere." This does not seem to have been intended as a loosening of the connection between Camphill and anthroposophy; indeed, Community members were now free to join a Christian Community congregation and an Anthroposophical Society branch as *individuals*, rather than simply as members of the Camphill Community. But the change did reflect König's deepening understanding of Rudolf Steiner's "Threefold" social theory, according to which absolute freedom must be honored in the spiritual realm. The intent of the Second Memorandum was to place the Camphill Community clearly within the spiritual realm, so that its members could pursue their common spiritual tasks in entire freedom. By contrast, decision-making bodies such as the Schools Community Meeting and Camphill Movement were located in the "middle sphere," where equal rights held supreme value. This differentiation of spheres has allowed Camphill to welcome a wide range of individuals to participate in the economic and rights spheres, even as the spiritual sphere of the Community remains committed to anthroposophy.

There is a paradox here, for the Threefolding theory itself, which has implications for all three spheres, is rooted in Steiner's own spiritual experiences. Indeed, though the inner Community has withdrawn from the day-to-day administration, it continues to be responsible for preserving the essential identity of Camphill. For the most part this paradox has been fruitful rather than destructive, because Camphill's economic and social practices are transparent enough that non-anthroposophists (both spiritual seekers and those committed to another spiritual path) can readily discern whether they wish to participate. These practices are also stable enough that the Camphill Community has rarely, if ever, had to intervene to prevent a community from abandoning its identity.

The paradox is compounded by the fact that "religious" rituals, insofar as they have a social dimension, cannot be confined to the sphere of free spiritual life. When König urged that "our life [be] permeated by religion, permeated by the grace of the Sacraments," he made a point of adding that "religion permeates the sphere of rights, builds the basis for the sphere of work, as well as for the sphere of the free spiritual life." When König identified the weekly "Bible evening" as one of the three "pillars" of Camphill, moreover, he associated it primarily with the rights sphere, insofar as all members of the community would meet as equals in their discussion of the Bible. (The "college meeting," with its educational emphasis, was the "pillar" corresponding to the free spiritual sphere.) König thus did not imagine that he was violating his companions' spiritual freedom by expecting them to attend Bible evenings and sacramental services; such attendance was simply necessary to knit together the social fabric of the village. An increasing number of contemporary Camphillers, by contrast, see services and Bible evenings as spiritual practices that should be left to the free choice of each individual.[18]

Given these paradoxes, and the resulting tensions, many Camphills struggle to articulate their Christian identity in terms that are comprehensible to the general public, including those who have not even visited a school or village. These challenges are evident in the self-descriptions that Camphill places write for their Web sites, brochures, or listings in directories such as the one produced by the Fellowship for Intentional Community. The ten Camphills included in the 2000 edition offered self-descriptions ranging from "living and working together" and "live with special needs adults" to "Spiritual Social Renewal Care" and "anthroposophy." Camphill Soltane wrote that "ours is a spiritual and service community with a reverence for life, for cooperation, and for celebration," while Camphill Triform said that the movement's "hallmark is a genuine recognition of the spiritual integrity of the individual regardless of ability." Five mentioned anthroposophy and seven mentioned Steiner, describing him as a philosopher, scientist, educator, and humanitarian. Such self-descriptions reflect a fear of being perceived as "sectarian," and appropriately emphasize the fact that all sorts of people are welcome to be part of Camphill. But some also create the unfortunate impression that Camphill life is shaped by a vague "spirituality in general," rather than by the specific (if noncoercive) perspectives of anthroposophy.[19]

For those who do spend time at Camphill, its Christian identity appears most clearly in the way the cycles of the day, week, and year are observed. Every meal begins with prayer, often accompanied by a Bible passage (drawn from a special Camphill lectionary) or a meditative verse from Rudolf Steiner's "Calendar of the Soul." Using evocative language, these verses draw connections between biblical themes and the natural processes associated with each season of the year. A steadily declining number of Camphill households observe a "Bible Evening" on Saturday, in which participants reflect on the connections between the week's Bible passage and their own experiences. Different Camphills make different arrangements for Sunday worship. At Camphill Village Minnesota the lay-officiated Service of Offering is celebrated just once a month. On other Sundays, Camphillers go to worship services at nearby churches or join for a spiritually eclectic "gathering" hosted by one of the households. Camphill Copake, on the other hand, makes the sacraments of the Christian Community regularly available, and a large segment of the community participates.

There is a strong expectation, though not a formal requirement, that Camphillers participate in seasonal festivals that combine spiritual content with drama, dancing, and fun. Few are inclined to complain about this expectation, because the festivals truly serve a social function by drawing the entire village or school together. They are drawn from the traditional Christian liturgical year, though much is made of some holidays that are neglected by non-anthroposophical Christians. Michaelmas, or the feast of the Archangel Michael, is a major event because of the anthroposophical understanding that Michael is the guardian of the present astrological age. Camphillers gather on each of the twelve days of Christmas to light candles on the tree, tell stories, and perhaps hear a lecture on the spiritual significance of the slowly lengthening days. In almost every case, festival observances are designed to connect participants to the spiritual realities underlying natural phenomena. At Camphill Beaver Run, students celebrate the Ascension of Christ by climbing a mountain or flying kites at the park; the villagers at Camphill Kimberton Hills sing carols to their cows on Christmas Eve. Water is a major theme of the festival of Saint John the Baptist, and on one occasion at Camphill Village Minnesota a walk to the village's spring was marked by a hailstorm. Most interpreted it, tongue half in cheek, as a sign of the saint's presence among us.

As I conducted interviews, I heard equal praise for the festivals from committed anthroposophists and from those whose relationship to anthroposophy was ambivalent at best. David Spears of the Lukas Community explained that festivals "serve as the heart of the community," meeting the "social" needs of those who enjoy baking cookies and singing Christmas carols at the same time as they bring "religious content, leading thoughts from anthroposophy and other religious orientations as well." Douglas Elmquist, who had grown up at Copake but was uncertain about anthroposophy, said that for him the festivals "bring us back together. . . . It's more of a feeling of the community coming together, doing something. Getting up on Easter morning and going up and watching the sun rise. . . . We're doing something together, and it feels special. I can't tell you that it's spiritual."

The Camphillers' praise for the festivals is echoed in the words of both Camphillers and Catholic Workers when asked about the contribution that Christian identity makes to community life. "It has struck me," wrote Jim Levinson after several years as a Catholic Worker, "that when we in community worshipped together, we were fine. And when we weren't fine, we didn't worship together." [20] "I think basically everybody needs some sort of spiritual foundation," Sheila Russell of Community Homestead told me. "I think that holds a lot of people together and I think without that they're really lost." Camphill, added Ben Cownap of Kimberton Hills, "wouldn't be able to continue without some people carrying anthroposophy as the leading image." The individuals just quoted were quite diverse in their personal spiritual identities. Jim Levinson is Jewish; Ben Cownap told me that his personal spiritual path "needs work," while Sheila Russell said she wasn't even a "spiritual seeker." This juxtaposition of personal diversity with a strong commitment to the Christian identity of the community points to a common thread among these communities. Each has affirmed, again and again, that spiritual practices are essential to the health of a community, *and* that personal freedom is essential to healthy spiritual practices. The paradox involved in these paired principles cannot readily be reduced to the static formula of a creed. But when it is grappled with in an ongoing way, it can be a source of great vitality for shared life.

Welcoming the Stranger

Perhaps the most important way in which Camphill and Catholic Worker communities have honored the paradox of Christian identity and personal freedom has been by "welcoming the stranger" who does not share the spiritual identity of the community. Indeed, each movement has gone out of its way to make such persons feel welcome. Camphill and Catholic Worker advertisements stress that they "accept people of all spiritual paths" or "embrace volunteers of many beliefs and faiths."[21] One member of the Des Moines Catholic Worker told me that "there are more Baptists and Quakers here than Catholics." After a quick count revealed that this wasn't quite true, cofounder Frank Cordaro observed that "we're probably as Catholic and Christian as we have [ever been], because there are times when you couldn't find a Catholic in the crowd." Virtually all the long-term coworkers at Camphill Copake are students of anthroposophy, but their village is designed to give honor to other religious traditions: the overall layout mirrors the mandala shapes of Buddhist monasteries, while the community's "holy of holies, our place of the spirit" is named for the Native American religious leader Black Elk. "Here we experience a closeness to those beings of nature which were honored by the Native American peoples," wrote Penny Roberts in explanation.[22]

In each case, the expressions of welcome are rooted in core spiritual principles. The Catholic Worker both anticipated and embraced the inclusivist ecclesiology of Vatican II, according to which people of all faiths may be in partial "communion" with the saving work of the Catholic Church. Anthroposophy is also best understood as an "inclusivist" tradition insofar as it interprets other religions in light of the centrality of the Christ event while affirming the importance of each individual's unique spiritual journey. Applying this anthroposophical principle to the spiritual diversity present at Camphill Village Minnesota, Lois Smith reflected that "I don't want an anthroposophical world, in that I want everything to look a certain way or sound a certain way or be spoken out in a certain language. I want us all to make that ultimate breakthrough to the spirit, from whatever ways will be right for each person."

Each movement has a history of special connection to one or more "outside" groups. At the time of the Catholic Worker's founding, the most prominent promoter of Catholic social teaching in the United States was Father Charles Coughlin, whose calls for "social justice" were laced with bitter attacks on the Jews. But Day had many Jewish socialist friends (including at least one, Mike Gold, who was still volunteering at the Oakland Catholic Worker in the 1960s), while Maurin wrote of "the presence of Jews all over the world" as "a reminder to the world of the coming of Christ." They rebuffed Coughlinite overtures, castigated the United States for failing to respond to early instances of Nazi genocide, published a woodcut in which the Christ Child wore a Star of David, and helped launch the Committee of Catholics to Fight Anti-Semitism. These early expressions of solidarity inspired a steady stream of Jews to affiliate themselves with the Catholic Worker, including the Jewish liberation theologian Marc Ellis and the Quaker artist Fritz Eichenberg, an ethnic Jew who left Germany at the beginning of the Nazi era. More recently, Catholic Workers have challenged subtle forms of anti-Semitism within the peace and justice movement, such as the tendency to blame modern oppression on Jewish purity laws.[23]

The Catholic Worker's social vision also inspired ecumenical and interfaith connections. The movement has always stressed the connections between liturgy and social justice, and this interest led a few Workers to the Orthodox Church or Byzantine Rite Catholicism. Ammon Hennacy introduced the Worker to the Doukhobors, a Russian sect with a radical peace witness, and persistently made connections with other peace churches and even the communal heritage of the Mormons. But perhaps the most admired non-Catholic in the Worker movement has been Mohandas Gandhi. Gandhi figured prominently in the early Worker retreats as a "reproach to the West" because of his fidelity to Jesus' teachings on nonviolence. When he died, the *Worker* virtually canonized him in an obituary: "There is no public figure who has more conformed his life to the life of Jesus Christ than Gandhi, there is no man who has carried about him more consistently the aura of divinized humanity, who has added his sacrifice to the sacrifice of Christ. . . . In him we have a new intercessor with Christ, a modern Francis, a pacifist martyr."[24] In later years, the Worker sponsored frequent conferences on Gandhian nonviolence, while calling attention to the distinctive perspectives of Buddhist, Native American, and Muslim practitioners of Gandhi's methods.

Camphill's early relationship to Judaism was even more intimate than the Catholic Worker's, insofar as many of the founders were ethnic Jews who would likely have died in the Holocaust had they not escaped to Scotland. Their original vision of Camphill life was deeply indebted to the semicommunal ethos of the Jewish ghetto, and Camphillers have since paid close attention to the evolution of the Jewish kibbutz movement. Karl König's parents, still observant Jews, resided at Camphill for its first decades, and he himself spent the last years of his life reflecting on the meaning of the Holocaust and his own Jewish heritage.[25] When Camphill first arrived in

North America, most of the villagers were children of Jewish parents who felt a strong sense of solidarity with the founders of Camphill, and a secular Jewish culture is still tangibly present at Copake.

Such connections help Camphill and the Catholic Worker offer clear gestures of welcome to the diverse individuals who make their way to their doors. In some cases, these people were drawn to the practice of community life almost in spite of the spiritual principles that inform it. At Camphill Village Minnesota, Trudy Pax told me that she had "visited a lot of communities where I liked the theory but not the practice. At Camphill, I didn't like the theory but the practice really worked." David Stein made a similar point even more provocatively, telling Rosalie Riegle Troester that "I don't see the Catholic Worker as having the remotest thing to do with being Catholic. I justify it on logical and rational terms. . . . The Catholic Worker makes so much sense to me on all those levels that I don't see a religious justification as necessary."[26]

Others are spiritual seekers or eclectics who affirm the principles of their chosen community in general terms, but feel little need to affiliate with any one tradition. Sara Thomsen and Paula Williams told me half-seriously that their time at the Loaves and Fishes Catholic Worker had solidified their identity as "Benedictine witches." At the Lukas Community, Joy Dean told me that "I think more of myself as a spiritual being having a human experience. . . . I don't specifically have a religion other than honoring the divine in everything." This perspective allowed her to immerse herself in the Steiner study groups sponsored by Lukas. Steiner's "observations and insights are just phenomenal," Dean explained. "All it does is add to my experience because he was such a great teacher." At Camphill Copake, Frank LeBar expressed a similar appreciation for the "adventure" of learning more about Steiner. "I think the more you read Steiner," said LeBar, "the more you realize that many things that we're saying nowadays . . . are things that he said way back in the 1920s or earlier." At the same time, LeBar dissented from some of Steiner's ideas and observed that "to my way of thinking, Jesus and Buddha and all the rest of them were talking about pretty much the same thing."

Perhaps the most vocal group of "strangers" are those who find that community life offers an ideal niche for their personal spiritual path, even though it is different from that of their community mates. Tom Farr and Mary Davis were for several years members of Camphill Village Minnesota and devoted followers of A Course in Miracles. Both testified to the ways in which community life deepened their spiritual practice. Forgiving oneself and others is the heart of A Course in Miracles, Tom explained, and "everyday Camphill provides another opportunity to forgive." At Camphill, Mary added, "the work is always giving me an opportunity to be in a new situation or new encounter that's always reflecting back to me what I can see about myself. It's all like a huge mirror. And if I want to I can look in a way that allows me to see myself and also see others."

Jim Levinson was even more emphatic about the way the Catholic Worker deepened his Jewish faith. The "attention paid to things spiritual," he told Rosalie Riegle Troester, had helped him do "new and deeper things within Judaism. My grandfather had been a cantor and his ancestors back through the generations. And now I am a cantor, also." Even David Stein, who seemed so dismissive of the Catholicity of the Worker, acknowledged that the movement had helped him connect with the heart of his own tradition: "I define Judaism as the repudiation of idolatry, period. This society makes an idol of money, status, power, clout, military supremacy, luxury, fashion—many, many things. To live in a place like the Catholic Worker is to renounce those idols."[27]

Perhaps the most striking example of the ways in which outsiders can find a spiritual niche in community is the experience of Buddhists at Haley House. At the time of my visit, I was struck by the prints of *bodhisattvas* alongside the traditional Catholic Worker woodcuts and by the Zen haiku on the cover of a street magazine published at the house. Community member Matt Daloisio shared a newsletter featuring a collection of Christian, Jewish, and Buddhist responses to September 11, all written by community members. Haley House's evolution toward Buddhism was a gradual process, shaped in part by founder Kathe McKenna's personal journey and in part by the ways in which the practices of community life encouraged individuals who were exploring Buddhism. Beth Ingham, for example, came to Haley House in 1980 as a twenty-year-old just back from the Peace Corps in South Korea, and as a seeker exploring her attraction to Buddhism. She found that the simple tasks of hospitality resonated with Buddhism's emphasis on "daily practice": "The daily practice of arising at dawn to prepare breakfast, of shelving boxes filled with cans and of sorting through bags of clothing in the ever chaotic basement, the daily encounter with hundreds of guests and volunteers meeting each other's 'needs,' the struggle of community decision making, and the often violent encounters between the guests began to change me."[28] Beth and others led the community gradually to incorporate Buddhist practices of reflection into its shared life, even as it continued to welcome new "strangers," including an Israeli rabbi who came to Haley House specifically to study Buddhism.

Community life empowers Beth Ingham and other "strangers" to share the riches of their tradition. Haley House's Matt Daloisio, himself a devout Catholic, told me that he had learned a lot from the Buddhist emphasis on mindfulness and "understanding yourself and why you're doing things, before you can even look outward." Each week, a Catholic nun with Buddhist training came to the community to do "listening sessions," in which the whole community attended deeply to the experiences and beliefs of just one member. These sessions helped the community come to terms with extremely contentious issues, including the members' diverse positions on abortion. "In the first week," Matt said, "if you'd told me I'd have to sit around and talk to people just for the sake of doing it, it would have been contrary to anything I would have understood as being important. But it's incredibly valuable."

At Camphill Copake, similarly, an American Buddhist neighbor helped arrange for the visit of two Tibetan lamas who created a sand mandala ceremony for the community. "There was a whole ceremony, creating it," recalled Roswitha Imegwu, "and they did it in total silence. And when it was all done and they had done certain prayers, and I guess they had invited the god to come and be there, or the gods. And then when that was completed they let them go and then the whole thing was dissolved and everyone got a little sand and was able to take it away. It was really amazing." Roswitha, who is married to an Indian, also mentioned a time when she had incorporated a reading from the Bhagavad Gita into her household's traditional Bible evening. She had noticed a parallel between the Gita and the text from Saint Paul assigned for that day, and she invited two Indian guests to read the text in Sanskrit after she had read it in English. "It was a wonderful affirmation—again, finding a common ground."

The practices of welcome that bring these gifts to community can create tensions, though these are rarely the consequence of religious differences per se. Both Camphill and the Catholic Worker have struggled more with volunteers who are indifferent to the spiritual identity of the community than with those who are fervent adherents of a different faith. Few Camphillers, for example, would complain about Roswitha Imegwu's incorporation of a Hindu text into the Bible evening, but many are distressed that few young coworkers find any meaning in the Bible evening at all. Similarly, Frank Cordaro told me of the "bad times" the Des Moines Catholic Worker experienced just before its fifteenth anniversary. Frank had left the community about eight years before, and gradually all the members with a grounding in the Catholic tradition also moved out. The house was left to a small group of young volunteers with "no affinity for the church or faith." When Frank and others approached them with plans for an anniversary celebration, they resisted. "When I pressed them on," Frank says, "let's start a dialogue or discussion on the tradition and Dorothy Day and some of the religious aspects, and they would say, we're anarchists, we don't have to."

Despite the fact that the young volunteers "did some pretty good hospitality," Frank found the situation unacceptable. Still, he realized that the only way to restore the community's Catholic identity was to be willing to do "the work." Standing on the outside, he had no moral authority to tell the Workers to be more Catholic: "If you're going to regain the community, have some influence on the community, you've got to move into the community, pay your price, you've got to put your time in, you've got to put the sweat equity of leadership, and once you've done that, then you can say your piece." Frank recruited a dedicated volunteer from the Los Angeles Catholic Worker, Joanne Kennedy, to bring a more consciously Catholic perspective to the Des Moines house, and shortly thereafter moved back into the community himself. A decade later, the community was thriving and had a renewed sense of connection to its Catholic roots, but was still home to as many non-Catholics as Catholics.

"You don't have to be a Catholic Christian to be part of this," Frank concluded. "What you've got to do is buy into the hospitality and respect the larger tradition, which in part is the Catholic Church. And that's, let's say, the envelope in which it comes." Others from both Camphill and the Catholic Worker echoed his view that a shared commitment to spiritually based work can hold even a spiritually diverse community together. When I asked Christine Elmquist about spiritual diversity at Community Homestead, she replied that "some people are very centered on anthroposophy, some are not really interested but all are committed and pulling for this community." Hartford Catholic Worker Brian Kavanagh affirmed that "if you're doing God's work, you're God's people, even if you call yourself an atheist," then cited the Gospel parable of the two sons to support his position: "The father says to his son, go out and do thus and so. And the son says, no way, I'm not going to do it. And then repents and does the work. And the other one says, sure Dad, I'll do it, and then goes off with his buddies and doesn't do the work. Who's the one that does the father's will? . . . It's the first one."

In short, in order to "welcome the stranger" a community must have a sufficiently clear sense of its shared "work" *and* include at least some members who can articulate the connections between that work and the founding spiritual tradition. At Camphill, the tasks of curative education and social therapy are connected to anthroposophy because anthroposophy teaches that each individual has a unique spiritual destiny, and that the world is impoverished if people with special needs are not able to share their gifts with others. The work of hospitality is connected to Catholicism because of Jesus' teaching that "whatever you did for the least of these, you did for me" (Matthew 25:40). In both cases, the link is so intimate that lifesharing can be seen as anthroposophical work regardless of who does it, and hospitality can be seen as Catholic work regardless of who does it. Community members who don't share these spiritualities must, of course, be prepared to accept that some of their housemates will understand things in this way. Atheists at the Hartford Catholic Worker, for example, would have to accept that Brian Kavanagh would regard them as part of "God's people"!

Communities must also wrestle with the question of just how many members they need who are able to articulate the connection between the community's work and its spiritual roots. After expressing her profound appreciation for the spiritual diversity at Camphill Minnesota, for example, Jan Zuzalek acknowledged that she worries about what would happen if the number of committed anthroposophists slipped below half of the long-term coworkers. At Community Homestead, Mark Steinrueck speculated that some Camphills are no longer "renewing themselves" spiritually, but are simply living on the "inertia" of previous generations' spirituality. Matt Daloisio, despite his appreciation for the Buddhist spirituality at Haley House, eventually moved to the New York Catholic Worker in hopes of finding a more nurturing environment for his own Catholic spirituality. Still, most would agree that there is no magic formula for maintaining the creative balance of diversity and identity. Rather, the tension between the two makes "precarity" a central community value. "It's got to be a catch-all for everything and the more diverse we are the better we are," summed up Frank Cordaro. "The spirit of the Worker—you know, it's not dogma. . . . You start making a dogmatics, then you've lost it." Without a dogmatics, the only way to preserve identity is through the work.

Honoring the Journey

The spiritual "precarity" of community life does not apply only to those "strangers" who are clearly outside their community's dominant spirituality. In some ways it appeals even more to those Catholic Workers and Camphillers who are lifelong Catholics and anthroposophists, or converts to those traditions. Almost every Camphiller and Catholic Worker can tell of the meandering path that led them to a new spiritual identity or to a rediscovery of their childhood roots. For many, life in community does not offer an "end" to the journey, but simply opens new vistas to be explored. At their best, each community movement has encouraged such individual journeys, even when their implications for the life of the community are unclear.

In both movements, the experience of the founders contributed to this wayward ethos of conversion. The pivot of Dorothy Day's autobiography is her account of how she was drawn to the Catholic Church both by the "natural happiness" of giving birth to a child and by her intuitive sense that Catholicism was "the Church of the poor." The constant retelling of this story makes Catholic Workers especially attentive to the dynamics of conversion, even though a relatively small percentage of them are converts to Catholicism in the literal sense.[29] Karl König, like Dorothy Day, could trace the roots of his adult conversion to incidents in his childhood: when he was eleven he kept a picture of Jesus hidden in a cabinet, and he began attending Catholic services at a time when he still dreamed of being a rabbi. His story of conversion is less frequently retold than Day's, but for the early Camphillers it provided an important model of openness to personal transformation. König, Anke Weihs recalled, "taught us not to live by theory alone but to regard every hour of the day as an opportunity to develop reverence, modesty, creativity and the will to transform oneself." König's biographer has also suggested that his Judaism allowed him to experience the "Christ event . . . as a direct personal message of liberation and salvation which was neither limited nor burdened by the traditions of the Christian denominations," and this may explain Camphill's appeal for seekers who feel alienated from their Christian upbringings.[30]

Indeed, the conversion stories of many Camphillers and Catholic Workers begin with dissatisfaction with conventional religiosity. The Christian faith of his parents, explained Peter Madsen of Camphill Copake, "didn't tickle what I would call my spirituality. It tickled a sense maybe of obligation, of history, all different strange things, but none of it was incredibly moving." Peter's dissatisfaction led him to explore Buddhism and Hinduism in high school, "dabbling in all these various religions" before anthroposophy offered him a new way of understanding Christianity. Similarly, the Jewish rituals of Lois Smith's childhood were meaningful family time, but for her "it wasn't a holy experience." Her sense of the holy was kindled when college art and music classes exposed her to Handel's *Messiah*, Bach's Mass in B Minor, and the great works of Christian art—though she wasn't fully conscious of the meaning of these experiences until she encountered anthroposophy at Camphill.

While Camphillers typically point to a lack of spirituality in the religions of their youth, many Catholic Workers were more distressed by the lack of a social conscience. Prior to coming to the Catholic Worker, said Scott Mathern-Jacobson, he had experienced Christianity as "a lot of great words but not a lot of action." The Catholic Worker opened up a new understanding of Christianity because "this experience was living it." Similarly, Claire Schaeffer-Duffy of Saints Francis and Thérèse Catholic Worker told me that in high school she had been "taken with" the evangelical movement. But in college she started volunteering at a battered women's shelter, and when she talked about that experience with her evangelical friends she encountered a disconnect. "The question of accepting Christ verbally or not . . . seemed an odd one to ask a woman facing possible death." Her desire for an alternative led her to write an undergraduate thesis on the Catholic Worker, and to visit Catholic peace activists in Europe. "There was this kind of automatic synthesis of politics and faith in these young people, which I hadn't seen amongst my friends in the US, and it was what I was reading about in the Catholic Worker. And it seemed to be that the Catholics were the ones making that synthesis."

Few of these converts would have come to anthroposophy or Catholicism simply by reading books or attending church services. What made the difference for them was that the daily rhythms of shared life allowed them to see that life and faith could be integrated in a way that had not previously seemed possible. It also allowed them to bypass their intellectual resistance to "joining" by gradually leading them to a place where they realized they had somehow already joined. When Jan Zuzalek first arrived at Camphill, for example, she said to herself, "I'm never going to join anything. I'm not going to become an anthroposophist or become this or that." Indeed, she had been drawn more to Hinduism and Buddhism than Christianity. But gradually she came to accept that "for some reason I'm not in a Buddhist community. And I do want a spiritual life." Practicing the anthroposophical meditations and becoming a Camphill Community member allowed her to deepen both her spiritual life and her sense of connection to her friends in community. Christine Elmquist, who arrived at Camphill Copake several years after Jan Zuzalek, came with a theological education and an even greater degree of resistance to what she called "God-squaddy" spirituality. But the contrasting personalities of her two houseparents helped her to grapple with anthroposophical ideas at a personal rather than an academic level. "He was very down to earth, and he didn't have anything really to do with anthroposophy, kind of flaky stuff, he was from Maine. . . . And she was from a very anthroposophical family, and was really holding that whole thing. So when they said it, it made sense to me, I could hear it. And they would just let drip little things. And every bit I heard was stuff that made perfect sense to me."

"I know that I never would have [become] a Catholic," Louise Cochran told Rosalie Riegle Troester, "if I hadn't come through the left door of the Catholic Worker." She told the story in greater length in a prose poem published in the Haley House newsletter. A Presbyterian pastor's daughter, she had first felt her faith "come alive" while visiting a Tibetan Buddhist monastery where "I experienced the combination of authentic spiritual (as opposed to moral) teachings and MYSTERY." In the midst of her attraction to Buddhism, though, she "kept getting 'Christian interference,'" so she enrolled at Harvard Divinity School in preparation for ordination in the United Church of Christ. When she dropped out to join the Haley House community, she insisted that she was not becoming a Catholic; indeed, "the thought had never entered my mind." Within a year she was attending daily Mass and thinking of conversion. "My new Catholic friends said, 'Are you insane? You can have the Mass, the silent retreats and spiritual direction without becoming a Catholic—without an institutional affiliation.'" Her only explanation was "that it had become clear to me that the Church is my Home and that I could, of course, continue to visit, but I wanted to move in." Her confirmation was nontraditional, held in the soup kitchen with her Jewish husband singing the Exalte, and she continued to struggle to put words to the experience. "Today when people ask me why I did it, I still have to say, 'It is a mystery.'"[31]

As this tentative note suggests, community-based conversion does not necessarily offer a sense of finality. Though Peter Madsen struck me as both well-informed about anthroposophy and deeply committed to it, when I first asked him how he identified himself spiritually, he said, "struggling. Struggling to realize my spiritual identity." He added that both he and other Camphillers often miss the opportunities that community life provides for spiritual growth. The danger confronting Camphill, Peter said, is not that the numbers of professed anthroposophists will fall too low, but that "anthroposophy is taken on as a cloak that might make me more acceptable to the community at large," rather than as a genuine spiritual path. "The test of a true anthroposophist," Peter concluded, is to recognize that anthroposophy does not have a monopoly on truth and "to be so spiritually awake to recognize where the light is shining."

The experience of conversion also does not always erase the reservations these people once had about institutional religion. Christine Elmquist readily acknowledged that reading Steiner "just left me cold and still leaves me a little cold" because of his preoccupation with the details of the spiritual hierarchies.

"It's more the truth of it" that she values, "and not all the little layers—that's guy stuff." Louise Cochran told Rosalie Riegle Troester that she still dissents from the Catholic policy on ordination, noting that "I know some very gifted women who would be wonderful priests."[32] "I love the church, and I love the faith," said Scott Mathern-Jacobson, "but it's a mixed bag." Soon after his conversion he realized that the Catholic Worker was "definitely the fringe" of the church in North America, and he continues to struggle with mainstream Catholicism.

What community life does is to place these reservations in a new context. Christine Elmquist doesn't need to enjoy reading Steiner so long as she lives in a community that puts his ideas directly into practice. Scott Mathern-Jacobson may not like much of what he sees in the North American church, but the Catholic Worker movement makes him aware of more promising developments around the globe. "The Catholic Church is the church of the people," he said. "South of the border, in South America you're finding people that . . . have more of a Catholic Worker idea. . . . The East Timorese, faithful people, that have gone through so much, largely are Catholic, faithful Roman Catholic people too. So those are the inspirations for me to stay in the church." Louise Cochran's experience in a Catholic Worker community that is profoundly interreligious allowed her to set aside her institutional critiques and focus instead on "talking to people about their journeys toward God. . . . Different paths are right for different people. But there are barriers on the different paths, also, and some people can't get past them, so they try another path."[33] Her own experience of conversion to Catholicism, in other words, provided a vantage point from which she could honor even the person who converts *from* Catholicism to Buddhism or another tradition.

This sort of recontextualization is even more apparent in the testimony of people who rediscovered their childhood faith when they came to community. When Joel Kilgour came to the Loaves and Fishes Catholic Worker, for example, he "had abandoned Christianity as a religion of oppression." Joel had grown up in what he called "a nice parish," but he "just couldn't reconcile my political beliefs with what I understood of the church." His Catholic high school's emphasis on academic and economic success turned him off so much that he still takes pride in having reduced his graduating class's college acceptance rate from 98 percent to 96 percent. But the witness of his fellow Catholic Workers forced him to read the Gospels seriously for the first time. "They didn't tie me down to a chair and read them to me. [But] all of a sudden I was here in a community of Christians who were unlike any Christians that I'd met before. And I didn't quite understand where they got their crazy

Christian ideas from, because it sure wasn't what I was hearing from the church." As he read the Gospels, Joel discovered both the revolutionary power of nonviolence and the liberating message of a Jesus who would not condemn him because of his attraction to other men. Perhaps most importantly, Joel's growing faith in the Resurrection allowed him to move beyond the angry activism of his youth. The Resurrection, Joel told me, "means that I can be a realist and also hopeful. I can know how bad things are. I can know that thirty-six thousand children starve to death every day, and I can really know that and I can really feel that and I can want to scream about it, and sometimes feel like there's no hope for this world" and yet trust that both those children and their killers may be in paradise together. For Joel, the Resurrection is "the only thing that keeps me going sometimes."

Joanne Kennedy came from a privileged Catholic background similar to Joel's, and like him she had largely abandoned the church when she first encountered the Catholic Worker. Even her experience at a women's Catholic college had only deepened her opposition to the male hierarchy of the church. But when a friend "dragged" her to the Los Angeles Catholic Worker, she realized that it "wasn't too hierarchical" and found that "interesting." Even more importantly, the Worker's soup line "struck me as Eucharist" in an authentic way that she had missed when attending liturgies in college. Even so, her spiritual life didn't really deepen until she moved into a Worker house, where she "did 'the work' every day and was so happy doing it." After that, she gained a real appreciation for those traditional Catholics who could immerse themselves in studying the lives of the saints, and even opened up a new conversation with her ultraconservative Catholic sisters.

Even those who have not strayed so far can find their faith renewed through community life. My former student Mike Sersch, for example, was a serious Catholic throughout college, living in an intentional student community that emphasized faith-based work for peace and justice. But life at the Winona Catholic Worker challenged him "to delve deeper into Catholicism," and in particular to heed Dorothy Day's advice to attend daily Mass. "And now as a community we're almost all daily Mass goers," Mike told me. "It feels like our work just naturally grows out of that. . . . It's a way of nourishing yourself, that you go to the sacramental table and you go to the very physical table and the two are related. . . . There's not a disconnect, it's all tied together. And the walk from our place to the cathedral is almost a straight shot." Chuck Berendes, who was active at Place of Grace Catholic Worker in La Crosse, Wisconsin, during high school, added that his Catholic Worker experience made him "proud to be Catholic." "People are taking shots at the church a lot, people in the church are doing stupid stuff," Chuck explained, "but that hasn't been my experience really. My experience has been with regular people mostly who think being Catholic's important and their faith is important, and prayer is important, and working for justice is important."

Stories of the rediscovery of faith are less common at Camphill, simply because the percentage of birthright anthroposophists in Camphill mirrors their small numbers in society as a whole. But children of anthroposophists often report that the spiritual glimmerings of their childhood only began to make sense in the context of community life. Despite her parents' devotion to Steiner's ideas, Sylvia Bausman told me, she "stayed quite well away" from anthroposophy as a young adult. At a challenging moment in her parenting she picked up a book by an anthroposophical doctor. "I was astonished in reading the words in this book to find out that it was like my native language." Around the same time, her father introduced her to the work of Camphill, and soon she realized that it was her destiny to live out her ideals in community. Similarly, Roswitha Imegwu, who grew up in Camphill, only began to read Steiner when, as a young widow with small children, she was considering either an academic career or a return to Camphill. "There was one thing that really lit a spark in me. And that was when I read this Fundamental Social Law—that the well-being of a community is greater the more the proceeds of one person's work goes to support another. . . . I thought, wow, that's how it should be." This new insight into Steiner's spiritual and social teaching is what allowed Roswitha "to look at [Camphill] as something other than the home I had known," and eventually to join the community.

For both converts and returning prodigals, community life can provide powerful encouragement for the spiritual journey. But it rarely offers a clearly defined destination. Three years after we had discussed daily Mass in our interview, Mike Sersch told me that he felt "much more like an anarchist Christian and less a Catholic now." And Louise Cochran's conversion narrative ended on a deliberately open-ended note: "My story isn't finished yet. In fact, it's only just begun. This is the way I understand why I became a Catholic now. Ask me again in another five years—I'm curious myself to hear more of the story."[34]

As these words suggest, the spiritual journeys of some Catholic Workers and Camphillers defy categorization. "We've had people who have joined the Catholic Church here, who have become serious Catholics while they've been here," Haley House's Kathe McKenna told Rosalie Riegle Troester. "We've had people leave the Catholic Church. We've had people become serious Quakers while they've been involved with us; we've had people leave the

Quakers. . . . There are people involved with understanding what it means to be a witch. . . . If anybody is alive spiritually, they're searching."[35] At Camphill Kimberton Hills, similarly, one long-term housefather who had studied anthroposophy for years told me that he had recently begun to practice Tibetan Buddhism instead, while a more recent arrival reported that his Buddhist meditation had lapsed since he came to Camphill. Several of the people I interviewed for this book responded to transcripts and drafts by musing on their continued spiritual development and the fact that "you can't stick the same finger in the river twice."

Mark and Nicola Hobson came to Camphill as part of a long spiritual journey that has passed through Quakerism and both Theravada and Zen Buddhist traditions. They chose Camphill (and, later, the Lukas Community) because they wanted a spiritually based community that fully honored their marriage and family commitments. But initially, they struggled with the ideas of Rudolf Steiner. "We were drawn to this kind of work through what we saw, not by any intellectual affinity with anthroposophy," explained Nicola. "I thought, life is great here and the work is good but leave me alone with the Rudolf Steiner kind of thing. He seemed incredibly convoluted and complicated to say the most simple things." Eventually, though, she found ways to incorporate some of his insights into what she calls "an eclectic mix of Buddhism and Christianity and world religions." For his part, Mark called himself a "Christian Buddhist anthroposophist searcher," and distinguished his understanding of the spiritual journey from that of more conventional Christians. While many churches encourage their members to "believe that Jesus rose again and was the son of God and everything will be easy," Mark wanted "a practical way of trying to develop skills that would help me open my heart." He found this first in Buddhism, then discovered in anthroposophy a way of bridging the gap between Christianity and Buddhism.

"I guess at one time I was proud to say I was Catholic," Catholic Worker Brian Kavanagh told me, "and now it's just like I believe in God." He explained that his reading of such authors as Joseph Campbell and his encounters with other faiths have deepened his appreciation of the divine mystery and forced him out "of the little box I've lived in my whole life." He no longer accepts traditional doctrines such as the virgin birth, and he often feels more connected to God on his daily walk than he does at church. Brian is wary of people "that say they know all about [God] and they've got him in this nice neat package," but he also understands the appeal of that sort of spirituality. "I think maybe your faith's deeper when you start questioning and really searching. . . . But there is a certain niceness about having that feeling of safety when you just stay inside the nice four walls and the roof of the church, and your decisions are made for you and you just follow a few rules and regulations." Brian can maintain his faith without rules and regulations because community life has given him a deeper sense of connection to other people. He still attends Mass at the parish across the street from the Worker house "because I love the people that go there." But his understanding of Christ's sacramental presence is much broader. "I used to say I go to Mass only because that's where I get the Eucharist. Now I believe that in a very literal sense that if there's a bunch of people gathered around and we share a meal together, that's a valid Eucharist."

Many Catholic Workers assume that such spiritual explorations have been encouraged by their movement only since the death of Dorothy Day. But probably no Catholic Worker has been as intrepid or as wayward a spiritual pilgrim as Day's close friend Ammon Hennacy. Hennacy's activist career began when he was jailed for draft resistance during World War I. In prison, his reading of the Sermon on the Mount converted him to an anarchist Christianity. His gregarious spirit brought him to the Milwaukee Catholic Worker in the 1930s, and soon he was encouraging socialists, Protestants, and just about anyone he could find to attend that community's roundtable discussion. Indeed, Dorothy Day would later recall, "One of the great things that Ammon did for the Catholic Worker back in the thirties . . . was to increase our ecumenical spirit."[36] Hennacy continued his eclectic ecumenism after his move to New York, where his high regard for the Worker (and infatuation with Dorothy Day) led him to convert to Catholicism in 1952, to write a regular column for the *Worker*, and to found the Joe Hill House of Hospitality in Salt Lake City.

In 1965, however, Hennacy formally broke with the Catholic Church, in part because he wished to marry for a second time (though his new wife remained a Catholic) and in part because "after fifteen years in the Catholic church I find that any increase in spiritual emphasis that I have gained has been in spite of and not because of attendance at Mass and taking Communion." Affirming his true identity as a "non-church Christian," Hennacy dismissed the Bible as mostly folklore and called the Catholic Church "a reactionary organization" to which no Christian anarchist ought to belong. He saw "no reason for joining any other church for all churches support exploitation, and mostly they support war." Starting his own church was not an option, because "I sure don't want any Ammonites following me around." Still, Hennacy professed to "believe in the virgin birth of Christ and in personal immortality, in all of Christ's miracles and in the resurrection, and that we can be 'saved' from sin by following Him, whether we belong to any church or not." Reflecting his eclectic interests, he described both purgatory and re-incarnation as "logical," but declined to speculate on the details. "It is how you live that counts."[37]

In the face of such challenging testimony, Dorothy Day stood by her friend, continuing to publish his column and solicit donations for his house of hospitality. In articles written in response to his marriage, the publication of his autobiography, and his death, she wrestled with his "tone deaf" approach to theology, his "coarse" criticisms of bishops and priests, and his loss of "our daily supersubstantial bread, Jesus Christ become incarnate." But she excused many of his criticisms as evidence that "Ammon wanted so much to see priests and bishops and popes stand out strong and courageous against the sin and the horrors and the cruelty of the powers of this world," and re-joiced that he had found love in his marriage. Even as she hoped that "Ammon will one day see the wheat, not the tares, in the Church," she refused to pass definitive judgment on his choices. "Who can understand another, who can read another's heart," she wrote. "We cannot judge him, knowing so well his own strong and courageous will to fight the corruption of the world around him." Her own meandering path, coupled with her long years of experience in community, had given Day an awareness of "the many conversions we must all pass through," and so she could affirm those whose paths were quite dif-ferent from her own.[38]

Day's conclusion suggests some of the reasons life in community can encourage ongoing spiritual journeys. Though Camphill and the Catholic Worker have defined their identities more in terms of Christian "works" than Christian "faith," each has also created a context in which individuals feel free to share their personal faith journeys. The daily work of community, more-over, easily becomes ongoing spiritual experiment. For Catholic Workers, the "result" of that experiment is often a deeper ecumenical commitment, nourished by the daily experience of serving meals or protesting wars along-side persons of many Christian and non-Christian traditions. For Camphill-ers, the cultivation of esoteric practices in the midst of daily life can open doors to esoteric traditions outside anthroposophy.

Communitarians must also live in the tension between the ideals that drew them to community and the often murky realities of actual community life. The tension between the coming kingdom of God and the kingdom of God as already present among us is, of course, a perennial theme in Christianity. While many Christians avoid the tension by implicitly holding to a purely "futurist" eschatology, Camphillers and Catholic Workers take the idea of the present kingdom seriously, and the resulting tension forces them constantly to reexamine their assumptions about what that kingdom *is*. When Brian Kavanagh said that any shared meal is a valid Eucharist, for example, he touched on the wider Catholic Worker experience that the heavenly banquet symbolized by the Eucharist can be experienced more directly when Workers and guests gather around a common table. Such experiences, possible only in community, may inspire community members to return to "the world" with new fervor—and with powerful challenges to more traditional religious institutions.

Notes

1. König, *The Camphill Movement*, 38.

2. Cited in Troester, *Voices*, 219.

3. Dorothy Day to "Fellow Workers," 9 July 1939, Dorothy Day—Catholic Worker Collection, series W-1, box 1; Dorothy Day to "Fellow Workers in Christ," 22 July 1941, Dorothy Day—Catholic Worker Collection, series W-1, box 1; Dorothy Gauchat, cited in Troester, *Voices*, 19; Meg Hyre, "St. Joseph House," *Catholic Worker* 52/5A (August 1985) 2; Gary Donatelli and Robbie Gamble, "On the 'Famous Retreat,'" *Catholic Worker* 52/7 (October–November 1985) 4; and e-mail from Phillip Runkel to Dan McKanan, 18 July 2005.

4. Day, *Loaves and Fishes*, 123; and Dorothy Day, "On Pilgrimage," *Catholic Worker* 13/5 (June 1946) 8.

5. Peter Maurin, "The Law of Holiness," in *Easy Essays*, 137–8; Day, "Counsels and Precepts," *Catholic Worker* 8/9 (July–August 1941) 2; Furfey, "Maximum—Minimum," *Catholic Worker* 3 (May 1935) 5; and Hugo, "In the Vineyard," *Catholic Worker* 8/10 (September 1941) 1, 5, 8. The first quote, taken from a papal encyclical, appears frequently in issues of the *Catholic Worker*.

6. Ruth Heaney, cited in Troester, *Voices*, 105; Day, *Loaves and Fishes*, 32; and Day, "More About Cuba," in *On Pilgrimage: The Sixties*, 94.

7. Cited in Geoffrey Gneuhs, "Radical Orthodoxy: Dorothy Day's Challenge to Liberal America," in Thorn, Runkel, Mountin, *Dorothy Day*, 218.

8. Tom Cornell, cited in Troester, *Voices*, 39; and Jim Forest, cited in Troester, *Voices*, 36.

9. Dorothy Day, *On Pilgrimage: The Sixties*, 13.

10. Ann O'Connor and Peter King, "What's Catholic about the Catholic Worker Movement? Then and Now," in Thorn, Runkel, Mountin, *Dorothy Day*, 142; and Mark and Louise Zwick, "Roots of the Catholic Worker Movement: Saints and Philosophers Who Influenced Dorothy Day and Peter Maurin," in Thorn, Runkel, Mountin, *Dorothy Day*, 62.

11. Jane Sammon, "The Church Is All of You," *Catholic Worker* 51/7 (October–November 1984) 1.

12. "Developments at Haley House," *Haley House Newsletter*, Hiroshima-Nagasaki-Feast of the Transfiguration 1985, 6–7, in Dorothy Day—Catholic Worker Collection, series W-19, box 1, folder 12; Kathe McKenna, interview with Rosalie Troester, 9 June 1988, Dorothy Day—Catholic Worker Collection, series W-9, box 6, folder 9, p. 62; *The Catholic Worker—Saint Catherine of Genoa*, Chicago, 2/2 [*sic*] (June 1990) 6; *Loaves and Fishes* (Winter 2002) 2; and *Catholic Worker Grapevine*, July 11, 1993, in Dorothy Day—Catholic Worker Collection, series W-54, box 1, folder 6.

13. [Ammon Hennacy], "Our Positions," *Catholic Worker* 21/10 (May 1955) 5; and "'Making a path from things as they are to things as they should be'—Peter Maurin," *Catholic Worker* 45/4 (May 1979) 4–5.

14. Sarah Jeglosky, "Who We Are," *The Catholic Radical*, August 1986, p. 1, in Dorothy Day—Catholic Worker Collection, series W-51, box 1, folder 2.

15. König, *The Camphill Movement*, 38, 35.

16. For the relationship between anthroposophy and the Christian Community, I am indebted to my interview with David Spears of the Lukas Community, but readers may wish to consult James H. Hindes, *Renewing Christianity* (Hudson, NY: Anthroposophic Press, 1996).

17. Müller-Wiedemann, *Karl König*, 152, 222–6, and 198.

18. König, *In Need of Special Understanding*, 186.

19. *Communities Directory*, 3d. ed. (Rutledge, MO: Fellowship for Intentional Community, 2000).

20. Jim Levinson, "A Dozen Years at Haley House and Noonday Farm," *Haley House Newsletter*, Summer/Fall 1995.

21. Advertisement for Camphill Village Minnesota, *Communities* #113 (Winter 2001) 71; and listing for Dorothy Day House, Berkeley, California, at catholicworker.org/.

22. Penelope Roberts, "An Imagination of Camphill Village," in Hunt, *Shining Lights*, 23.

23. Dorothy Day, "On Pilgrimage," *Catholic Worker* 31/9 (April 1965) 5, in *On Pilgrimage: The Sixties*, 220; Peter Maurin, "Let's Keep the Jews for Christ's Sake," *Catholic Worker* 6/12 (July–August 1939) 1; Dorothy Day to "Fellow Workers," 9 July 1939, Dorothy Day—Catholic Worker Collection, series 1, box 1; "Salvation Is from the Jews," *Catholic Worker* 55/1 (January–February 1988) 1; and Jane Sammon, "Why Vilify God's Chosen," *Catholic Worker* 57/4 (June–July 1990) 1. For a detailed analysis of the Catholic Worker's relation to Judaism, see Marc Ellis, "The Catholic Worker, the Jews, and the Future of Ecumenical Religiosity," in Thorn, Runkel, and Mountin, eds., *Dorothy Day*, 494–514.

24. "Notes on Retreat," *Catholic Worker* 11/10 (December 1944) 2; and "We Mourn Death of Gandhi, Non Violent Revolutionary," *Catholic Worker* 14/11 (February 1948) 1. The first quote is the earliest reference to Gandhi that I found in the New York *Catholic Worker*. But Dorothy Day later recalled that during the Spanish Civil War, almost a decade earlier, "We were not, of course, pro-Franco but pacifists, followers of Gandhi in our struggle to build a spirit of nonviolence." See Dorothy Day, "Michael Gold," *Catholic Worker* 33/6 (June 1967) 8.

25. Christie, *Beyond Loneliness*, 63; and Müller-Wiedemann, *Karl König*, 416–29.

26. David Stein, cited in Troester, *Voices*, 415.

27. Jim Levinson, interviewed by Rosalie Riegle Troester, *Voices*, 154; and David Stein, interviewed by Rosalie Riegle Troester, *Voices*, 415–6.

28. Beth Ingham, "Then and Now," *Haley House Newsletter*, Winter 93–4, 96–7, in Dorothy Day—Catholic Worker Collection, series W-19, unboxed folder.

29. Dorothy Day, *The Long Loneliness*, 150; and Rosalie Riegle, "A Long Loneliness: Metaphors of Conversion within the Catholic Worker Movement," in Thorn, Runkel, and Mountin, *Dorothy Day*, 564.

30. Müller-Wiedemann, *Karl König*, 17, 152, 61.

31. Louise Cochran, cited in Troester, *Voices*, 513; and Louise Cochran, "The Beginning of the Story: Why I Became a Catholic," *Haley House Newsletter*, Feast of Catherine of Siena, 29 April 1986, 9–12, in Dorothy Day—Catholic Worker Collection, series W-19, box 1, folder 12.

32. Louise Cochran, cited in Troester, *Voices*, 514.

33. Ibid.

34. Louise Cochran, "The Beginning of the Story."

35. Kathe McKenna, interviewed by Rosalie Riegle Troester, Dorothy Day—Catholic Worker Collection, series W-9, box 6, folder 9.

36. Dorothy Day, "Ammon Hennacy—'Non-Church' Christian," *Catholic Worker* 36/2 (February 1970) 2.

37. Ammon Hennacy, *The Book of Ammon*, second edition edited by Jim Missey and Joan Thomas (Baltimore: Fortkamp Publishing Company, 1994) 474–6.

38. Dorothy Day, "What Does Ammon Mean?" *Catholic Worker* 31/11 (June 1965) 3, 7; Dorothy Day, "On Pilgrimage," *Catholic Worker* 34/3 (March 1968) 8; and Dorothy Day, "Ammon Hennacy—'Non-Church' Christian," *Catholic Worker* 36/2 (February 1970) 2.

Dying and Rising

No spiritual movement in our time can flourish if its aims are specialized in any way . . . it is purely and simply a spiritual law: if a spiritual movement is to help humanity to progress it must be generally human in intention and character.

—*Rudolf Steiner*[1]

The most important outcome of establishing a community is not how long it lasts, but rather that it was created at all. Experiences can last a lifetime for someone who was deeply touched during a single visit. And I believe God remembers even a single act of kindness.

—*Joe DaVia*[2]

Every community that wishes to touch the world must also be open to the possibility of death. There is an inescapable tension between sustaining an institution and reaching out to the larger world, and Catholic Workers and Camphills have consistently emphasized the latter. The practices I have described in previous chapters—encouraging the unfolding of individual vocations, embracing the developmental processes of family life, celebrating the diversity of faith journeys—can all disrupt stable communities. At their best, these communities have embraced the disruptions in the faith that the work of touching the world will go on, even if it takes new forms in each generation.

This is not to suggest that communities that touch the world are fated to brief lives. Camphill and the Catholic Worker have sustained themselves over three generations—a notable achievement in the history of intentional communities—and are still going strong. In large part, this is because of their embrace of concrete service missions and their less grandiose expectations of sweeping social change. But "success," if measured in terms of longevity, carries its own dangers. An enduring institution is likely to devote an increasing share of its resources to self-preservation, and may become fearful of any risks that could undermine stability. In Steiner's words, it may become less "generally human" and thus less capable of touching society as a whole. To their credit, Camphills and Catholic Workers continue to ask if their existing forms are the best ones for the world, even as they celebrate silver and golden anniversaries.

Of course, not every community death is a good thing, or likely to usher in a speedy resurrection. Individuals who have experienced the death of a community, whether after one year or two decades, typically compare the experience to that of a divorce. Such negative experiences are especially pronounced in communities that fail to achieve a regular rhythm of shared life before they begin to collapse, or for relative newcomers who cannot yet imagine how to translate community values into a less structured environment. The lesson to be learned from such experiences, however, is not that permanence must be pursued at all costs, but rather that the pain of death can be softened if it is faced openly from the beginning.

There are two distinct, though certainly related, reasons that communities should be willing to live in the face of death. One is that such willingness makes it easier to risk investing resources in touching the world. The other is to remain open to the possibility of resurrection—the possibility, that is, that the community's deepest values can find full expression only after the collapse of its institutional form. This latter reason is rooted in Christian faith, yet the idea of resurrection is not a Christian monopoly. Indeed, Christians have always recognized the logic of resurrection in both natural and social phenomena. "Unless a grain of wheat falls to the ground and dies," Jesus reminded his followers, "it remains just a grain of wheat; but if it dies, it produces much fruit" (John 12:24).

Success and Failure

The complexity of the issue of communal death is highlighted by several recent scholarly reflections on community "success." Should success be measured by the longevity of individual communities or community movements? What other measures are available? Much of this discussion responds to Rosabeth Moss Kanter's groundbreaking *Commitment and Community*, published in 1972 and still the most influential sociological study of both nineteenth-century utopianism and twentieth-century communalism. A sympathetic observer of 1960s communes, Kanter set out to see what those movements could learn from earlier communities. What "mechanisms of commitment" allowed some communities to hold together while others collapsed? She chose a sample of thirty nineteenth-century communities and classified them as "successful" or "unsuccessful" based on longevity, with a twenty-five-year lifespan qualifying as success. Next, she identified practices that occurred more frequently in successful rather than unsuccessful communities, and grouped these under the themes of sacrifice, investment, renunciation, communion, mortification, and transcendence. Her book includes a handy chart for each theme, listing specific commitment mechanisms and their relative frequencies.[3]

Kanter's catalogue of "successful" practices reads like a mirror image of the world-touching practices I have celebrated in this book. The "sacrifice" chart, for example, lists such items as celibacy, present at all the successful utopias but only two of twenty-one unsuccessful communities. "Renunciation" includes the use of uniforms, restrictions on interaction with outsiders, and the separation of parents from children. "Transcendence" includes the use of doctrinal tests of faith as well as the maintenance of hierarchical authority. The practice of requiring members to renounce all private property upon admission, and then destroying the records to discourage them from leaving, appears in two charts. Such items suggest that a successful community must subordinate individual freedom to the welfare of the group, discourage any loyalties, even to biological kin, that might compete with group loyalty, insist on absolute ideological commitment, and place high walls between itself and the world.

Neither Camphills nor Catholic Workers could follow such advice without sacrificing their deeply held ideals of individual freedom and connection to the world. But neither can they simply dismiss her analysis of the unsettling consequences of those ideals. Many individual Catholic Worker houses have collapsed quickly; others have achieved intergenerational continuity only by recruiting a steady stream of very short-term members. Camphill historically has been more successful in retaining long-term members, but it also is becoming more and more a "revolving door" community. Both Camphill and the Catholic Worker, moreover, have consistently failed to achieve economic self-sufficiency, relying on individual donations or governmental support for the lion's share of their funding. Both movements, in short, are challenged by Kanter to take seriously the connections between their ideals and their instability.

The best response, I believe, is to embrace a certain degree of instability and define success more clearly in terms of one's ideals. One community theorist who provides a helpful model for doing this is Donald Pitzer, who articulated his own theory of "developmental communalism" in response to Kanter. Communal groups, Pitzer suggests, must be judged not by longevity but "in terms of how well they achieve their own objectives, service the needs of their own members, and influence the general society." Often, communities are better understood as incubators of ideals than as ends in themselves: people create communities in order to achieve certain goals or realize certain values, and often they dissolve their communities for the sake of these same goals and values. Communal organization may be called for when a group is getting started or facing persecution, but may lead to stagnation or inflexibility later on. The relevant question is not longevity, but whether a community begins and ends in fidelity to its larger goals.[4]

Pitzer's theory applies most obviously to religious communities devoted to a specific revelation or new teaching. From his perspective, the Mormons "succeeded" by abandoning their communal economy when it impeded expansion, while the Shakers perhaps "failed" because they preserved communalism even after it became a significant obstacle to recruitment. But in those cases, the communal "goal" can easily be identified as the promulgation of the distinctive teachings of Joseph Smith or Mother Ann Lee. Camphill and the Catholic Workers represent somewhat different cases. Neither has a distinctive revelation to share with the world, and both tend to treat community life more as an end in itself rather than as a means to a more narrowly "religious" end. But they fit into Pitzer's paradigm insofar as they distinguish the value of communal sharing in general from its specific institutional forms. At their best, Camphillers and Catholic Workers are willing to see their own institutions dissolve for the sake of the larger values of community.

They also disavow conventional definitions of "success." "What we do is so little we may seem to be constantly failing," wrote Dorothy Day in an early version of the Worker's "Aims and Purposes." "But so did He fail. He met with apparent failure on the Cross. But unless the seed falls into the earth and die, there is no harvest."[5] Harry Murray, a sociologist and Catholic Worker, similarly drew on Henri Nouwen's distinction between "efficacy" and "fruitfulness." Rather than measuring success in terms of immediate effects, a fruitful community will "attempt to live virtuously and to adhere to values, trusting that God will utilize our efforts in ways we could never predict."[6] The practice of hospitality, for Murray, is the ultimate expression of fruitfulness because it does not attempt to impose any specific effects on the guest. Camphillers might say much the same for their own practices of social therapy and lifesharing.

Still, it is relatively easy to say that worldly success is of little or no importance. It is quite another thing to devote years of one's life to the building up of a community with a particular institutional form, only to see that form dissolve in acrimony or resignation. Christians can affirm that resurrection always comes after death, but it is nevertheless the case that resurrection is usually unimaginable at the moment of death. Easter may follow Good Friday, but Good Friday nevertheless has its own story to tell. In this section, consequently, it is important to honor fully the stories of Good Friday before turning to those of Easter.

The Good Fridays of the Catholic Worker

The Catholic Worker has certainly had its share of Good Fridays. The first and most notable occurred during World War II, when the vast majority of Catholic Worker houses closed their doors—some because of disagreements with the New York community's staunch pacifism, some because essential volunteers were either drafted or sent to conscientious objector camps, some simply because the wartime economy had generated virtually full employment and reduced the need for hospitality. Even Dorothy Day announced in 1943 that she would take a yearlong sabbatical, forcing the other editors to issue pointed denials of press reports that the entire movement was collapsing.[7]

In many cities, Catholic Workers were too busy trying to preserve their houses to reflect on the significance of their deaths—or, at least, to send their reflections on to the *Catholic Worker* paper, which sometimes published notices of house closings without any explanation. In other cases, Workers managed to share theological reflections that built on the Gospel themes of death and resurrection. Jim Rogan wrote poignantly that a house closing meant that he could go ten days without lice, then turned serious: "It has been the will of God that St. Anthony's House in Baltimore be closed." While the guests were either sad or indifferent, Rogan claimed, the volunteers—most of whom had been ordered to conscientious objector camps—"could not feel troubled because it was so clearly an indication of God's will." This confidence allowed them to reflect on the gifts of the past, without worrying too much about what might come next. "We all considered it a great privilege, blessing and joy to be chosen by God to minister to the poor. . . . There was much grief, much suffering. But we learned that there is no love without suffering and we tried to teach it to the poor. We tried to be fools for Christ. No one doubted that we were fools but many wondered why." Rogan concluded with a hint of resurrection, noting that "God is pruning us so that later we can bring forth some fruit."[8]

Rogan's confidence in Providence partly reflected the momentous historical context: World War II was transforming all American institutions, and it would have made little sense for Catholic Workers to ascribe their own closings to local or personal factors. Still, Dorothy Day was chastened when she took stock in 1948. They had had thirty-two houses before the war; now they had nine. Even the New York community had been reduced to "a few older men" during the war, though they had since attracted "three or four young ones." The other houses struggled to regain their footing, even as observers asked "when we were going to open houses again throughout the west." Day's response to such inquiries put her theology of resurrection front and center. "Unless the seed falls into the ground and die, itself remaineth alone," she began. "But if it die it bringeth forth much fruit. So I don't expect any success in anything we are trying to do, either in getting out a paper, running houses of hospitality or farming groups, or retreat houses on the land. I expect that everything we do be attended with human conflicts, and the suffering that goes with it, and that this suffering will water the seed to make it grow in the future."[9] And perhaps it was the suffering of the World War II years that prepared the soil for the movement's remarkable growth in the 1960s and beyond.

Various factors helped the Worker avoid complete collapse. The war galvanized the commitment of the most ardent pacifists, some of whom returned to the Worker after stints in conscientious objector camps. The New York motherhouse remained strong, partly by absorbing seasoned volunteers from defunct houses. At the same time, Dorothy Day continued to encourage fledgling efforts, even when they departed in significant ways from the New York model. This was important, because those communities that managed to survive the crisis of the 1940s broke with the New York model in significant ways—Rochester by accepting nonprofit status, Detroit and Cleveland by coalescing around an anchor family. Day wisely recognized both the uniqueness of New York City (where the problem of homelessness demanded public attention even in the best of economic times) and her own gifts as a publicist and fundraiser. She redistributed excess donations received by the New York community to other houses, and sympathized when those houses made decisions she would not have contemplated. She also corresponded with former Workers who enlisted in the Army, ensuring that many of these individuals would remain loyal members of the Catholic Worker extended community.

Since the 1950s, the Catholic Worker experience has been marked by steady growth rather than "boom and bust." Yet even in this period, perhaps half of all new Catholic worker communities have folded within a few years. Each of these communities can tell its own "death story," yet too often they fail to take the opportunity to do so. At the Catholic Worker Archives, the records of many communities end with a last, desperate plea for new volunteers, rather than with a remembrance of the gifts and challenges of the years (or months!) gone by. The pages of the New York *Catholic Worker* are filled with obituaries of leaders from the 1930s and 1940s, but only occasionally is there an "obituary" for an entire community. In part, this reflects the "precarity" that has always been a part of the Catholic Worker movement. Given the small size of Catholic Worker communities, and their reliance on spontaneous donations and short-term volunteers, almost every community faces the possibility of death on an annual if not daily basis. It is hard to predict which communities will actually close their doors—indeed, one of the most thoughtful "obituaries" I found was written at a discouraging moment just a few years into Viva House's nearly forty-year history.[10] By the time a community's death is inevitable, it is often home to only a handful of recently arrived volunteers. With little connection either to their community's history or to the Catholic Worker movement as a whole, these volunteers often fail to pull together a closing celebration or even compose a meaningful obituary.

One recent Catholic Worker death story is that of Bethlehem Peace Farm, which affiliated with Tacoma's Guadalupe House Catholic Worker in the early 1990s. From its beginnings, Bethlehem struggled with a dilemma typical of Catholic Worker farms: was it primarily an agricultural enterprise or a rural house of hospitality? A series of live-in volunteers struggled to find the right balance. After several years anchoring the farm, for example, Jim and Katrina Plato realized that their interests had shifted from agriculture to the arts, and from hospitality to care for their own children. After a series of discussions, they decided the best gift they could offer the community would be to leave in such a way as to make room for others with new vision and energy. Katrina explained the decision in an elegiac essay in the community's newsletter. "A couple months ago," she wrote, "a strong wind blew through the farm pulling up the Bethlehem Farm sign at the end of the driveway. A fitting symbol of movement and transformation." She went on to describe her family's decision to move on, then concluded that "This farm is calling for passionate farmers. Jim and I move to a new community and new hospitality, making room for evolving community and a fresh vision here. . . . A new sign will be put up by the new community made of different wood and fresh paint."[11]

This essay put a hopeful face on what was apparently a painful process of discernment. By sharing their own process, the Platos reminded the farm's supporters of the value of vocation: they were willing to risk Bethlehem's institutional future in order to be faithful to their own callings. At the same time, their emphasis on their own decision may have prevented them from reflecting deeply on the dynamics that had challenged and would continue to challenge the farm itself. Just before the Platos' departure, a young Worker named Gary Brever had arrived with lots of energy for "evolving community and a fresh vision." Gary galvanized a lively extended community, including a nearby family who planned to make their draft horses available for plowing and planting, and "opened the doors wide" for hospitality. But Gary never managed to attract other long-term volunteers or the support of seasoned Workers, and he quickly realized that Bethlehem's shady location and clay soil were not well suited to his own vocation as a farmer. "I remember at one point we did a diagram," Gary told me, "[with me] in the middle, juggling all these things." After a little more than a year, Gary was burned out, and he left to start a family and his own organic farm.

The short-term volunteers who succeeded Gary had little connection to the Catholic Worker heritage, and none were prepared to make a real investment in the community's future. In 2001 a remnant wrote a letter to farm supporters that struck a very different tone from Katrina Plato's 1998 essay. The farm, they wrote, "is facing an unsure future and the possibility of closing down" but also "looking for core community members." The "all-consuming" work of building community, they admitted, was "creating more dysfunction in everyone's lives," to the point that they had decided to stop offering hospitality. Yet they reiterated the call for new members, without clarifying whether they were hoping for people to join their own process of community-building or for newcomers to bring an entirely new vision after they left. It is hard to imagine who would respond to such an ambiguous invitation, and so it is unsurprising that this is the last record of the community in the archives.[12]

Undoubtedly, there is more to this story than can be found on paper. I gained additional insight into the dynamics of closing a Catholic Worker house when I spoke to Mike Sersch, then the only live-in member of the Winona Catholic Worker community. "I'm a one-person community," said Mike ruefully. "That's really tough because for me, community comes first." In such a situation, Mike explained, it was important to make clear personal decisions, and to be willing to live with their implications. He had decided not to offer overnight hospitality, because "I can't do that sustainably, personally. I might do a meal, like an evening meal, and whoever can come can come, and maybe some pantry stuff. I'd be open three hours a day." Mike added that while he was "hoping and praying" for new Workers, he had decided to leave Winona if they did not arrive within a year, even if that meant letting the community die. "It's really sad to see a community die," he explained. "But . . . community shouldn't be on life support. . . . Winona either is going to die or it's going to be reborn as something different. We won't be who we used to be. Because who we used to be is no longer living there." As it turned out, Mike did leave Winona about a year later, just before two of his college classmates (among others) arrived to lead the Worker house into its next stage of life.

Both Mike Sersch and the final community members at Bethlehem Farm found themselves in the difficult position of contemplating the death of a community within a short time of their own arrival. Jim Levinson had a longer perspective when he reflected on "A Dozen Years at Haley House and Noonday Farm" in 1995. Though neither community had closed, Levinson's essay was in a sense an obituary for the specific circle of people with whom he had lived, and a searingly honest account of the difficulties they had experienced. A "remarkable bunch" of Workers, he wrote, saw themselves as "lights unto the nations," but "there were times during the past two years when I wondered if we, far from being a light unto the nations, were behaving even a notch better than the national average." Again and again, friendships eroded as people held one another to impossibly high standards. "When I came to Noonday Farm," Levinson wrote ruefully, "I was deeply committed . . . to environmental issues. . . . After a few lectures by the self-appointed garbage monitors on no-no's that had been found in my garbage, I became just a notch less committed." Reflecting on community of goods in the apostolic church, Levinson mused that community might be easiest in times of persecution. "Is it unrealistic to suggest that when the immediate threat passed and Christianity became a notch more respectable, the apostles and their descendants found other ways of living that, if less holy, were not quite as difficult?"[13]

Far from throwing water on the entire project of intentional community, Levinson's larger goal was to suggest that communal values might find new life in the larger society. "My challenge, as we leave the farm, is to find ways of reclaiming these beliefs from which I have become somewhat distanced." Though many of his friendships had suffered at the farm, he had already experienced that in most cases "relationships improved just as soon as we stopped living together." This experience of renewed energy persuaded him that community life was worthwhile, even if it could not be sustained over a lifetime. "Despite all the problems and all the difficult learning involved, there was so much richness that I wouldn't have given up the community experience for the world. . . . And I would never say a word to discourage a young person—or an old person—from experiencing the richness that I experienced in community." In the death of community life, Levinson discerned its enduring value.

My own first experience of the Catholic Worker was with a community in the midst of an equally intentional death process. As a graduate student, I cooked a weekly meal at Saint Catherine of Genoa Catholic Worker on Chicago's South Side. Founded in late 1988, Saint Catherine's originally provided transitional housing for homeless people with AIDS. This hospitality effort was challenged by the "changing face of AIDS" and the cumulative toll of disease, drug addiction, and death. But for Tom Heuser, who was the central community member during its final years, this was not as significant a factor in Saint Catherine's closing as the changing face of the community itself.[14]

During the early 1990s, Saint Catherine's proximity to the University of Chicago and several theological seminaries had made it easy to attract community members who were also full-time students—and who were not always fully committed to the Worker vision. But in 1995 the community decided to accept only individuals able to make the Worker their first priority. Describing the situation as a "crossroads" or even a "precipice," Tom Heuser wrote in the community newsletter that "we've decided to forgo what seems readily available to us (students who express an interest in living here) and hold out for those interested in coming here simply to do our work and to form an intentional community living in voluntary poverty." The immediate implication, he admitted, was that he would be the only Worker at Saint Catherine's until others arrived. Still, Tom insisted, the decision was consistent with the Worker ethos: "I've heard the word 'crisis' used, but I feel little sense of urgency. . . . If God intends, the Workers and resources will continue to come to us. We need only carry on with faith."[15]

Initially, Tom's faith was rewarded: new Workers did arrive, and the work continued for another two years. But while the newcomers were fully committed for the short term, they were not prepared to take responsibility for the community's ongoing direction. "When I came to Saint Catherine," Tom recalled, "what drew me there was the collegial sense of responsibility that I found there." This ideal of shared leadership led him to push for the ban on part-time Workers, but he continued to feel "that I was much more of a house manager than I was comfortable being. . . . While I was willing to take on that role on an interim basis when needed, I felt it was becoming more of a permanent characteristic. And at that point I decided it was time for me to move on."

Saint Catherine's extended community recognized that Tom's departure meant the end of the community, and they responded with a farewell gathering and an elegiac final newsletter. Both present and past Workers reflected on their differing responses to the closing. "When Tom let drop . . . one evening that St. Catherine's was indeed closing," mused Lillian Larsen, "I found myself immediately suffused with sadness. . . . In reflecting on that conversation, I could not help but be struck by the dramatically different emotions we were experiencing—my sadness, his joy." Though she could embrace Tom's decision, she still felt sad that the world has so "few houses of refuge where there is room for everyone."[16] Tom's own contribution, meanwhile, struck a joyful tone: "How mysterious that Spirit is! What a miracle it wrought at the Catherine of Genoa Catholic Worker! I've always felt this place a blessed gift and wondered at the beauty of God's profligate goodness. And so, while this time of taking down and packing up has its sobering aspects—it's another death, really—I can't help but also feel a deep sense of gratitude, yes, celebration, for what has been here. It's magnificent to behold!"[17]

Two aspects of this death story stand out. One is the fact that the community was able to honor the primacy of individual discernment, even in the face of crisis. Tom made his own decision first, and this decision was honored even by those who were saddened by it. No one, apparently, tried to cajole or guilt-trip Tom into staying on, and for his own part Tom did not try to cajole others into taking up the work that he was leaving. Once it was clear that Saint Catherine's would indeed close, Tom and Lillian were able to acknowledge one another's different emotions. The second is that the community was able truly to look back, rather than forward, at the moment of death. Though the closing reflections hint at the possibility of resurrection, their primary emphasis is on the divine gifts they had already received. At least intuitively, the Workers at Saint Catherine's understood that one must truly experience death in order to be open to resurrection.

Good Fridays in Camphill

Camphill has rarely had to face the death of an entire community: to my knowledge, all of the Camphills founded in North America are still integral parts of the network, though elsewhere a few communities have folded. Yet the very founding of Camphill was itself a Good Friday of sorts. As a war refugee and near victim of the Nazi genocide, Karl König, like his Viennese associates, had felt "alone, a drop in the vast human sea of a city, a stranger, a foreigner," upon his arrival in Great Britain. He thought of the future with despair: "Will it be possible to turn this lonely life into order and shape again?" For König, the war was both a personal crisis and the death of a precious cosmopolitan ideal. Austria had been "overrun and conquered by men who had betrayed the very essence of the destiny of Europe," and Camphill was founded in the hope of resurrection. "Could we not take a morsel of the true European destiny and make it into a seed so that some of its real task might be preserved: a piece of its humanity, of its inner freedom, of its longing for peace, of its dignity?"[18]

This formative experience has shaped the Camphill experience in many ways, especially by making coworkers more attentive to the villagers' experiences of "exile" from mainstream society. In addition, many Camphills have faced significant crises that might be described as "near death" experiences. In 1978 Camphill Beaver Run experienced such a crisis when New York auditors decided to cut off state funding for Beaver Run students. The officials expected that their decision would cause the village to close, and some Camphillers briefly thought the same thing. The majority, however, quickly decided to take constructive action. "It was a serious decision," recalled cofounder Ursel Pietzner. "We decided we would fight." The auditors had said so many "untruthful and nasty things," added Bernie Wolf, that the Camphillers resolved to "establish some credibility, some acceptability on a broader framework. We certainly were well accepted by those parents and agencies that sent children to us. [But we] wanted a more universal statement that we're okay." To shore up relations with the Pennsylvania government, they sent many American coworkers to school for special education certification. This increased the workload of other coworkers, but it was also an opportunity for the community to rally. "It was very exciting, dramatic," recalled Wolf, while Pietzner described the episode as an "inwardly and spiritually strong time."

One consequence of the crisis was that Beaver Run steadily built up connections to a variety of individuals and organizations beyond the village. The parents who rallied to Beaver Run's defense became more involved in all aspects of its life. The community reached out to new supporters in order to provide financial aid for students who could not get government support. Perhaps most importantly, the Camphillers who pursued special education certification built friendships with professors first at West Chester University, and then at Immaculata University and other schools. Today these connections are bearing fruit in Beaver Run's effort to provide formal college credit for its curative education seminar. Through a partnership with the State University of New York's Program on Noncollegiate Sponsored Instruction, the village hopes to allow coworkers to combine the seminar with a modest number of outside classes to earn a bachelor's degree. Such initiatives provide many opportunities for Camphillers to share their movement's wisdom even as they learn from more conventional practitioners of special education. "The only way to allow our work to influence the work that goes on around us in the disabilities field," explained Guy Alma, "is for people to know us. . . . There's a growing realization that we'd like to have an effect on the outside world."

A similar crisis came to Beaver Run's neighbor, Kimberton Hills, about a decade later. The county mental health officials were "just the best friends you could possibly have wanted," recalled Helen Zipperlen, and supported the village's understanding of itself as a community rather than as an institution. But state officials intervened in the late 1980s with demands that the "facility" be properly licensed. Zipperlen responded with feistiness. "As far as we know," she told the licensers, "we're not a facility." When the officials said they were serving people with low IQs, she replied that "we don't play IQs. I can't tell you the truth about that." She then showed them the community's files, in which "villagers" and "coworkers" (terms Helen prefers not to use) were intermingled. Kimberton's board agreed to resist the pressure for formal licensure, and to this day the community maintains its independence by "living up to pretty high standards."

Kimberton's response to the challenge might seem the polar opposite of Beaver Run's. But in both cases, a challenge from outside forced the community to find creative ways of engaging society. Even Kimberton's refusal to be licensed was a chance for dialogue with the inspectors. "They would come down," recalled Helen Zipperlen, "and we would be very hospitable and offer coffee and walk around. They would usually depart totally confused." With the support of a sympathetic official, Helen even got a federal grant to write a report on less bureaucratic strategies for keeping people safe and healthy. Inspectors, Helen insisted, are "never the bad guy. These are human beings trying to do a job, and you can help them by being challenging." The crisis also forced the village to contemplate the (remote) possibility of its death, and at least Helen found this to be a very good thing. Again and again, she asked the other Camphillers to think about what they would do if the government forcibly took away all the persons with special needs. Would they simply go their separate ways, or would they find other ways to keep the Camphill spirit of community alive? Helen relishes every opportunity she gets to ask this question. "I'm never happy," she said, "when the question isn't there."

A similar question is inescapably present at Camphill Village Minnesota because it has experienced a gradual but steady decline in its population of both coworkers and villagers. Entire houses have at times been closed, standing as visible reminders of the possibility that the community might not live forever. As the "carrying" members of the community (the long-term coworkers with enough experience to attend to the big picture) grow older, they have asked hard questions about what might happen if younger people do not arrive to take their places. The board has discussed everything from the possibility of raising an endowment large enough to sustain the entire community to the question of how to tell when it is time to die. The coworkers, meanwhile, have asked more intimate questions. What would it mean to become a community of just two or three households? Is it possible to stop grieving the loss of "what Camphill has always been" and look more closely at the interests and desires of the people who are actually there? "People are attracted to a certain place at a certain time," mused Jan Zuzalek, and if they are no longer attracted to Camphill Minnesota there might be a reason. "You don't have to despair. It might mean something new is supposed to come about."

The situation of Camphill Copake may seem diametrically opposed: a steady stream of new villagers and coworkers means that Copake is always hard at work on its next new residence. But it has had to confront another sort of "near death" experience: its very prosperity makes it a different community than it was a generation ago, as people who grew up there often point out. Originally there were no dishwashers, and people with limited skills could find meaning in the work of dishwashing; eventually dishwashers were brought in to ensure that everything was sterilized properly. Once people had to drive five miles to the nearest gas station, and so were more inclined to walk around the village; when a village gas pump was put in, they walked less. "The danger," said Mark Steinrueck, making clear that he does not necessarily see this as the current reality, is that "people will come for whom it's just a comfortable life. . . . Everything's taken care of. . . . So they're not really interested in what it took to create this." Many of Copake's current residents expressed similar concerns with a slightly different tone. "I'm still of the opinion that it's just a little too big," said Peter Madsen, noting that it is very rare to see the entire village come together, either for a common meeting or a festival. But it is very difficult, he acknowledged, when there are so many administrative people whose schedules are set more by the larger society than by the rhythms of village life.

At both Copake and Minnesota, these "near death" experiences bring new opportunities to touch the world. Camphill Minnesota's recruitment difficulties stem in large part from the fact that it is located very far from the centers of the anthroposophical subculture, in a rural area with no Waldorf school and few cultural activities of the sort that Copakers take for granted. But its isolation has allowed—or forced—the village to forge partnerships with local farmers, who are now beginning to use Camphill's processing kitchen to diversify their own enterprises, and even with the Amish, whose youngsters help hunt the pocket gophers that bedevil Camphill's fields. Copake's prosperity, on the other hand, is the result of its proximity to the wealthy philanthropic and artistic communities of New York City. Many of the villagers there have wealthy parents, and musicians ranging from Pete Seeger to the New York Philharmonic are regular guests at the village. Mark Steinrueck may be right to worry that it is not entirely healthy to take for granted that one can "just wander along a little footpath, end up in this beautiful hall and have some of the world's best musicians come and play music for you." But this also means that "some of the world's best musicians" are challenged to consider the possibility of living in a nonhierarchical community in which a person who is unable to speak or bathe herself may be valued as much as a world-class violinist.

The struggle to touch the world is related to another sort of "near death" at Camphill. As villages rely more and more on nonresident paid staff, the sense of solidarity is breaking down, or at least changing its shape. Some German Camphills have abandoned income-sharing: both resident and nonresident staff people are free to spend their salaries as they see fit. No North American Camphill has taken this step, but Beaver Run now has about as many employees as resident coworkers, and the employees include several who were previously resident coworkers. One Camphiller who experienced such shifts at both Beaver Run and Brachenreuthe in Germany told me that they can change "the whole dynamic of the community." As fewer teachers participate in the life of the houses, for example, there is more division between school life and home life. Given the reality of different schedules inside and outside the community, it has also been more difficult to bring the whole village together for cultural events.

Yet such changes bring opportunities as well as threats. Camphill, said Beaver Run's Claus Sproll, is currently entering its third generation—something that rarely happens to a community movement. This "means now we are pioneering and we have to redefine community." To encourage its nonresident employees to "carry" more of the communal spirit, Beaver Run has incorporated them into its educational activities and provided several with free memberships in the Anthroposophical Society. Claus is convinced that these initiatives will help Camphill avoid the fate of communal groups, such as the Shakers, that responded to generational transitions by withdrawing from the larger society. "The skin has got to be broken open," Claus explained. "The outreach and connecting [is] the health-giving thing." Instead of asking "what have we lost," a third generation must "go through the eye of the needle" by embracing new forms of membership and new styles of commitment.

Claus's hope is that by integrating its employees more fully, Beaver Run will actually deepen and expand its sense of shared life. It remains to be seen if that will be the case. It may be, as other Camphillers fear, that increasing reliance on employees will gradually transform Camphills into more conventional group homes and special schools. But such risks are part of Camphill's creative dialogue with society as a whole. Because both Camphills and Catholic Workers have consistently chosen the risky path of engagement rather than the death-denying path of self-preservation, Diedra Heitzman's description of Kimberton Hills would apply equally to most communities in both movements: "We are extremely strong and extremely fragile at the same time."

Personal Death Stories

The stories of communal death and near-death are intertwined with the deaths, literal or metaphorical, experienced by individuals. The deaths of community founders can be particularly significant. When Dorothy Day died in 1980, observers wondered if the movement would survive. The residents of the New York Catholic Worker felt quite "testy" about the number of times they were asked, "What will happen to the Catholic Worker now that Dorothy is gone?" But around the nation, Catholic Workers were too busy creating new houses of hospitality to be much troubled by the question. Six months after her death, the *Catholic Worker* could memorialize Day by profiling new houses in such diverse locations as rural Virginia and California, Memphis, Saint Louis, and Davenport, Iowa. In the quarter century since, the movement has experienced friendly debates about whether to support Day's canonization, and about the degree to which her views should still be binding on the movement. But almost all would endorse Peggy Scherer's conclusion that "we may have lost Dorothy, but we still have the gospel."[19]

Karl König's death marked an even more profound turning point. Regula Stolz, who lived in community with König for many years, was present at the time of his death and recalled it as "an incredible turnaround." Especially for the originally Camphillers, König was both "a brother to all of us" and "kind of the king and the person who . . . just knew what the next step was." Though König did not always exercise direct authority over the movement, he offered advice freely and "when he said it, one would have the confidence he knew what you had to do, and you would go to Africa or you would go to Norway or whatever. You would just do it. And then all that of course fell away and we knew then that with his death that things would really change."

Fortunately for the movement, König had provided a safeguard against a power struggle by designating specific individuals, many of whom shared his charismatic gifts, to take leadership of the various regions. In North America, people turned to Carlo Pietzner in much the way they had turned to König, trusting that "he just knew" and would encourage the right next step. Through his constant traveling and lecturing, Pietzner was (in the words of his widow) "the inspirer of the whole region"; he also left an artistic legacy that is still present nearly everywhere one looks at both Copake and Beaver Run. But he also continued König's work of dispersing authority more widely for future generations. By the time of his death, Pietzner had passed most of his concrete responsibilities to various other people, and these leaders were able to continue their work without significant disruption. "I don't recall anything like a crisis," said Bernie Wolf of Pietzner's death. "I think other people . . . who had been so inspired by him and had relied so much on some of his leading thoughts and ideas felt bereft."

Without such leaders as König or Pietzner, Regula Stolz told me, Camphillers gained a new sense that "every individual matters so much. We can't depend on the other one or rely on the other one. We can only do it together." Losing Pietzner and his sister-in-law Renate Sachs, echoed Sylvia Bausman, was "like growing up. The light gets brighter around you. There aren't these cozy moments . . . [when] I could always depend on the consciousness of the whole. Now I have to take my consciousness and try to bring it together with others. . . . It doesn't happen easily." "I would say it's much more exciting now," added Richard Neal, who was present during Copake's early years and returned after the deaths. "These were very special people. . . . It's very natural that a community starts off with one or two people who have a very strong vision. . . . After a while those people aren't there. And for me that's when it starts getting really interesting. If we have a real disagreement in our circle, we're the only ones who can work it out. And that's good. It's also a challenge, and it can be frightening, but as a process it's good."

Even the deaths of ordinary people can transform a community. Roswitha Imegwu told me the story of Jack Acker, a member of Copake's extended community who had organized a concert series to benefit Copake, and also got the Camphillers involved in a walkathon for Habitat for Humanity. "He was really a ball of energy," recalled Roswitha, but when he contracted terminal cancer he realized that he needed "the spiritual support of the community" to "nourish his soul." "I think it was on Easter Monday," she went on, "he moved into this house. He sat in this living room with us, looking very weak, very very thin, but very bright, and then he went upstairs and he never came down after that. . . . People came and they played music for him, they sang for him, they played the lyre for him, the choir came and sang under his window. His family came in and out, we fed them all. It was just amazing." During that last week of Jack's life, his once-wary daughter forged a friendship with the village. And a few months later Roswitha's grandson was born in the room where Jack had died.

Camphill Kimberton Hills has also cultivated an honest appreciation of death. "One of the achievements of Kimberton Hills that I'm most proud of," Helen Zipperlen told me, "is how we have . . . changed certain people's attitude to death." When someone dies, Helen explained, "they spend three days in the Blue Room, and then there's a wonderful funeral. During the three days anybody can come in and read to them, sing to them, bring a flower, just be. The whole thing is open and aboveboard, very beautiful." In keeping with the anthroposophical teaching that death is a "threshold" to a new and freer form of existence, Helen said, Camphillers recognize death as "a wonderful change of state." She also said that this practice has helped the community stay connected to those who have died. "The invisible community here is sometimes almost tangible. And that's been tremendously healing for many, many people."

During my time at Camphill Minnesota, I also heard stories of more metaphorical deaths, and their transformative effects. Long-term community leaders Bill and Laura Briggs recalled the crisis they experienced in 1992, after more than a decade at Camphill Copake. They were responsible for six villagers, two or three young volunteers, and their four young children, and Laura was recovering from a serious car accident. When she realized that communal demands made healing impossible, the Briggs family decided to "take some time as a family" by moving to Santa Rosa, California, where Bill's parents lived. The California economy was "in shambles" at the time, but the support of other Copakers led them to stick to their decision. After a period of difficult job hunting, Bill found meaningful employment, and they settled in to what became a two-year sabbatical.

The real experience of death came when the Briggs family planned for their return to Copake. Their understanding, and that of several members of the community, was that they would be automatically readmitted after their time away. Others, however, saw the family's request to return as an opportunity to try out a more critical and searching process of mutual discernment—despite the fact that they were three thousand miles away and in precarious economic circumstances. Questions and concerns that had not been voiced for a dozen years were communicated to them in a series of upsetting letters. Eventually, the Briggs family managed to address the concerns, and Camphill Copake extended an invitation for them to return. But by that time the emotional damage was too great. "It was painful," says Laura, "for us to experience their feeling that had been carried for many years and never voiced. . . . After hearing all that, at least for me, there was no way that I could go back." Despite their abiding love for Camphill, and real uncertainty about what their future might hold, the Briggs family turned down Copake's invitation.

Around the same time, Tom and Trudy Pax-Farr arrived at Camphill Village Minnesota with their two young sons. They had recently experienced the failure of another attempt at community building, and were delighted when they visited Camphill Minnesota and discovered that it seemed to be just what everyone in the family wanted. But their sons' enthusiasm waned as they realized what it meant to share their parents with four developmentally disabled adults. The situation was especially challenging for Daniel, who is mildly disabled himself, and soon a special "support group" was formed to help him explore alternatives. "It was us, his family, plus a few other people," said Trudy, "and we just sat and talked about what we thought would be the best for him." Everyone agreed that Daniel needed some distance from his parents, and so he was placed in another house. That worked for a time, but after a "couple big explosions" the group began talking about Triform, a Camphill in New York that works specifically with young adults. After several meetings, Daniel agreed to a trial stay at Triform.

The decision was upsetting at several levels. At sixteen, Daniel was younger than most Triform villagers, so Trudy and Tom worried that he might not fit in. If he were to be sent away from Triform, would this new rejection only compound his difficulties? Trudy, especially, wondered if sending her son away from home was evidence that she had somehow failed as a parent. Such things are rarely done outside intentional communities! "It was sort of unorthodox," Tom allowed, "that we would even try this out. In society's eyes I don't think it's too cool to farm your kid out when he's sixteen years old." To a degree, the Camphill network felt like an extended family that could be entrusted with Daniel's care. But Triform was far away and unfamiliar to Trudy and Tom. Perhaps most worrisome was the fact that Daniel had not, as the group hoped, fully embraced the decision as his own choice. "He felt a bit kicked out," said Trudy. "We really wanted him to be able to come to that decision with us. And he did, sort of."

As Trudy and Tom saw their son depart for New York, they felt a great deal of trepidation. But, like the Briggs family, they let go of their original vision for family life in community in the hope that by letting go, by truly experiencing the death of their dream, something new might come about. On a more intimate scale, both these families relived the experiences of so many early Catholic Workers, of Tom Heuser when he made the decisions that led to the closing of Saint Catherine's, of Karl König when he arrived alone in the unfamiliar land of Britain, and of countless other communitarians. Probably every person who has been drawn to Camphill or the Catholic Worker has at one time or another had to face the death of a community dream. Yet many of these same people have also learned that resurrection often follows death.

Stories of Resurrection

For the Briggs and Pax-Farr families, resurrection came relatively quickly. Even as the Briggses were smarting from the near rejection of Copake, they received an invitation to move to Camphill Village Minnesota. This was attractive in part because several of their friends from Copake had since moved to Minnesota, but mostly because of the tone of the invitation. Bill recalled "We had an absolutely open invitation to come here without any strings. . . . It was just like, come and be with us, we'd love to have you." Once they accepted Minnesota's invitation, things came together for the Briggs family in dramatic ways. Before leaving California, they were able to play a role in planning a new village in Santa Cruz, where people were "really hungering and thirsty for community life." Once in Minnesota, they emerged as leaders of a young community, exercising some of the gifts that had been questioned at Copake. They also realized that they had played an important, if painful, role in the development of the Copake community. "We were a catalyst," said Laura, "of a lot of things that they needed to work on. . . . But it also opened a number of doors for us that we didn't see prior to the doors being closed on us."

For Trudy and Tom, the surprise of resurrection came when they realized that Daniel was not having the difficult time they had worried he might have at Triform. Instead, he thrived there. "He just transformed completely," said Trudy. Her son Nick returned from a visit to Daniel and told her, "Mom, you wouldn't believe the things they tell him to do and he does it." The resurrection experience blossomed in 1999 when Daniel returned to spend an entire summer at Camphill Minnesota. During that summer, his mother recalled, Daniel was a "shining person" who brightened the lives of almost everyone in the village. Community members who recalled Daniel's troubles were amazed to discover his gift for breaking down barriers between villagers and coworkers. The same summer was my first at Camphill Minnesota, and I recall especially how Daniel's twenty-first birthday party drew the community together. The village itself is roughly the same age as Daniel, and the deeply serious joy he took in his coming of age helped the community think about its own passage from adolescence to adulthood.

Of course, experiences of resurrection are not always so obvious or so immediate. But a closer look reveals that Camphill and Catholic Worker communities are often resurrected in the creative work of people who were briefly touched by community life. "The gold moves on and the dross remains," Dorothy Day liked to say, alluding in part to her community's many prominent "alumni." Marc Ellis wrote a provocative memoir of his year at the New York Worker, then went on to become the foremost proponent of a Jewish theology of liberation. Michael Harrington spent two years at the Worker in the 1950s because it "was as far left as I could go and still be in the church." Ultimately he left both church and Worker, but his experiences of urban poverty shaped his writing of *The Other America*, which in turn inspired Lyndon Johnson's War on Poverty. "Though he broke with the Church," recalled Eileen Egan in a memorial, "he never broke with the Catholic Worker, and came to talk at our Friday evening meetings whenever we invited him." Senator Eugene McCarthy also left the Worker for politics. When he bumped into Dorothy Day on a train platform years later, he said, "You don't like me now, Dorothy, because I'm in politics." But she replied that "God puts people where they ought to be in life—although how far we go in that place is up to us."[20]

Day's clarity about the Worker's own mission allowed it to be resurrected in movements with other missions. When associate editor Tom Coddington complained that the Worker should focus on labor organizing rather than direct service, Day encouraged him to do so—but insisted that he move off the Worker premises and find his own funding. Though this split was bitter, other Workers who were deeply involved in the seamen's strike organized the Association of Catholic Trade Unionists while sitting "around the table in the Catholic Worker." ACTU leaders such as John Cort distanced themselves from the Worker's extreme idealism, but retained a fierce loyalty to the inspiration they had received from Dorothy Day. "Many of us," recalled Cort, "didn't buy the whole thing: the agrarianism, the total pacifism, the anarchism or personalism. . . . But [the Catholic Worker] got me interested, for instance, in the cooperative movement, in the trade union movement. A lot of people were like that." The Association of Catholic Conscientious Objectors and Catholic Peace Fellowship were founded under similar auspices, and maintained ties of both ideology and affection to the Catholic Worker.[21]

Camphill cannot point to as many famous alumni as the Catholic Worker. Yet, in quieter ways, many Camphill alumni have sought to take lessons learned in community into more conventional settings. People at Camphill Village Minnesota are quite excited by the work their former companion Kristin Wilson has done in building up the Whole Farm Co-op and thus helping local farmers remain solvent by providing them with new markets for sustainably raised products. Other Camphills have sponsored or spun off community supported gardens, in which customers purchase a weekly "share" of fresh produce. Indeed, Camphill Copake has sometimes claimed to have been the initiator of the Community Supported Agriculture movement in the United States, making it the great-grandfather of around one thousand "CSAs" across North America.[22]

Camphill Kimberton Hills has an especially strong commitment to supporting related initiatives, even if these draw off the energies of longtime coworkers. Early on, Helen Zipperlen and others forged friendships with the staff of Pennhurst, a nearby state institution that was "deinstitutionalizing" three thousand adults with developmental disabilities. Though the Camphillers might have seen this as an opportunity to recruit villagers and coworkers, they instead helped the staff develop their own new initiatives. For a time, they worked with others who hoped to bring a L'Arche community to their county. Out of this grew Orion Communities, a network of household communities that evolved into a wide-ranging service and advocacy organization for persons with disabilities. Though Orion required energies that might have been devoted to Kimberton Hills itself, Helen is certain that it was worthwhile. "In developing our vision, we were all the time thinking and listening with [others]."

Indeed, both Camphill and the Catholic Worker have done their best work by thinking and listening with others. The fruits can be hard to see— and I may have failed to see the most important ones—but they are as significant as the communities' more public works. The organic farms, worker cooperatives, and grassroots peace groups that are among the most hopeful aspects of American society today have sprung up, in part, from the fertile seeds of Camphill and the Catholic Worker.

Resurrection in New Communities

The unaffiliated communities that surround both the Catholic Worker and Camphill movements can also be understood as "resurrected" forms of those movements. When Mike Miles and Barb Kass moved from Jonah House to rural Wisconsin, for example, they were inspired by Peter Maurin's agrarian vision and anticipated that their farm would be part of the Catholic Worker movement. But the companions who were willing to make a long-term commitment to the community had their spiritual roots not in Catholicism but in Gandhian nonviolence and Native American spirituality. It made little sense to impose a Catholic Worker identity on such a diverse group, and so the community was born as the Anathoth Community Farm. Still, the Miles/Kass household is decorated with Catholic Worker woodcuts; Anathoth is listed on the Catholic Worker Web site; and several veteran Workers have moved back and forth between Anathoth and the Loaves and Fishes Catholic Worker in Duluth.

Anathoth's flexible relationship to the Catholic Worker movement has given them the freedom to engage the larger society in a variety of ways. Mike's brother and sister-in-law raised their family on an adjoining, privately owned farm, participating in some but not all of the community's activities. Mike and Barb have made an especially strong commitment to keeping their community open to their neighbors in Luck, Wisconsin, where Barb works in a local social service program and Mike coaches track at the local school. Looking at the community's tire swing, Mike commented that "by the time Phil is a senior I'll have pushed every kid in the school in that swing." Such ties have made it easier for other parents to seek Mike and Barb's views on America's wars in Kosovo and Iraq. More recently, Mike has broken slightly from the longstanding Catholic Worker tradition of anarchism by running for Congress on the Green Party ticket. He couched his reasons for the campaign in terms that underscored a desire to touch the world. "For me," he mused, "it is much easier to walk up a driveway and go to jail than to walk into a bar festooned with red, white and blue buntings and talk with locals about why war is a bad idea and that there is no money for health care because the Pentagon has it all." Mike received more votes than any other Green congressional candidate in the nation.

Not far from Anathoth, Community Homestead offers a similar model of how a community movement can be "resurrected" in ways that allow greater interaction with the larger society. Community Homestead's variation on the model of Camphill has been profoundly shaped by its founders' youthful experiences at Camphill Copake. Richard Elmquist and Sophia Steinrueck (now Wertmann) were staff kids at Copake in the 1970s, while their spouses arrived there as young coworkers in the 1980s. After marrying, both couples left Camphill to pursue more traditional careers: Richard worked as an aerospace engineer, his spouse Christine as a teacher, and Adrian and Sophia worked on biodynamic farms. By the early 1990s, the two couples felt a hunger for community and service, even though Camphill itself wasn't "quite what we were looking for." As children they had borne the brunt of occasional tensions between Copake and its neighbors, and so they wanted a community that was open to the larger society. They also had witnessed the pioneering community of their youth grow into a prosperous village, perhaps a bit too dependent on donations from wealthy benefactors. So they began casting around for a new model of shared life that would give them "a certain amount of freedom to allow things to refresh themselves." As this model developed, it attracted Richard's brother Douglas and Sophia's brother Mark.[23]

The process of imagining a sort of "second generation" of Camphill was partly unconscious. "What we've done in Community Homestead," admitted Richard, "is really based in large part upon the perceptions of the young person, particularly teenagers, growing up in Camphill. So that's not always very, necessarily, insightful. It's much more an emotional thing than an intellectual thing." The three founders who had spent their childhoods in Camphill, in particular, were frustrated by the fact that they could "feel what a community should be like" but had trouble "intellectually understanding what that was." Wanting a community based in intention rather than habit, they decided to reenact much of Camphill's founding process, putting aside such Camphill "pillars" as the weekly Bible evening. "We don't like to be told what to do," added Christine, "so we have to run along and make our own mistakes. . . . The biggest way to tick people off in this community . . . is to say, well, I think this is the way we should do things, because this is the way it's written in a book."

Community Homestead has sought to recover the pioneering spirit that brought their parents to Camphill a generation before. "Without a doubt for all of us, there's a certain amount of pride in struggling," said Douglas Elmquist. He recalled with nostalgia his mother's stories of carrying bread dough three-quarters of a mile to the one house at Copake that had a proper oven, then noted ruefully that Copake today has the best bakery "that money can buy." "I understand that there's this natural evolution of the place," said Douglas, but "I like the feeling that you know that if the weeds are getting carried away that our meetings move out to the garden." This pioneering spirit is reflected in the community's name, with "Homestead" deliberately evoking the pioneering period of American (and Wisconsin) history. It also entails a commitment to "prioritizing the economic" and avoiding the large gifts and endowments on which many Camphills rely. "Big grants . . . do have a corrupting power," explained Douglas Elmquist. "When Camphill talks about fundraising they talk three to five million. When we get a twenty thousand-dollar check . . . [we] throw a party." Douglas went on to acknowledge that this is just his perspective as someone on the outside, and that the concern doesn't detract from the good work done by Camphill. "I have absolute respect for what they're doing, don't get me wrong."

As an alternative to endowment building, the founders decided that at least some of them would work outside the community. At the time of my visit, Richard worked part time as an engineer, Garth Riegel worked full time at a Waldorf School, and Douglas was making a transition from full time outside work to greater involvement in the community. Each contributed his entire salary to the community, which then distributed all income, Camphill-style, according to individual needs. In considering the admission of new coworkers, moreover, the community has consistently asked, "what was that person going to add to the economy of Community Homestead?" When Mark Steinrueck joined, for example, he brought the expertise he had gained running an urban bakery and coffee shop, and as result the community has begun selling its own label of coffee.

Though Garth Riegel admitted that holding a full-time job while living in community is "not the best of both worlds," this practice helps Community Homestead stay connected to the larger society. Indeed, probably the most important way in which it has differentiated itself from Camphill is in its emphasis on bridge building. Compared to Camphill, said Christine Elmquist, Community Homestead is "a little more interconnected with the world. We are not saying we are separate from the world or somehow sheltered from the world or better than the world, or—because we are the world. We're a part of it." Several of the villagers hold part-time jobs in town, while others volunteer to clean the public library. Most years, at least two community members coach local soccer teams, in which several of the community kids also participate. Adrian Wertmann has emerged as an important leader in the local farming community, and the community's garden draws many people who come to buy produce. Remembering Copake's occasional conflicts with its neighbors over taxation, Community Homestead even decided to pay local sales and property taxes, despite their nonprofit status.

Community Homesteaders see their approach as an evolution of Camphill's vision, rather than a stark alternative. When Camphill came to the

United States, explained Mark Steinrueck, "there was a real feeling that this was something so foreign and alien to the world that they really had to protect it, the way you protect a small child." By the 1980s, by contrast, "at least certain elements in society" were more open both to persons with disabilities and to intentional community. The Community Homesteaders felt, in Richard's words, that Camphill "had evolved enough that it didn't need to be sheltered and hidden away in valleys or whatever. That it could actually now blossom and be available to the greater world." So they bought existing houses within a small rural subdivision, as well as a nearby farmstead. They encouraged new families to join the community gradually, living nearby and participating in the village's cultural life for a few years before making a permanent commitment. These new patterns of residential life allow Community Homestead to prod the larger society toward even greater acceptance. "Hopefully in another fifty years," said Christine, "even Community Homestead will seem too distant from the rest of society. As everyone learns to embrace the gifts of people with special needs, and to restore a healthier connection to the land, it will be possible for the community simply to be the town."

Parallel efforts exist within Camphill itself, and one indicator of increasing openness is the fact that Community Homesteaders have felt the consistent support of the Camphill movement. Early in their planning process, they sought guidance from several experienced Camphillers, and—"probably rightly" according to Richard Elmquist—received enthusiasm, encouragement, but no actual advice. The Camphillers saw the value of an autonomous initiative and refused to compromise it. The sense of shared vision was confirmed when Richard and Douglas's parents retired to Community Homestead after spending nearly fifty years at Copake and other Camphills. That gesture reversed the usual logic of homecoming and provided the occasion for the larger Camphill movement to honor the new direction taken by Community Homestead. In a report published in Copake's anniversary volume, the senior Elmquists assured their former community mates that they weren't "leaving Camphill, but rather going to Camphill in a different form," and that the Camphill impulse was alive and well in the "many places fostered by the Camphill spirit."[24]

Communities without Signs

Despite their differences from the communities that preceded them, Anathoth Community Farm and Community Homestead are readily visible *as* communities. In other cases, the spirit of community is resurrected in less obvious forms. At dozens of what might be called "communities without signs," people live in close proximity, sharing the joys and sorrows of daily life, but see little need to announce themselves to the world as intentional communities. Though these communities neither seek nor receive many accolades for their efforts, their integration into the larger society makes them an essential vanguard for any movement that is committed to "touching the world."

The most common Camphills "without signs" are "lifesharing" households, in which a family simply welcomes one or two or three adults with disabilities into their home. This was the original model of the Orion Communities, initiated by a large group of friends of Camphill Kimberton Hills who sought new forms of lifesharing and mutual support. Though Orion ultimately evolved in a different direction, many of the families continued to share their homes with special-needs persons after moving to New England. Western Massachusetts is now home to the Cadmus Lifesharing Association, a loose network of families organized by Nick and Andrea Stanton, former leaders at Camphill Beaver Run. Each participating household maintains its own nonprofit status, while Cadmus itself is a nonprofit whose "members" are the various households. "We believe," explains the Web site, "that, in a community, interdependence can only be achieved where the members are first of all independent."[25]

Yet another creative adaptation of the Camphill vision is House of Peace in Ipswich, Massachusetts. Founder Carrie Schuchardt spent many years at Camphill Kimberton Hills, during which time she developed a strong interest in work with Vietnamese boat people. After taking a few teenaged refugees into her home at Camphill, she decided (along with two Kimberton villagers) to make this her life's work. She relocated to Massachusetts and married John Schuchardt, a lawyer with strong ties to Catholic Workers and other war resisters in New England. House of Peace is thus unusual in blending wisdom from both Camphill and the Catholic Worker. Drawing on the special gifts of persons with developmental disabilities, it creates a welcoming environment for newcomers to the United States. "These individuals," wrote one observer, "often severely functionally limited, are brilliant in the field of making people feel at home and binding people together."[26]

A similar spirit is present in Catholic Worker reflection on the ideal of the "Christ room." The patristic bishop and theologian John Chrysostom, Dorothy Day recalled, had counseled the early Christians to "have a room to which Christ may come," and she encouraged her admirers to maintain "Christ rooms" in their own households. Formal houses of hospitality like those in New York City were really a compromise, she explained in a 1936 editorial. "We emphasize again the necessity of smallness. . . . The idea[1] . . . would be that each Christian . . . should take in one of the homeless as an honored guest, remembering Christ's words, 'Inasmuch as ye have done it unto the least of these, ye have done it unto me.' . . . Those of our readers who are interested in Houses of Hospitality might first of all try to take some one into their homes." In keeping with this principle, Catholic Workers have sometimes answered, "what about your house?" when receiving a call from a social worker looking for a space for a homeless person.[27]

Examples of the Christ room spirit have appeared throughout the Catholic Worker's history. One of the founders of the first Milwaukee community, for example, subsequently lived in an African American neighborhood in Chicago that was also home to Catholic Worker sympathizers Gordon Zahn and Don Klein. Her bookshop, which served as a meeting place for activists of many stripes, inspired Dorothy Day to write that "she is as much a Catholic Worker as ever and her works of mercy reach out in all directions. She has an understanding of poverty and of destitution and always a readiness to share in the one and to alleviate the other." "We are always hearing," Day observed, about informal Catholic Worker farms. "But I hesitate to name their localities, because there is such a hunger for community, there are so many wandering monks and scholars . . . that I would not want to be responsible for disturbing their privacy."[28]

At least three Minnesota farms have taken the Catholic Worker spirit in new directions. A year at the Loaves and Fishes Catholic Worker inspired Paula Williams to start a community-supported flower farm just outside Duluth, while her former housemates Hans Peterson and Heidi Morlock moved to a southern Minnesota farm owned by Heidi's family. With another family in residence and an active extended community, they are building "Seven Story Farm" into an inspiring model of intentional community and sustainable agriculture, though it is not an "official" Catholic Worker farm. Farther west, Gary Brever drew on his experience at Bethlehem Peace Farm when he started a Community Supported Agriculture project called Plough Share Farm. Because the intense hospitality practiced at Bethlehem left him burned out, for example, he is determined to preserve "sacred space" for his growing family. During the summers, they share noon meals with a community of interns, but preserve supper as family time.

Gary is clear that Plough Share Farm is "first and foremost a business." Indeed, he argues, the best way to promote a more sustainable rural economy is simply to "be an example that survives. . . . As we are surviving they get more interested in what we are doing in organic farming." As a Catholic Worker, Gary was frustrated by the movement's tendency to criticize the "system" rather than offering constructive alternatives; he also felt that the demands of hospitality were so intense that he was always "begging" for support from the larger society rather than giving back in a neighborly way. At Plough Share Farm, he has the opportunity to be "reciprocal to other people's needs," whether by providing produce shares to low-income families, volunteering at church, or simply shoveling a neighbor's driveway. At the same time, he is grateful to the Catholic Worker for instilling in him a critical understanding of the military industrial complex, and the ways it distorts American agriculture. As his children get older, moreover, Gary hopes to renew his connection to the Worker tradition of solidarity with the poor.

Even as former Workers are renewing the rural economy, urban houses of hospitality are often surrounded by "satellite" families. Within a few blocks of the Loaves and Fishes Catholic Worker in Duluth, one can find the homes of about a half-dozen former Workers, many of whom have sustained deep, long-term relationships with former guests of Loaves and Fishes. During my interview with Steve O'Neil and Angie Miller, for example, one former guest dropped by their home to say hello, and they told me of a recent trip they had taken with another to plant potatoes at Anathoth Community Farm. There are also several people in Worcester, Massachusetts, who once lived in "official" Catholic Worker communities but now simply practice hospitality and resistance in the context of traditional family life. Among the most articulate is Mike Boover, who was once part of the live-in community at Worcester's Mustard Seed Catholic Worker. Since the time of his marriage, Mike told me, he has tried to take the Catholic Worker vision and "bring it in little ways into more so-called normal life." As manager of a residential program for people with mental illnesses, he hired former Workers and helped them discern whether to choose radical community or conventional employment in the social services. He parlayed his role as an unofficial Catholic Worker archivist into a doctor of ministry dissertation and a teaching job at Anna Maria College, where he shares the Catholic Worker vision with new generations of students.

At home, Mike and his wife Diane maintain what is outwardly a traditional single-family home they call Annunciation House. Next to the house is an old barn that Mike relocated from the Mustard Seed and converted into a chapel called the Hound of Heaven. Behind the chapel is a grape arbor for discussions, and then a garden and chicken coop. Echoing a slogan of Peter Maurin's, Mike said, "It's all in a row, cult, culture, and cultivation." In this inviting space, Mike and Diane practice several forms of hospitality. Mike uses the Hound of Heaven to host a meditation group called the Lazy Bums, and dreams about expanding this work to include a small-scale folk school. Mike and Diane have hosted homeless individuals for months at a time, though they have also honored their children's requests for periods of family-only time. They open their home frequently for shared meals: during the day I spent with them, they hosted two families from their parish for lunch, and for supper they had two friends who had been homeless guests at the Mustard Seed decades before. In the midst of all this activity, Mike and Diane maintain a restful spirit that is not easy to find in a Catholic Worker. Annunciation House, Mike concluded, "is a translation. . . . I think a lot of us translate the Worker vision into a new language in order to work in so-called normal society. . . . You need to grant the vision some room."

Even when they carry names like "Annunciation House" or "Cadmus Lifesharing Association," households that resurrect community values on a small scale often go unnoticed by the journalists and scholars who gravitate to the New York Catholic Worker or Camphill Village Copake. Too often, even the people who live in such households describe their efforts as "compromises" or marginal to the work done by the "real" communities. Yet they embody an ideal that is at the heart of the Camphill and Catholic Worker traditions. If the ultimate goal is "social renewal" or "creating a new society within the shell of the old," communities that stand apart from mainstream society can play at best a transitional role. The most essential work of Camphill and the Catholic Worker is not building up a village or a house of hospitality, but living in a new way—a way marked by sharing, hospitality, and the recognition of diverse gifts—and blending that new way with the full range of vocations and family situations present in society.

Another way to make this point is to consider the relationship of Camphill and the Catholic Worker to the communal ideal expressed in the book of Acts. Virtually all Christian communities have drawn inspiration from that text's description of the Jerusalem church: "All who believed were together and had all things in common" (Acts 2:44). This text is authoritative for such movements as the Hutterites and Bruderhof, who believe that all Christians have an obligation to practice complete community of goods. More mainstream Christians, on the other hand, dismiss it as an illustration of the apostles' pragmatic response to circumstances unique to the first century. They may be grateful to the apostles for using communal sharing to safeguard the vulnerable flame of the Gospel, but see no need to imitate the practice in the modern age.

Camphill and the Catholic Worker suggest a third alternative to these polarized principles. In reflecting on the early church, they have sought to imitate the spirit rather than the precise structures of the apostles. The fate of the Jerusalem church, significantly, was not that different from the fate of many early Worker communities. Without clear rules that mandated sharing, its external structures faded away almost as soon as they had begun, yet they were replaced by a "spirit" that has inspired new ventures in Christian community from Saint Benedict to the present. Likewise, the spirit of Camphill and the Catholic Worker may live on in sharing households and sustainable farms long after their names have passed from the lips of scholars, visitors, and friends.

The most important "resurrection" of any community is thus the invisible, spiritual one. When individual vocations and family commitments provide a bridge to wider sharing, when everyone honors the vulnerable stranger as they would honor Christ, and when the abilities of even the most "disabled" person are recognized as gifts from the spiritual world, then the work of Camphill and the Catholic Worker will be complete, even if both movements have passed from the earth. Indeed, it may be that the death of each movement, as a distinct institutional reality, may be a necessary step on the path to a renewed society.

Notes

1. Rudolf Steiner, "Spiritual Principle," cited in Michael and Jane Luxford, *A Sense for Community*, 178.

2. Joe DaVia, "DMCW 25th Anniversary Photos and Reflection," *via pacis* 25/3 (October 2001).

3. Kanter, *Commitment*, 80, 82, 92, 104, 112, 124–5.

4. Donald E. Pitzer, "Introduction," in Donald E. Pitzer, ed., *America's Communal Utopias* (Chapel Hill, NC: University of North Carolina Press, 1997) 3–13.

5. Dorothy Day, "Aims and Purposes," *Catholic Worker* 7/6 (February 1940) 7.

6. Murray, *Hospitality*, 252.

7. Peter Maurin, Clarence Duffy, Arthur Sheehan, and David Mason, "We Carry On," *Catholic Worker* 10/10 (October 1943) 2.

8. Jim Rogan, "Baltimore House Closes," *Catholic Worker* 9/4 (February 1942) 5.

9. Dorothy Day, "Letter on Hospices," *Catholic Worker* 14/10 (January 1948) 2.

10. Joe Lynch, Willa and Brendan Walsh, "Viva House," *Catholic Worker* 38/9 (December 1972) 7.

11. Katrina Plato, "Changing of the Bethlehem Farm Sign," *Bethlehem Peace Farm* 1/1 (May 1998) 1–2, Dorothy Day—Catholic Worker Collection, series W-4, box 17, folder 13.

12. "Dear Friend," ca. March 2001, Dorothy Day—Catholic Worker Collection, series W-4, box 17, folder 13.

13. Jim Levinson, "A Dozen Years at Haley House and Noonday Farm," *Haley House Newsletter* (Summer/Fall 1995).

14. "A Brief History of Saint Catherine of Genoa Catholic Worker," Dorothy Day—Catholic Worker Collection, series W-63.

15. Tom Heuser, "Another Crossroad," *The Catholic Worker—Saint Catherine of Genoa*, Chicago 7/2 (May 1995) 1.

16. Lillian Larsen, "It Has Been Home," *The Catholic Worker—Saint Catherine of Genoa*, Chicago 9/2 (Summer 1997) 5.

17. Tom Heuser, "Time to Say Farewell," *The Catholic Worker—Saint Catherine of Genoa*, Chicago 9/2 (Summer 1997) 1.

18. König, *Camphill Movement*, 13–4.

19. Jane Sammon, "Living Fully for Others," *Catholic Worker* 46/9 (December 1980) 11; *Catholic Worker* 47/4 (May 1981) 1; and Peggy Scherer, cited in Riegle, *Dorothy Day*, 189.

20. Troester, *Voices*, 120–33; Eileen Egan, "Michael Harrington," *Catholic Worker* 56/8 (December 1989) 5; and Bruce Cook, "The Real Dorothy Day," *U. S. Catholic* 21 (April 1966) 29, cited in Marilyn L. Klein, "Families in the Catholic Worker Movement," M.A. thesis, Graduate Theological Union, 1991, Dorothy Day—Catholic Worker Collection, Series W-7.1, box 4, folder 2, p. 67.

21. John Cort, cited in Troester, *Voices*, 12–4.

22. Michael and Jane Luxford, *A Sense for Community*, 113.

23. There are other instances of coworker children who have started initiatives that resemble Camphill but remain unaffiliated. The daughter of Carlo and Ursel Pietzner, for example, founded a youth guidance community in Norway that includes many Camphillers but does not use the name.

24. "A Visit from Mary and Asger Elmquist," in Hunt, *Shining Lights*, 75.

25. See www.cadmuslife.org/.

26. Matthew Perry, "A Recipe for Renewal," *Spirit Working*. See www.spiritworking.org/featuredcolumnist/featured_6.html.

27. Day, "Houses of Hospitality," *Catholic Worker* 4/8 (December 1936) 4; Miller, *Harsh and Dreadful Love*, 204, and David Stein, "Direct Action," *Via pacis* 7/3 (June/July 1983) 9.

28. Day, *On Pilgrimage—The Sixties*, 28; and Day, *Loaves and Fishes*, 206.

Acknowledgments

My work on this book began in 1999, when I was finishing my first year as a college professor and looking for a meaningful way to spend my summer vacation. The people of Camphill Village Minnesota made an exception to their usual policy when they agreed to let me stay for just one month, and they made the same exception in each of the next three summers! I am deeply grateful for their flexibility, and even more so for the light and joy I experienced in the houses, garden, and summer kitchen of that community. The hospitality of every person at Camphill Minnesota provided the good soil in which the seed of this book germinated.

My interest in intentional Christian communities was sparked even earlier, as a result of my encounters with Habitat for Humanity, the Lutheran Volunteer Corps, Saint Catherine of Genoa Catholic Worker in Chicago, and the Community of Saint Martin in Minneapolis. I am grateful for the example and commitment of the countless people who have been a part of each of these spirit-filled communities.

As I conducted my research, I experienced again and again the hospitality that is a hallmark of both Camphill and the Catholic Worker. In addition to the persons named below, I would like to thank Eddie Bloomer, Christina Bould, Monica Cornell, Maria Rosa Costa i Alandi, Mary Elmquist, and Asger Elmquist for the kindness and care they extended to me during my visits to their communities. I am also grateful to Chris Gamm, who conducted several of the earliest interviews as my research assistant during the summer of 2000, and to Phillip Runkel, who shepherded my brief stay at the Dorothy Day—Catholic Worker Collection at Marquette University.

My greatest debt is to the many Camphillers and Catholic Workers who shared their experiences and wisdom with me in formal interviews. The following individuals agreed to be quoted by name in this book: Sonja Adams

(Camphill Special School, Beaver Run, Pennsylvania, 4 May 2005); Christopher Allen-Doucot (Saint Martin de Porres Catholic Worker, Hartford, Connecticut, 4 January 2002); Guy Alma (Camphill Special School, 2 May 2005); Sylvia Bausman (Camphill Village USA, Copake, New York, 9 August 2002); Chuck Berendes (Place of Grace Catholic Worker, La Crosse, Wisconsin, 10 April 2002); Rose Berger (Sojourners Community, Washington, D.C., 26 May 2000); Sylvia and Harry Bingham (Camphill Village USA, 6 August 2002); Greg Boertje-Obed (Loaves and Fishes Catholic Worker, Duluth, Minnesota, 24 August 2002); Mike Boover (Annunciation House, Worcester, Massachusetts, 6 January 2002); Jeremy and Liz Brett (Lukas Community, Temple, New Hampshire, 7 January 2002); Gary Brever (Bethlehem Peace Farm, Chehalis, Washington, 22 April 2005); Bill, Laura, Angela, and Joseph Briggs (Camphill Village Minnesota, Long Prairie, Minnesota, 30 July 2000); Frank Cordaro (Des Moines Catholic Worker, Des Moines, Iowa, 2 February 2002); Tom Cornell (Peter Maurin Farm, Marlboro, New York, 23 May 2000 and 3 October 2004); Ben Cownap (Camphill Village Kimberton Hills, Kimberton, Pennsylvania, 6 May 2005); Matt Daloisio (Haley House Catholic Worker, Boston, Massachusetts, 3 January 2002); Mary Davis (Camphill Village Minnesota, 29 June 2002); Carla Dawson (Des Moines Catholic Worker, 20 August 2000); Joy Dean (Lukas Community, 7 January 2002); Scot and Linda de Graf (Sojourners and Circle Communities, Washington, D.C., 26 May 2000); Christine and Richard Elmquist (Community Homestead, Osceola, Wisconsin, 16–17 March 2002); Douglas Elmquist (Community Homestead, 17 March 2002); Dietmar Emmert (Maple Hill Farm, Temple, New Hampshire, 8 January 2002); Suzette Ermler (New York Catholic Worker Community, 23 May 2000); Tom Farr (Camphill Village Minnesota, 22 July 2000); the Focus Group (Camphill Special School, 2 May 2005); Jan Goeschel (Camphill Special School, 4 May 2005); Diedra Heitzman (Camphill Village Kimberton Hills, Kimberton, Pennsylvania, 6 May 2005); Tom Heuser (Saint Catherine of Genoa Catholic Worker, Chicago, Illinois, 24 November 2001); Mark and Nicola Hobson (Lukas Community, 7 January 2002); Nadine Holder (Community Homestead, 16 March 2002); Donna Howard (Loaves and Fishes Catholic Worker, 24 August 2002); Bob Hulteen (Sojourners, 6 May 2000); Roswitha Imegwu (Camphill Village USA, 8 August 2002); Barb Kass (Anathoth Community Farm, Luck, Wisconsin, 21–22 August 2000); Brian Kavanagh (Saint Martin de Porres Catholic Worker, 4 January 2002); Betsy Keenan (Strangers and Guests Catholic Worker, Maloy, Iowa, 19 August 2000); Joanne Kennedy (New York Catholic Worker, 23 May

2000); Joel Kilgour (Loaves and Fishes Catholic Worker, 25 August 2002); Karen Lattea (Sojourners, 26 May 2000); Frank LeBar (Camphill Village USA, 9 August 2002); Peter Madsen (Camphill Village USA, 6 August 2002); Paul and Astrid Martin (Four Winds Community, Temple, New Hampshire, 8 January 2002); Susan Masters (Sojourners, 6 May 2000); Reba and Scott Mathern-Jacobson (Loaves and Fishes Catholic Worker, 22 July 2000); Billy and Lindsey McLaughlin (Sojourners and Circle, 26 May 2000); Jerry Mechtenberg-Berrigan (Anathoth Community Farm, 14 May 2000); Mike Miles (Anathoth Community Farm, 21–22 August 2000); Angie Miller (Loaves and Fishes Catholic Worker, 25 August 2002); Michele Naar-Obed (Loaves and Fishes Catholic Worker, 24 August 2002); Richard Neal (Camphill Village USA, 9 August 2002); Steve O'Neil (Loaves and Fishes Catholic Worker, 25 August 2002); Trudy Pax (Camphill Village Minnesota, 22 July 2000); Ursel Pietzner (Camphill Special School, Beaver Run, Pennsylvania, 3 May 2005); Nancy and Steve Potter (Camphill Village Minnesota, 27 July 2000); Lawrence Purcell (Redwood City Catholic Worker, Redwood City, California, 14 July 2000); Claire Quiner (Des Moines Catholic Worker, Des Moines, Iowa, 2 February 2002); Jim Rice (Sojourners and Circle, 26 May 2000); Garth Riegel (Community Homestead, 16 March 2002); Bill Roskind (Camphill Village USA, 8 August 2002); Sheila Russell (Community Homestead, 17 March 2002); Jim Rice (Sojourners and Circle, 26 May 2000); Bob and Jackie Sabath (Sojourners and Circle, 26 May 2000); Melanie Sabra (Camp-hill Special School, 3 May 2005); Claire, Scott, and Patrick Schaeffer-Duffy (Saints Francis and Thérèse Catholic Worker, Worcester, Massachusetts, 5–6 January 2002); Mike Sersch (Winona Catholic Worker, Winona, Minnesota, 12 April 2002); Lois Smith (Camphill Village Minnesota, 4 June 2002); Rob Soley (Sojourners and Circle, 26 May 2000); Anitra Sorensen (Maple Hill Farm, 8 January 2002); David Spears (Lukas Community, 8 January 2002); Ed Spivey Jr. (Sojourners and Circle, 26 May 2000); Claus Sproll (Camphill Special School, 4 May 2005); Johanna Steinrueck (Camp-hill Village USA, 9 September 2000); Mark Steinrueck (Community Homestead, 16 March 2002); Regula Stolz (Camphill Village USA, 7 August 2002); Jim and Barb Tamialis (Sojourners, 27 May 2000); Brian Terrell (Strangers and Guests Catholic Worker, 19 August 2000 and 13 March 2005); Clara Terrell (Strangers and Guests Catholic Worker, 19 August 2000); Sara Thomsen (Loaves and Fishes Catholic Worker, 24 August 2002); Ted Walker (Des Moines Catholic Worker, 2 February 2002); Karen Wallstein (Camphill Village USA, 8 August 2002); Brendan and Willa Walsh-Bickham (Viva House Catholic Worker, Baltimore, Maryland,

25 May 2000); Kate and Dave Walsh-Little (Viva House, 25 May 2000); Paula Williams (Loaves and Fishes Catholic Worker, 24 August 2002); Don and Kristin Wilson (Camphill Village Minnesota, 10 September 2000); Bernie Wolf (Camphill Special School, 4 May 2005); Helen Zipperlen (Camphill Village Kimberton Hills, 6 May 2005); and Jan Zuzalek (Camphill Village Minnesota, 20 May 2002). All contributed enormously to the book, though not all are actually quoted. I am also deeply grateful to those individuals who shared their wisdom with me but chose not to be quoted by name.

As I transformed my visits and interviews into a book, I benefited greatly from the financial support of the College of Saint Benedict and Saint John's University, which granted me a series of research releases and a full-year sabbatical in 2004–2005. I also thank the Henry Luce Foundation and the Association of Theological Schools for extending me a Henry Luce III Fellowship during my sabbatical year. The Communal Studies Association, International Communal Studies Association, and American Academy of Religion all provided sympathetic venues for me to share early versions of the ideas contained in this book.

I am also grateful to the first publishers of the following articles, who have given permission for portions of them to be incorporated into this book: "Intentional Individuals: Growing Up in Radical Christian Communities," *Communal Societies* 23 (2003) 129–44; "'Doing the Work': Can a Community Be Spiritually Diverse and Still Maintain Its Identity?" *Communities: Journal of Cooperative Living* #124 (Fall 2004) 50–54; and "Honoring the Journey: The Wayward Paths of Conversion in the Catholic Worker and Camphill Movements," *Journal of the American Academy of Religion* 74 (November 2006) 926–53.

I met my spouse, Tammy, relatively early in the process of writing this book. For the past five years she has been the fiercest champion of the project, and every page bears marks of her insight and commitment. Tammy's clarity about the ways communities can go wrong, in particular, has shaped my understanding of what is right about both Camphill and the Catholic Worker. Our daughter, Oriana, enlivened my sabbatical year by accompanying me to the park after I finished each morning's writing. On her behalf, I would like to thank the quilt-makers of Community Homestead. We won a ladybug quilt at their annual festival, and during my sabbatical each day ended with Oriana's plea to be tucked in beneath her beloved "Bugs."

Learning More about Camphill and the Catholic Worker

Almost all Camphillers and Catholic Workers would say that the best way to get to know their communities is to visit them. Visitors should call or write in advance; contact information for individual communities is readily available at www.catholicworker.org and www.camphill.org. Information on most of the unaffiliated communities mentioned in this book can be found either on these Web sites or through a quick Web search.

Those who wish to read more about the Catholic Worker might begin with Dorothy Day's frequently reprinted writings, especially *Loaves and Fishes* (Maryknoll, NY: Orbis, 1983) and *The Long Loneliness* (San Francisco: Harper San Francisco, 1997). The best general histories of the movement are Mel Piehl, *Breaking Bread: The Catholic Worker and the Origins of Catholic Radicalism in America* (Philadelphia: Temple University Press, 1982) and William D. Miller, *A Harsh and Dreadful Love: Dorothy Day and the Catholic Worker Movement* (New York: Liveright Publishing, 1973), but both were published too early to come to terms with the explosion of the movement since Day's death. The contemporary flavor of the Worker is more visible in Patrick G. Coy, ed., *A Revolution of the Heart: Essays on the Catholic Worker* (Philadelphia: Temple University Press, 1988); William J. Thorn, Phillip Runkel, and Susan Mountin, eds., *Dorothy Day and the Catholic Worker Movement: Centenary Essays* (Milwaukee: Marquette University Press, 2001); and Rosalie Riegle Troester's outstanding oral history, *Voices from the Catholic Worker* (Philadelphia: Temple University Press, 1993). Those who wish to do serious research on the movement should most certainly visit the Dorothy Day—Catholic Worker Collection at Marquette University.

There is much less formal scholarship about Camphill than about the Catholic Worker, but the movement itself has produced several helpful overviews. Karl König, *The Camphill Movement*, 2d edition (Botton Village: Camphill Books, 1993) is the best introduction to the founding ideals, while Cornelius Pietzner, ed., *A Candle on the Hill: Images of Camphill Life* (Hudson, NY: Anthroposophic Press, 1990) provides a comprehensive picture of the movement. Other useful studies include Hans Müller-Wiedemann, *Karl König: A Central-European Biography of the Twentieth-Century*, trans. Simon Blaxland-de Lange (Botton Village, U.K.: Camphill Books, 1996); Michael and Jane Luxford, *A Sense for Community: A Five Steps Research Paper 2003* (Whitby, U.K.: Camphill Books, 2003); and Nils Christie, *Beyond Loneliness and Institutions* (Oslo: Norwegian University Press, 1989). Those who wish to explore the spiritual roots of Camphill should begin with the writings of Rudolf Steiner, especially *How to Know Higher Worlds: A Modern Path of Initiation*, trans. Christopher Bamford (Hudson, NY: Anthroposophic Press, 1994); *Theosophy: An Introduction to the Supersensible Knowledge of the World and the Destination of Man*, trans. Henry B. Monges (Hudson, NY: Anthroposophic Press, 1971); and *An Outline of Occult Science*, trans. Catherine E. Creeger (Hudson, NY: Anthroposophic Press, 1997). A brief but very helpful overview of Steiner's ideas is Robert A. McDermott, "Rudolf Steiner and anthroposophy," in Antoine Faivre and Jacob Needleman, eds., *Modern Esoteric Spirituality*, vol. 21 of *World Spirituality: An Encyclopedic History of the Religious Quest*, ed. Ewert Cousins (New York: Crossroad, 1992) 288–310. A more sociologically oriented study is Geoffrey Ahern's *Sun at Midnight: The Rudolf Steiner Movement and the Western Esoteric Tradition* (Wellingborough, Northamptonshire: Aquarian Press, 1984).